BEARING LIFE

BEARING LIFE

WOMEN'S WRITINGS ON CHILDLESSNESS

Edited by

Rochelle Ratner

The Feminist Press
at The City University of New York

Published by The Feminist Press at The City University of New York
365 Fifth Avenue, New York, NY 10016
www.feministpress.org

First edition, 2000

Library of Congress Cataloging-in-Publication Data

Bearing life : women's writings on childlessness / edited by Rochelle Ratner.
     p. cm.
    ISBN 1-55861-236-X (alk. paper)
    1. Childlessness—Literary collections.   2. American literature—Women
    authors.   3. American literature—20th century.   4. Women—Literary collections.
    I. Ratner, Rochelle.
    PS509.C5157B43   2000
    810.8'0353—dc21   99-41438
                                               CIP

The Feminist Press would also like to thank Mariam Chamberlain, Florence Howe, Joanne Markell, Caroline Urvater, and Genevieve Vaughan for their generosity in supporting this publication.

Text design and composition by V&M Graphics, New York.
Printed on acid-free paper by Haddon Craftsmen, Bloomsburg, Pennsylvania.
Manufactured in the United States of America.

05 04 03 02 01 00   5 4 3 2 1

Contents

Acknowledgments, vi

Introduction, 1

Part One FACING CHOICE, 13

EVELYN C. ROSSER   January 1953, 15

DENISE DUHAMEL   Reminded of My Biological Clock—
                        While Looking at Georgia
                        O'Keeffe's Pelvis One, 16

IRENA KLEPFISZ   Women Without Children/Women
                        Without Families/Women Alone, 19

MARY MACKEY   This Is a Question I Do Not
                        Answer, 29

RITA MAE BROWN   *From* Rita Will, 31

SANDRA CISNEROS   Old Maids, 36

MARGE PIERCY   The daughter of fur, 38

ELISSA RAFFA   The Vow, 40

JODI SH. DOFF   Tie Me Up, Tie Me Off, 48

HETTIE JONES   Minor Surgery, 51

AMY TAN   *From* The Joy Luck Club, 60

SUZANNE OSTRO   Antisocial Baby Notes, 64

AMY HEMPEL   Pretty Story, 67

DEBORAH BOE   Something I Forgot to Tell You, 69

VICKI LINDNER   Meditations on Childlessness, 70

JOY WILLIAMS   The Case Against Babies, 77

LYNDA SCHOR   The Arm Baby, 84

PATRICIA FOSTER   Outside the Hive: A Meditation
                        on Childlessness, 92

Part Two KNOWING LOSS, 103

DIANE DI PRIMA   I Get My Period, September 1964, 105

PAULETTE BATES ALDEN   *From* Crossing the Moon, 106

WENDY ROSE   Forty, Trembling, 112

PAMELA WALKER   The Wash House, 113

CHITRA BANERJEE DIVAKARUNI Outside Pisa, 120

TORY DENT   The Deferred Dream, 122

BECKY BIRTHA   The Childless Woman Poems, 131

JOYCE CAROL OATES   The Mother, 134

SANDRA SCOFIELD   Cutting My Heart Out: Notes
Toward a Novel, 136

KIT REED   The Weremother, 140

ROCHELLE RATNER   Stork Talk, 144

JANICE EIDUS   Mother and Two Daughters, 147

DANIELA GIOSEFFI   Taking the Train to Harmon, 155

JUDEE NORTON   Norton #59900, 157

MINNIE BRUCE PRATT   The Child Taken from the Mother, 163

GRACE PALEY   In the Garden, 165

LUCI TAPAHONSO   All the Colors of Sunset, 168

LINDA HOGAN   Nothing, 172

NAOMI SHIHAB NYE   Mother of Nothing, 173

Part Three   BEARING LIFE, 175

KATHLEEN NORRIS   Land of the Living, 177

REBECCA MCCLANAHAN   Liferower, 179

VALERIE MINER   You Remember Sophia, 182

JOY KOGAWA   *From* Obasan, 185

ANA CASTILLO   A Lifetime, 188

MARGARET ATWOOD   Hairball, 190

NIKKI DILLON   Chick Without Children: The
Latest Celebrity Interview, 200

SHYLAH BOYD   Cherry-Shiree, 204

DONNA BROOK   Parent As a Verb, 209

JANE RULE   The Question of Children, 211

ELIZABETH MARRAFFINO-REES   All My Kids, 213

JULIA ALVAREZ   Imagining Motherhood, 218

BELL HOOKS   *From* Black Woman Artist
Becoming, 222

MAY SARTON   *From* Journal of a Solitude, 226

MOLLY PEACOCK   Upbringing, 231

About the Authors, 233
Further Reading, 242
Credits, 244

Acknowledgments

I want to thank Shelley Roth, my agent, who helped me enormously in developing the proposal for this book and was persistent in her efforts to get it published; Elaine Gill, of The Crossing Press, who first suggested I pull together an anthology; those friends and contributors who were continually suggesting the work of others and offering advice on editing anthologies (including Daniela Gioseffi and Janice Eidus); all those writers who not only agreed to write specific pieces for this volume, but delivered them well within deadline, and many others (writers, agents, and pubishers) who generously extended permission to use their work; and my husband, Ken Thorp, for putting up with me during what became a seven-year editing job.

R. R.
New York City
October 1999

In Memorium
Esther Tischler Ratner
1910–1995

Introduction

"I don't want children," the nine-year-old narrator in Evelyn C. Rosser's "January 1953" proclaims. "I want a mink coat, a red convertible, and a big house on the beach." I can just picture adults tittering in the background. Give her a few years, they say, and of course she'll change her mind.

In beginning this volume with Rosser's diary entry, I feel as if I'm embarking on an autobiographical journey. Growing up in the 1950s, I encountered, at an early age, the assumption that being female meant being—some day—a mother. I must have been five or six when my mother, giving me a bath, explained the importance of washing the belly button—"because that's where babies come from." I recall later, while bathing myself, purposely leaving my navel unwashed, so determined was I that I didn't want babies.

I also learned the "shame" of childlessness first hand. The whispers I heard concerned my grandfather, who had outlived three wives and married his fourth two years before I was born. For thirty years he'd had a house full of children: his, hers, and theirs. The last thing he wanted was more children. Although Rae, his fourth wife, was a widow, she was childless. But because the Jewish religion teaches it's a sin to marry a barren woman, the family concocted a story about her having had a son who died in infancy. (Years later, I gained further insight into how creativity might help a woman avoid the stigma of childlessness. Perhaps because I never had children, I am more comfortable teaching in senior centers and hospitals than in schools. I recall a woman who was probably the best writer in one particular class; she often wrote vivid poems to and about her grandson, David, reflecting on their outings and conversations. It was only after I'd been teaching the workshop for several months that I discovered she'd never married and never had children.)

My own commitment to childlessness remained virtually unbroken as I grew from child to adolescent to adult to non-parent. But *why*? Why, in the face of powerful social expectations and pressures, have I—and millions of other women—elected to remain "without child"?

As soon as we address the question of childlessness, we are thrust into the realm of cliché and mythology, where no one is protected from the false assumptions: women won't grow up until they're mothers; women who don't have children are selfish, cold; childless women must have been abused when they were growing up. Friends caution that you're missing out on life's most exhilarating pleasure or reason that your partner won't feel any ties to a childless relationship. Some myths are even more disturbing: the persistent notion that lesbians—not to mention poor women, women with prison records, or women with HIV—are categorically unfit to be mothers.

There are, of course, the easy replies to superficial questioning (or self-questioning): I adore my sister's children; I haven't been in the right relationship; this apartment is too small; I'm too wrapped up in my career (or my art); I don't want to clone a little image of myself; I want children, but my partner doesn't; I have a difficult time relating to children; the world doesn't need more children.

In fact, there are as many reasons for childlessness as there are childless women. My own rationalization as a teenager was that I hated my parents, hated them for having brought me into this troubled and friendless world, and I could never live with myself if my own child felt that way. On better days I added that I might be willing to adopt a child already born, but I could never be responsible for that birth. By the time I learned such feelings were a part of normal adolescence I had moved to New York, my apartment was too small, I wasn't in the right relationship and, because I had no siblings, nieces, or nephews, I had a difficult time relating to children.

As the only child in a middle-class family, in a tourist town 120 miles from New York and 60 miles from Philadelphia, I felt completely alone, isolated, alienated. My parents and others related as best they could. If I wanted to write (as I had since at least the seventh grade), they assumed I would become a journalist. Journalism was the only writing my family could relate to (though my father subscribed to Readers Digest Condensed Books when I was a teenager). I knew there was another sort of person out there, someone who would understand the thrill of reading and writing fiction or poetry, but I had no idea how to reach such a person. I did, however, manage to get my hands on some volumes of poetry.

At the same time, I was being told by most of those around me that *all* women wanted children, just as all women wanted wall-to-wall carpeting, dance lessons, biweekly trips to the beauty parlor, perfume, and another fifty things I've conveniently forgotten. Even the women poets whose work I had discovered—Denise Levertov, Adrienne Rich, Muriel Rukeyser—were all mothers, too. (Of course, when I was re-reading their poems in hopes of new inspiration, I simply skipped the poems about their children.) While their work could easily serve as a model for my writing, I still had no one on whom I could model my life. There was Gertrude Stein, and perhaps Anaïs Nin, but their lives frightened me, and their writing offered little inspiration at the time. No contemporary poet or novelist, as far as I knew, had produced a literature of childlessness, so there was no way to see my own feelings mirrored, no insights to be gained.

In the mid 1990s, when the proposal for this volume was making the rounds of publishing houses, one editor I respected made the comment that "children are in right now." That's precisely my point. After a woman has a miscarriage, she receives sympathy from everyone around her, along with urgings to try again and heartfelt stories of other people who miscarried but later had three children. If she's going for fertility treatments she will, again, hear all the wonderful success stories. After a woman has opted for abortion (unless she lives in a conservative or fundamentalist environment) she will most likely find a camaraderie among trusted friends and colleagues who will relate tales of their own (legal and illegal) abortions and assure her that there will be plenty of time to have children later, when she's more settled. But let a woman state that she has no desire for children, no wish to get pregnant, and no incentive to even explore adoption, and she will probably be met with silence—perhaps with an empty stare, perhaps with a hostile one.

These women desperately needed to talk, to realize they weren't the only women in the world who did not want children. And they needed to read about experiences and feelings that resembled—and thus validated—their own. I needed this myself. Because growing up—and even as a young woman living on my own in New York, reading widely and editing a review of contemporary literature—I had no belief that such women really existed.

In 1990, I chanced upon Irena Klepfisz's essay "Women Without Children/ Women Without Families/Women Alone," which candidly explored the fear and guilt her decision to remain childless has caused her. Written from the viewpoint of a Jew whose father was killed in the Holocaust, it had a resonance and poignancy that ignited my search for what others had written on the concept of child-free existence. But I was busy with other projects, and it was a lackadaisical search, at best.

Then I heard Molly Peacock read her poem "Upbringing." It was shortly before the 1992 presidential election, ironically enough at a benefit reading for Planned Parenthood. She prefaced the poem by recounting some of the grim details of abused children that had recently been flooding New York newspapers. The contrast of this poem with my memory of Klepfisz's essay reawakened my interest in the subject. I decided that a volume of women's writing about childlessness might yet be possible—an anthology exploring the lives, fears, and dreams of childless women, juxtaposing the works of writers I respected. And if it could be printed and bound, and distributed to bookstores and classrooms around the country, then perhaps the next childless woman might not feel so alone.

At the start, I wondered if this anthology should include both writing by women who had *chosen* not to have children and women who—through infertility, death, discrimination, or a variety of other losses—had been *denied* children. But how different, really, is Julia Alvarez's decision not to mother from Paulette Bates Alden's decision to give up fertility treatments, or from the decision by Pamela Walker's character to symbolically bury her lost infant? All three describe themselves mainly in relation to the mothers around them. All three writers eventually come to terms with their childlessness and get on with their lives. (In a way, even women who are mothers face similar challenges; the mother of a teenaged daughter recently told me that during an argument her daughter shouted, "Get a life!") As women, mothers and nonmothers, we find ourselves having to *let go*—of the physical child as well as of the desire for children.

In fact, I believe it is a virtue of this collection that the writers in these pages reflect a broad variety of experiences and perspectives, and even that they tend to contradict one another, or themselves; it testifies to the social and emotional complexity that surrounds the issue of childlessness. But at the same time this collection, taken as a whole, reveals much common ground: each writer deals with living as a woman without children, in a world that continues to consider motherhood a condition inseparable from womanhood.

Not all of the contributors—or their characters—are physically childless. Hettie Jones describes a mother accompanying her daughter to the abortion clinic. There are the pieces written by mothers who don't mention their children, such as Diane di Prima and Grace Paley. Nor does being childless prevent you from writing about children. Joyce Carol Oates, childless herself, presents an all-too-familiar portrait of an adolescent son shutting his mother out of his life. (It is often noted that the painter Mary Cassatt, famous for her portraits of mothers and children, was never a mother.)

It was not necessary that the selections included here be true stories (and many are not)—just deeply felt and vividly presented. Every writer who contributed an essay or memoir is also a poet or fiction writer, and when it came to making the final selections, art, as well as message, was a deciding factor.

Earlier, I mentioned my grandfather inventing a son for his childless wife. This was in 1947, and the family myth persisted well into the 1950s. Even though my grandfather had emigrated to the United States shortly after the turn of the century, he, like thousands of other immigrants from Poland, Russia, Italy, and a host of other countries, brought their old-world customs along with them. As this generation died out, the rigid insistence on childbearing became more and more flexible (although today we sometimes find the situation reversed: as Nikki Dillon points out, for example, some contemporary Italian American families view childbearing in much stricter terms than do their Italian counterparts). Even ultra-orthodox Judaism has relaxed to the point where a woman's remaining childless is no longer a sin (although a man is still bound by the commandment to "be fruitful and multiply"). But my memory of the traditions and attitudes my grandfather brought with him from his village, and my consciousness of all the different traditions and attitudes that must confront childless women around the world, served as a warning for me: Don't venture too far from territory you haven't intimately experienced.

While looking for work to include, I came across pieces by women from other countries, many of them extremely strong. But I did not feel I understood either comparative literature or the general living conditions that prompted these works well enough to create a truly international anthology on the subject of childlessness (a monumental task, and one I hope some other ambitious editor will take on). I chose instead to impose strict geographic limits. *Bearing Life* thus contains work by writers from the United States and Canada. I felt, too, that there was some virtue to these limits, in terms of the cohesiveness of the collection: The experience of being childless, the ability to choose childlessness, the response of family, friends, and others—all are tremendously affected by the environment in which a woman lives. I therefore hoped to achieve diversity and dialogue by including in the anthology women from many different cultural and socioeconomic backgrounds living in the United States and Canada.

In shaping the boundaries of this anthology, I also had to decide what historical period it would cover. Should it be a contemporary collection, or should it seek to include examples of women's writing on the subject of childlessness from earlier decades, even centuries? In fact, I spent time looking for literature from the nineteenth and early twentieth centuries. I cannot claim that my search was exhaustive (and of course, a good deal of women's writing, especially women's popular writing from these periods, remains out-of-print and unavailable), but the resulting impressions are perhaps worth noting.

Women's literature in English contains no shortage of novels, from Jane Austen to Jane Rule, in which mothers and motherhood are viewed with a critical eye, and in which women seem destined to live happy child-free lives. I did not find any early novel that made the issue of childlessness its central theme, but I did find stories in which characters—and authors—questioned or rebelled against the equation of motherhood with female destiny.

In Rebecca Harding Davis's 1861 story "Anne," a widow with loving children and grandchildren dreams of the glamorous life she once considered: a singing career, a romance with a man who later became a famous author. Without warning, she sets off to recoup the life she might have lived—but quickly comes to her senses and returns home. Charlotte Perkins Gilman's supposedly bereaved mother, in her 1889 story "The Widow's Might," proves more resolute. As her children debate her future, "Mother" makes her own choice: now that she has raised these "adults" and been dutiful for thirty years to a cold husband, she is off to travel, to *live*.

The stories by Gilman's contemporary Mary Wilkins Freeman are replete with aging "spinsters" who have no regrets and ask for nothing but their independence. (Many women writers of her time were, of course, "spinsters" themselves.) And the slave narratives of the nineteenth century offer an altogether different, devastating view of women whose childlessness was anything but a choice: tales of children forcibly removed and sold, mothers whipped if they dared to protest.

At the turn of the century, Edith Wharton, in "The Mission of Jane" (1904), presents an ironic counterpoint to the prevailing belief that a woman could not be "whole" without a child. The childless couple in the story adopts a little girl— only to find that their greatest relief comes when she is grown and out of the house, and they can again enjoy their time alone with each other.

Looking at the early years of the twentieth century, I found more literature by working-class women writers like Agnes Smedley, who depict the grinding strain of bearing and raising children in poverty—and, sometimes, assert that there are other ways for women to live. In her 1929 novel *Daughter of Earth*, Smedley's protagonist chooses to remain childless as part of her effort to escape the cycle that has destroyed her mother and so many of the other women around her.

But not surprisingly, literature directly exploring childlessness—particularly childlessness by choice—begins to emerge more visibly with the first stirrings of second-wave feminism, in the mid-1960s. In 1963, the year that Betty Friedan's *The Feminine Mystique* was published, Tillie Olsen delivered a lecture that would one day become part of *Silences*, her ground-breaking work on women writers, in which she acknowledged the challenge children present to women seeking the concentrated time and attention needed to pursue their art:

More than any other relationship, overwhelmingly more, motherhood means being instantly interruptible, responsive, responsible. Children need one *now*. . . . It is distraction, not meditation, that becomes habitual; interruption, not continuity; spasmodic, not constant toil.

Nineteen sixty-three was the same year that Sylvia Plath, living out the reality that Tillie Olsen described, woke at five o'clock every morning so she could concentrate on the startling poems in *Ariel* before the baby cried.

The following year, 1964, saw the publication of Jane Rule's novel *The Desert of the Heart* (reprinted 1985), which is, of all the novels I have read, the one that most boldly forefronts an image of women choosing, quite resolutely, *not* to have children. The protagonists in this emotionally complex story of love between two women are Ann, a casino-worker in Reno, who states flatly that "it's fertility that's a dirty word to me," and Evelyn, who is in Reno to get a divorce after a childless sixteen-year marriage, and comes to understand that the tragedy of her infertility is also a liberation. Not coincidentally, 1964 is also the date of the earliest piece in this volume, Diane di Prima's "I Get My Period: Summer 1964," a poem that embodies much of the ambiguity many women experienced at the time.

It seemed to me a logical choice to locate this book, in time, within the era that began with the contemporary women's movement in the West. In this era, feminists in general, and women writers in particular, have grappled quite directly with issues surrounding motherhood—and dared, as never before, to name childlessness as a viable choice. In her perceptive essay, "Motherhood—Reclaiming the Demon Texts," published in *Ms.* magazine (May/June 1991), Ann Snitow recalls writings from the contemporary feminist movement's first decade, such as Shulamith Firestone's *The Dialectic of Sex*, which attacked the institution of motherhood and its crippling effect on women. As Snitow reasonably points out, many of these works would be misinterpreted; these writers were lashing out at patriarchy, and not at women who were mothers. Yet they would be denounced as "mother-hating" texts, and while feminist writers would continue to examine motherhood, they would fail to sustain "a strong and clear critique of the prescription that all women must be mothers." This would become particularly true following the political shift of the early 1980s. Snitow writes:

It's been some time since feminists demanding abortion have put front and center the idea that one good use to which one might put this right is to choose not to have kids at all. Chastised in the Reagan years, pro-choice strategists understandably have emphasized the right to wait, to space one's children, to have each child wanted. They feared invoking any image that could be read as a female withdrawal from the role of nurturer. We are—in this period of reaction—elaborating, extending, reinstitutionalizing motherhood for ourselves. Never has the baby been so delicious. A feminist theorist tells me she is more proud of her new baby than of all her books.

Paula Weideger, in another *Ms.* magazine article called "Womb Worship" (February 1988) personalized this phenomenon, noting that the feminist movement had reversed itself on the question of childlessness by choice, and that she suddenly felt like a pitied outsider because she was holding her ground and not having children.

Yet the ideas of the women's movement in general, and the option to remain childless in particular, had entered the popular consciousness, and it could never be fully expunged. No matter how much rhetoric has been spewed concerning "family values," today even the most conservative women are aware of their options. The idea that women can be fulfilled without being mothers, that childlessness can even be a positive choice, seems to have seeped deep enough into the culture to weather the anti-feminist backlash. Snitow acknowledges that "however raggedly, women are already living out basically new story lines, making piecemeal changes." In the 1980s and 1990s, numerous articles in the popular press, and even several nonfiction books, defended the choice not to have children. And many others insisted upon the ability of involuntarily childless women to live rich and complete lives. (Admittedly, the Library of Congress has no subject heading that separates voluntary childlessness from "the heartbreak of infertility." University of Redlands librarian Angelynn King, who compiled much of the bibliography included here, lamented about how difficult this makes life for a researcher.)

The pieces collected in this anthology were scattered, not easy to find unless you were looking for them. But the fact is, they exist, as do a great many more not included here—some of them from the 1960s and 1970s, but most from the 1980s and 1990s. Other pieces were written expressly for this volume by women who welcomed the long-overdue opportunity to write on this subject. If, as I firmly believe, art imitates life, then we need no further proof that this issue is here to stay.

Politics aside, we seem to have reached the point where the experience of childlessness can be creatively explored. In 1998 Molly Peacock, whose poem "Upbringing" ends this volume, produced what is, to my knowledge, the first memoir to place the decision to remain childless at the heart of a woman's life story, *Paradise, Piece by Piece*. I hope that in the future many more full-length creative works—memoirs and novels—will focus on the issue; but I was encouraged that I found a rich enough stock of poems, stories, and essays to fill a volume. Judging by the responses I received when telling people about this project, it would seem we are finally breaking through the walls of silence. I believe it is only now, at the start of the new millennium, that *Bearing Life* could come into being.

"Facing Choice," the first section in this book, begins with work by or about women who for the most part are firm in their choice to remain childless, but who still feel the need to defend that choice. The opening pieces, Evelyn C. Rosser's "January 1953" and Denise Duhamel's "Reminded of My Biological Clock—While Looking At Georgia's O'Keeffe's Pelvis One," are the only two in the volume written from a child's point-of-view. Thousands of such youthful proclamations are no doubt heard every day—and are never, of course, taken seriously. But these girls were clearly serious, as their adult selves, looking back and reaffirming, attest.

Just listen to what I'm saying, nearly every writer in this section seems to plead. This feeling seems particularly powerful in the memoirs by Irena Klepfisz, Mary Mackey, and Rita Mae Brown. These writers are attempting to justify their choices, and in two cases their sexual orientation, to family, friends, even strangers, almost as if that external validation will help silence the questioning within. Klepfisz recalls her conventional acceptance, maintained in her twenties, that she would some day settle down and give her mother the grandchildren she so desperately wanted. When it becomes clear that this vision will not come to be, her family's disappointment exists beside her own fear of being alone, exemplified by the startling image of the "bag lady" on the streets or subway. The last person in her father's line, she doesn't want to face these issues, any more than Rita Mae Brown, still young and uncertain of her sexuality, wants to cause trouble between her mother and her aunt with rumors of her lesbianism and her probable childlessness. But these things come up; they can't be avoided. Mary Mackey, tired of explaining why she doesn't have children, states bluntly, "This is a question I do not answer"—but she is talking to strangers, people she is not concerned about hurting.

Because Vicki Lindner and Patricia Foster aren't called upon to answer for their decisions, their explorations seem more internal. In making her choice, Lindner understands and acknowledges what she is missing:

Few women's lives can be lived without regret, as every choice seems to preclude another. I don't regret not having a child, but sometimes I regret not wanting to have one. I regret drifting far from the stream of shared female concern; I regret not ever loving anybody *so much*. I regret my ongoing delight in solitude and freedom, because a "normal" woman does not want to be free or alone.

Foster, raised as "an honorary son," learns very young not only how important "success" is to her parents, but how a promising high school girl can get pregnant, elope, and suddenly "her life is over." Long after she is grown up, this powerful image reverberates.

With Sandra Cisneros's poem "Old Maids," we move into issues larger than the personal. Calmly, lyrically, without anger, Cisneros points out how she has learned from observing other marriages in her family that this simply isn't the life for her. She only hints at the details. With this subtlety, she permits readers to think about their own families, and the influences that have brought them to their own choices. Marge Piercy ("a suitable mother to orange cats") and Elissa A. Raffa are more specific about their family histories. Both works show women consciously breaking a heritage of familial oppression. The portrait Raffa paints might make readers recoil in horror. No wonder she doesn't want children, we say—to have grown up in a home such as that. But then we look closer, or look around us, and realize many people from similar backgrounds *have* built their own, reasonably content families (including Raffa's sisters). And we come to understand how important "The Vow" was to her, and how much it cost emotionally. Another high price is paid by Jodi Sh. Doff's narrator in "Tie Me Up, Tie Me Off," who, in order to remain firm in her choices, subjects her body to intentional abuse and, in doing so, loses the friendship of the woman she felt closest to.

Usually, hopefully, the very act of putting words on paper, having to harness and pace the thought process, helps the writer better understand her own situation, and, by placing it in context, appreciate it (perhaps one of the reasons that the journal form became important for professional and non-professional women writers in the 1960s and 1970s). Surprisingly, two of the strongest pieces about dysfunctional childhoods were withdrawn from inclusion here by their authors, who perhaps recognized they no longer feel the anger that their writing revealed just a few years ago.

Suzanne Ostro gives a far happier view of the connection between father and daughter. As one gathers from the tone of Ostro's memoir, we need not always take ourselves so seriously. The satiric riffs by Amy Hempel, Deborah Boe, and Joy Williams tease readers away from their own thoughts and fears. Nothing is sacred here—not the infant in the crib, not the marriage proposal, not the modern fertility industry or its clients. In Lynda Schor's surreal tale, a routine operation unexpectedly results in new perspectives on women as lovers and mothers, nurtured and nurturing. And Amy Tan's narrator even manages to turn ancient Chinese customs into a laughable tale, but gently, lovingly, respectfully.

Childless women are childless for many different reasons. Millions of women who desperately want children can't conceive or can't carry a child to term. Children are taken away in custody battles or placed in foster homes. Other children run in front of cars, or simply grow up and leave home. Regardless of the reason, for the writers and narrators in part two, "Knowing Loss," it's not a question of making decisions; it's a process of accepting reality.

Reality, for Paulette Bates Alden, presents itself as accepting what is, and valuing it—of realizing, as if hit by lightning, that "our life without a child seemed good to me." This statement comes near the end of a book about her longing for a child and the discouraging ordeal of fertility treatments. In "Nothing," Linda Hogan carries Alden's observation to the next level, showing a woman and her lover taking comfort in a body that too many others might think of as empty. Not so for the childless speaker in Chitra Banerjee Divakaruni's "Outside Pisa," who faces reality with the understanding that she might now have to cope with the end of a long, childless relationship. For Tory Dent, reality means facing up to the fact that she is HIV positive, that a child she would bear could have HIV, that as much as she might long for a child, she also feels she must abort the one she carries. But reality, in her case, still holds the faint hope that "maybe someday." Dent turns what could be an anguished chronicle into a poetic exploration. (Alden and Dent are among the privileged who have access to good medical care. There are, of course, probably thousands of women without insurance or savings, or on Medicaid, who do not have the opportunity to ponder such choices).

Speaking from her Native American background, Wendy Rose vividly imagines the ghosts of unborn children emerging from the empty womb, while the grandmother in Luci Tapahonso's story carries her ghost-baby in her arms. Yet both know that they themselves are part of the living. Pamela Walker, half-crazed by the baby which "lived and died inside me," abolishes her ghost through ritually burying its haunting proxy.

Other writers seek out the sensation of motherhood, as shown here in Becky Birtha's stunning poem sequence, "The Childless Woman Poems," or the woman addressed in Naomi Shihab Nye's "Mother of Nothing." Both poems portray a woman staring at a playground, taking comfort in other children while imagining a little girl or boy of her own. Birtha takes the masquerade further, imagining the childless woman in various other maternal situations.

Sometimes the ghosts take on human forms, the elusive and confusing presences that children can become. Daniela Gioseff explores her guilt in leaving her daughter with relatives so she can steal some time alone to write. Joyce Carol Oates describes an adolescent boy shutting his door, attempting to shut his mother out of his life—making her, suddenly, experience a loneliness as painful as any other form of unchosen childlessness. This story is memorable because of the vividness and poignancy with which Oates depicts a common occurrence between mother and child. While Oates' portrayal might make readers smile at the mother's needless worry, the daughters Sandra Scofield and Janice Eidus present us with earn their mothers our sympathy. Scofield's Jessica and Eidus's Ronelle are well past adolescence. Both daughters are from middle-class homes, but homes where something, somehow went wrong. One is mentally ill, the other wild, driven to crime. One or both may or may not be on drugs. What is unique about these two stories, however, is that both narrators restrain themselves, realizing there's only so much a mother can do. Another aspect of maternal restraint is presented by the woman in Kit Reed's "The Weremother," who pleads to be tied up before she can, under the guise of good parenting, harm a child. Just how much emotional damage a mother can unknowingly inflict is comically depicted in my own "Stork Talk."

While some women may judge themselves "unfit mothers," others have that judgment forced upon them—and their children forcibly removed. Judee Norton, who is in prison, is forbidden visits from her son, while the narrator of Minnie Bruce Pratt's poem faces a husband (and a judicial system) who see her lesbianism as just reason to deprive her of her child. The couple whose children are kidnaped, in Grace Paley's story, feel a similar anguish, made worse because they find it so unexpected, so arbitrary. Whereas Norton and Pratt heighten the already powerful drama by relating it from the mother's point of view, Paley distances readers from the mother by presenting the situation as seen by neighbors—thus suggesting that this isn't unique; it could happen to anyone. Any mother could suddenly find herself without child.

Once a woman has made the decision not to have children, or has reconciled herself to the fact that she probably won't, reasons no longer matter. The point is that the world doesn't end there: she has to get on with her life. Part three, "Bearing Life," introduces readers to women doing just that. Sometimes this concept is straightforward, as in the story by Valerie Miner, in which the protagonist realizes that she might not have children, "but she has a life." Joy Kogawa depicts a woman who is branded a "spinster" by the children she teaches, but who is lucky enough to have strong female role models in her extended family. Or, the conception can be outrageous, as in "Chick Without Children: The Latest Celebrity Interview" by Nikki Dillon, with its focus on the fictitious performance artist who has turned her childlessness into an art form all its own.

Margaret Atwood's vengeful "Hairball" was one of the first selections chosen for this anthology. With the same wild imagination often found in Atwood's other work, this story fulfills the revenge fantasies of many women involved with married men, or simply jilted. Atwood has been a pioneer in writing frankly and imaginatively about the social and emotional questions surrounding maternity and childlessness. Whether her novels are set in the past (*Alias Grace*), the present (*The Robber Bride*), or the future (*The Handmaid's Tale*), they address basic issues of the "haves" and the "have-nots." A very different but equally affecting image of a man with children encountered by a woman alone appears in Ana Castillo's sensitive story of a woman visiting her dying ex-husband.

Some childless women come to new understandings of themselves through encounters with women who are mothers. Shylah Boyd's tale of friendship has, like Margaret Atwood's piece, elements of malice just below the surface. "Cherry Shiree" takes us into the lives of two main characters, one with child, one without—and here questions of class come into play as well, as the childless narrator helps to empower a working-class woman to regain custody of her child. Indeed, there are many ways to make a difference in the life of a child, or to have relationships with children outside of the conventional definitions of motherhood, as Donna Brook and Jane Rule attest.

How a woman views her childlessness is often conditioned by the presence of sisters. This theme goes back to some of the works included in this books's first section. As Irena Klepfisz notes:

> A woman once told me how her sister, who had recently given birth, said to her that she was glad she had been able to provide their mother with the pleasure of seeing her first grandchild. The mother was dying. The woman felt hurt, not only because of her sister's insensitivity to her feelings, but because she had nothing comparable to offer her mother.

There are sisters in this section, also—in this case, sisters who offer solace. Kathleen Norris and Rebecca McClanahan chronicle the concern and love that often bonds them. For Norris, writing in a monastery, the picture of a sister and niece parallels that of the Madonna and Child (with surprising credibility and honesty, simply sharing an experience of life in which the author knows she will never participate). Julia Alvarez also tackles cultural concerns: of four sisters in her family, two have children, two don't. Then her third sister adopts. Alvarez wavers in the face of pressure—not from her family, but from herself—and finally comes to the understanding that she's content, as the title of her memoir states, "Imagining Motherhood"—and writing about it. Just how close imagination might be to reality is beautifully illustrated in Elizabeth Marraffino-Rees's "All My Kids."

Indeed, for many writers who don't have children, just putting words on paper—creating art rather than children—is enough. In journal segments, May Sarton and bell hooks, separated from one another by age, race, and background, face the same issues of loneliness, determination, and struggle that most of the writers within these pages deal with on a daily basis. Sarton from the perspective of old age, and hooks from the viewpoint of a woman nearing the final years of childbearing, look back over their lives and reaffirm that they wouldn't have done anything differently.

The book draws to a close with Molly Peacock's "Upbringing." Peacock recalls her own dysfunctional childhood and admits to the burden of becoming an adult alone—of just being a mother to the needy child within herself. Reading slightly between the lines (and here I go back to the first time I heard this poem read aloud), readers are enabled to view the decision of some women to remain childless as stemming from social consciousness as well as personal feelings or experiences.

Bearing Life contains over fifty contributors, and there are many more writers who might have been included in these pages. Women here assert their right to be non-mothers, child-free, childless—whatever they choose to call it—and to do so without shame or apology. In stories, essays, and poems, childless women may be heard, more and more, as strong voices.

These diverse pieces present alternatives to motherhood. They reveal women contemplating, enduring, enjoying, *living* lives without children. They explore—and in doing so legitimize—the experience of childlessness in the contemporary United States and Canada. This book is, in a profound sense of the term, a *pro-choice* book. But it is not a self-help book. It gives no instructions on how to overcome guilt, talk to a pregnant friend, or break the news to parents. Not every piece ends happily with a view of women finding fulfillment. Rather, the writers here face hard issues, and readers are permitted to share in their determination, frustration, fear, anguish, defiance, celebration and, sometimes, humor.

Reading these pages, we see ourselves, our friends, members of our families, and we take away something—love, understanding, maybe deeper knowledge—to pass on, if not to our own children, then to the children of others. It's an important legacy.

Part One

FACING CHOICE

January 1953

EVELYN C. ROSSER

I loved the doll I got for Christmas. Daddy broke it today. You see, it was an accident. My brothers took my doll from me and were throwing it back and forth to each other. When I ran to one brother, he threw it to another brother. I told Daddy to make them give it to me. He came into the bedroom and told them to stop throwing my doll. They didn't. He got angry. He snatched it from my brother and threw it to me. I didn't catch it. The doll hit the trunk. Its head was broken off. I cried. Daddy promised to buy me another doll. Mama told me to stop crying, because a nine-year-old girl was too old for dolls anyway. She said dolls only make girls want babies. She doesn't know me. I don't want a baby. I want a mink coat, a red convertible, and a big house on the beach. I'll have a funeral for my doll tomorrow, and I won't invite her.

Reminded of My Biological Clock—

While Looking at Georgia O'Keeffe's *Pelvis One*

(*Pelvis With Blue*, 1944)

DENISE DUHAMEL

I see so many things, a primitive ring,
a nest with a fallen-out bottom,
a white rubber band snapped into blue.
But mostly it's real memory
and the doctor holding up my x-ray
to the screen of light, a mini drive-in.
The bone was mine—big, oblong
and intact, even though my skin was purple,
my muscles sore. I'd fallen
off of Matthew's ten speed.
There were whispers that my hymen was probably gone,
first broken by the crossbar
that separates a boy's bike from a girl's,
rather than by Matthew himself. And now the x-rays
were showing my ready pelvis, an empty hammock,
just waiting for a sticky fetus sucking its thumb.
"It's beautiful," the doctor said
admiring my illuminated centerfold-skeleton
before he turned to me, the real—and therefore
less interesting—thing. He smiled:
"You have the perfect hip bones, Miss,
for carrying babies." To my mother, he said,
"If everything else inside her is OK, someday
she'll be in labor for no more than an hour."
I was thirteen and I wanted no baby,
only a boyfriend, only some petting.
I wasn't even sure how I felt
about tongues. My favorite game was
swimming deep under water, kicking through
a tent of spread legs, scissoring my thighs

in short quick ups and downs so I wouldn't lose
by booting someone in the crotch.
"But I don't want a baby, " I might have said aloud.
The doctor and my mother might have conspiratorially laughed.
My pelvis was as white as the ones Georgia painted,
except the weather surrounding hers
was robin egg-hopeful.
My bone was a whorl in an x-ray-gray storm.
My disembodied pelvis, like a melted hula hoop,
a coiling snake meeting itself, a lasso
without the rope of control to catch what I wanted.
"The women in our family are all Fertile Myrtles,"
my mother explained later, when I changed my
          mind, and tongues
and other appendages boys had
became more to my liking. "When I got
pregnant with you, I think I was just
looking at your father," she said as emphatically
as if she were telling me the truth. So I found out how to get
a diaphragm and pills and foams and condoms and used them
all at once, memorizing the percentages
of their individual effectiveness: 80, 82, 89.5.
"I'm pregnant, I just know it,"
I would panic every month, my pelvis
a nebulous halo, a loose-fitting noose.
Exasperated, my first real boyfriend would remind me,
"Impossible. We didn't even have intercourse last month.
Remember? You were too nervous." In the meantime,
my girlfriends, one by one, skipped their periods.
There were trips for abortions or quick marriages.
One young mother left high school
to become a cashier at the Stop & Shop.
While she was still nursing, she leaked milk
through her shirt and smock, leaving
something like a perspiration spot
every time a baby cried in her line.
This wasn't for me, though I felt guilty,
my pelvis being the right shape and all.
My mother watched her talk shows, sometimes
on the topic of childless women, and muttered,
"How can those career ladies be so selfish?
If they don't have babies now,
they'll grow old and die alone."
Sometimes in my dreams I'm back on Matthew's bike,
not falling this time, but riding off

into the orange-cowboy sunset. Other times,
though, a crown of thorns sprouts in my belly—
my nightmare grows dark.
It is always daylight around Georgia's *Pelvises*.
The sky is the blue that the child she might have had
might have seen when she was first born.
Sometimes I dream bluebirds land on my hipbone
as though I were a round limb
on a desert tree. I feed them anything
they desire. Then the mother birds
feed their youngsters, and I tell them
they can stay as long as they like.

Women Without Children; Women Without Families; Women Alone

Irena Klepfisz

This essay has grown out of my need to express some of my feelings and conflicts about being a woman who has chosen to remain childless, as well as to bear the silence surrounding the general issue of women without children.

That the silence has persisted despite the presence of the women's movement is both appalling and enigmatic, since the decision not to have a child shapes both a woman's view of herself and society's view of her. I have read a great deal about woman as mother, but virtually nothing about woman as non-mother, as if her choice should be taken for granted and her life were not an issue. and although I have heard strong support of the right of women to have choices and options, I have not seen any exploration of how the decision to remain childless is to be made, how one is to come to terms with it, how one is to learn to live with its consequences. If what follows seems at moments somewhat bleak, it is because I feel very strongly that in celebrating a woman's liberation from compulsory motherhood, we have neither recognized nor dealt with the pain that often accompanies such a decision.

My intent is to be neither objective nor exhaustive. I am aware that this issue evokes many other feelings than those expressed on the following pages, the feelings of women whose lives differ drastically from mine. I hope that they too will break the silence. [1977]

1. The Fantasy

At the center of my bleakest fantasy is the shopping-bag lady. I see her sitting on the subway, trudging along the highway, or crouched in a doorway at dusk. Invariably, she clutches her paper shopping bags close to her. From a distance her face looks blank, her skin gray. She is oblivious to the things around her, unresponsive to sounds and movements. She is particularly indifferent to people. Periodically she makes a quick motion, like an animal automatically brushing itself free from an irritation, a tic. Her gesture is loose, flabby, hardly aimed. It is, perhaps, the tremor of a muscle.

I keep my distance from her, though at times in my imagination I venture closer, detecting a faint stale odor, an odor distinctly communicating stagnation.

In reality, however, I have moved only close enough to discern the discolored skin, the broken blood vessels on her legs, stained purple bruises, barely healed wounds. I have eyed her socks and stockings, her shoes, her faded dress, the safety pins that hold her coat together. I have studied the surface content of her bags, seen the bits of material (clothing, perhaps), newspapers. I always wanted to know more, to know if the entire bag is filled with rags and papers, or if, deep inside, wrapped neatly and carefully in a clean cloth, lies an object from the past, a memento from a life like mine. But my desire to know has never overcome my real terror of her. So I have never ventured closer.

I have a distinct fear of contagion. But it is not necessarily of disease, though there is that too, the physical fear of being touched by such a creature. My greater fear is that she carries another kind of disease. On a subway, I watch as this creature sits, harmless, self-contained, oblivious to the other people in the car, while an invisible circle seems to form around her. No one will come near her, no one will sit close to her, no one will risk being touched by her. If she has succeeded in excluding us from her world, we must remember that our response to her reflects our equal determination to keep her out of ours. It is almost as if I, as if everyone else in the subway car, were determined to classify her as a species apart, to establish firmly that there is no connection between her and us. By keeping my distance, I affirm that she is not of my world, reassure myself that I could never be like her, that there is nothing she and I have in common—in short, that her disease is not communicable.

It is, I think, the most comfortable way of looking at her, for it deems her irrelevant to my life. Of course, if I were totally convinced, I would lose my fear of contagion. But this is not the case. More and more, I sense my connection to her, allow myself to absorb the fact that her world and mine overlap. More and more I dismiss as romantic the notion that some great, swift calamity, some sudden shock must have overtaken her and reduced her to her present condition. It is far more probable that her separateness, her isolation, resulted not from fire, nor from sudden death, nor from unexpected loss, but rather from a slow erosion, an imperceptible loosening of common connections and relations—a process to which I too am subject. Her disease is one to which I am and will remain vulnerable. She is not an anomaly, nor is her isolation from the rest of us a freak accident. She came from the same world I did, underwent the same life processes: she was born, grew up, lives.

So I remain in a state of terror and keep myself separate from her. I fear that I will not build up the proper immunity to resist the erosion; I am afraid I too will end up alone, disconnected, relating to no one, having no one to care for, being in turn forgotten, unwanted, and insignificant, my life a waste. In the grip of this terror, I can only anticipate a lonely, painful old age, an uncomforted death.

It is difficult to own up to this fantasy. I do so because it is true that I have it, but also because I know I am not unique in having it. I have heard many other women express it, perhaps not always in terms of shopping-bag ladies, but in terms of old age, insecurity. And it is not surprising because among my friends, many in their late thirties and early forties, these issues are becoming increasingly important. It is not surprising because we are living in a depression when everyone is worried about money and jobs, about the possibility of surviving in some decent way. For me, the shopping-bag lady epitomizes these fears, and though I often tell myself that she is an exaggerated example, equally often I think that she is not.

2. The Myths

For a long time I believed (and on some nonrational level still believe) that I could acquire immunity to the shopping-bag lady's disease by having a child. When depressed about the fragility and transiency of friendships, or the inconstancies of lovers, it was the myth of a child, a blood relation and what it could bring me, which seemed to be the only guarantee against loneliness and isolation, the only way of maintaining a connection to the rest of society. And certainly one of the difficulties for me, a woman who now knows that she will never bear children, is to let go of that myth without sinking into total despair.

That the myth is powerful is not surprising, since it is nurtured by everything around us, fostered by the media, by popular literature, by parents, by the questionnaires we fill out for jobs: *Are you married?* No. *Do you have children?* No. *Do you live alone?* Yes. *How many members in your household?* One. It is a myth perpetually reinforced by the assumption that only family and children provide us with a purpose and place, bestow upon us honor, respect, love and comfort. We are taught very early that blood relations, and only blood relations, can be a perpetual, unfluctuating source of affection, can be the foolproof guarantee that we will not be forgotten. This myth, and many others surrounding the traditional family, often make it both frightening and painful for women to think of themselves as remaining childless.

In reality, of course, I know that many shopping-bag ladies are mothers, have families, have children. What is obvious to any mature, rational woman is that children are not a medicine or a vaccine which stamps out loneliness or isolation, but rather that they are people, subject to the same weaknesses as friends and lovers. I have talked to many women whose ties to their families seem to be irrevocably broken. It is common to hear stories of the prodigal daughter going cross-country, returning home after fourteen, fifteen years to parents who are strangers. Expecting a traumatic, painful reunion, the woman returns numbed by the lack of connection, by her indifference to strangers. They are people with no special relation. They follow the accepted and expected rules, in a dire crisis write dutiful checks, and, upon their death, bequeath china to their unmarried daughters. But the emotional pull is not there from either side. There is no exchange of love, of comfort. Blood might indeed be thicker than water, but it, too, is capable of evaporating and drying up.

Yet despite this, despite having read Shakespeare's *King Lear* and Tillie Olsen's *Tell Me a Riddle,* despite having been taught by experience that children often come to love their ideals more than their parents (and vice versa), that children may take different roads, rejecting all ties to the past, despite all this, the myth retains its power and dominates my fantasy life. And there are important reasons why it does.

First, what I have just described is what I would like to believe is an extreme, an exception. There are, after all, many warm, loving relationships between parent and child. In these relationships, one can recognize genuine affection and ties among members of the family, even if often the very same relationships are fraught with tensions and painful encounters.

Once, when talking with a woman about our feelings about being childless, she began to tell me about her relationship with her mother, a relationship that for years had been filled with anger and pain. But I could sense that on some level the woman had a deep attachment, felt genuine concern and responsibility toward her mother, despite the fact that the relationship remained problematic, and many painful conflicts were still unresolved. While she was describing this to me, she suddenly revealed that her mother was on welfare and was receiving $180 a month. When I asked her how her mother could possibly manage on such an absurd amount, the woman laughed and said that, of course, she helped her out financially. We continued talking more generally about the issue, but then the woman suddenly said: "You know, it scares me. Being alone, without family. I think about my mother and what she would be doing now without me. I keep trying to think of her as just a woman, like me, trying to cope with the world. But there is a difference, a major difference between us. She has a daughter."

A second reason for the myth's ability to retain its hold on my fantasy life is that I have found no adequate subtitute for it. To discard it is to be left with nothing, to be faced with the void (or so I think in my most depressed moments). I admit this with some hesitancy, because certainly one aim of the lesbian/feminist movement has been to expose the superficiality of the family myth. The movement has consciously struggled to develop new alternatives for women, has, in a certain sense, offered itself as a new and better "home," a source of the support, affection, and security that many of us seek. I think, however, that for women who at one time or another were involved in various movement activities—support groups, collectives, business projects, experimental communes—for those women who, as a result of these activities and groups, experienced the first flush of excitement in their discovery of other women and in the sharing of feelings and goals, for those women who thought that they had indeed found new and permanent homes, alternate families—for them the disappointment has been quite keen. Too often, instead of providing a new and supportive home, the collective experiments ended in frustration, bitter anger, a hard silence that severed what everyone had hoped would be permanent ties. That this occurred, is repeatedly occurring, is not surprising. Because expectations were so high, because we wanted these groups to fulfill so many divergent needs, they were destined to disappoint. For me and for many other women it was a sobering experience, to say the least.

I do not mean to imply that nothing has worked or that we are standing in the midst of ruins. What I wish to emphasize is rather the sense of disillusionment and disappointment experienced by me and by many women with whom I have spoken, a sense that has contributed to a feeling of insecurity and, to some degree, pessimism. It is when these feelings become acute that I am most vulnerable, that my fantasy returns again to the concept of family and children. The old images resurface. But the difference between envisioning them now and envisioning them years ago is that now they hold no solace, they remain empty. Their uselessness in my life creates further pain, for I am without the alternatives that a few years ago, when I first became involved in the lesbian/feminist movement, I thought I had. I find the community's present and future only vaguely delineated; whatever community exists is still very young and rather shaky. The emptiness of the past, the vagueness of the future, leave me fearful, hesitant about my decision not to have a child.

Many women have had to face a similar issue on a more personal and more immediate level. They have had to face the fact that lesbian relationships are not instantly more stable, more secure, more permanent, than heterosexual ones. And because of this, the myth of motherhood takes on added power. A woman who thought she was about to break up with her lover told me, "For the first time in a really long time, I thought about having a child. I won't do it of course. But I did think about it." She was clearly expressing the idea that somehow a child would guarantee her a permanent relationship.

The emphasis is, of course, on *guarantee* and on *permanent*. If the parent is good, so the logic of the fantasy goes, then the relationship with the child will withstand shock, change, growth, poverty, differences in temperament and ideals—in short, anything and everything. The woman who dreams this way may acknowledge that such a relationship has yet to be realized, but she may be quick to add that she has learned a great deal from her own experience as a daughter, that with *her* child, she will avoid all the mistakes that her parents made with her. By learning from their errors, the woman now fantasizes, she will establish a far more perfect, loving, supportive relationship with her child and thereby guarantee for herself a permanent connection during her lifetime.

My fantasy of being a mother and my desire to have a child have been with me for a long time. It has taken me years to realize, however, that both the fantasy and the desire were to a great degree expressions of my dissatisfaction with my relationship with my own mother. It seems clear to me now that by becoming the calm, loving, patient, supportive mother that I have so often envisioned, I have hoped to annihilate the impatient, critical voice within myself, the voice that has kept me insecure and dissatisfied. Thus my desire to become the perfect mother, to act out that fantasy, has in reality nothing to do with having a child, but rather with my desire to experience something I wish I had experienced. It is not a child I wish to mother, it is myself.

In my fantasy, of course, the understanding, the patience, the support are always outwardly directed, because the myth of motherhood demands that they be so. According to the myth, if I do not have a child I will never experience that caring, that uncritical peace, that completely understanding sensibility. Only the role of mother will allow me that. This is clearly a wrong reason for having a child—one which can be ultimately disastrous.

This kind of thinking, however, points up another aspect of the myth about having children: that certain qualities can only be expressed through a relationship with a child. I am not saying that a relationship with a child is not unique. It is. But some of the qualities that we attribute to it are not limited to child-parent relationships. I would like to discuss just one of these qualities. Women expressing a desire to have a child often explain that they want their values and beliefs to be passed on. They feel that by having a child they can have some measure of control, some input into the future. A child, after all, can be molded and influenced; to a child can be passed on a whole way of life. That parents have tremendous influence over their children is, of course, self-evident. But the myth excludes the fact that they do not have total influence over their children, that they can never exert total control. As a woman once said to me about her child who was going to a day-care center, "Oh yes, I have great influence. I send her off in the morning looking like a human being, and she comes back in the evening wearing green nail polish because green nail polish is some teacher's idea of femininity."

There is something extraordinary in the idea of being able to participate so immediately in the shaping of another life, no matter how much other factors attempt to undermine that influence. Nevertheless, it is not only through a growing child that a woman can influence the world around her, though in the interest of the traditional family, women are taught to believe that it is the most direct and most meaningful way for them. Obviously, a woman taught to think this way will think that her life, her work, are totally useless and ineffectual if she does not have a child, an heir to her ideals and values. This is another real impasse for many women who decide to remain childless. I was interested in a conversation I had with a woman who told me she was considering adopting a child. One of her main reasons was the one I have just discussed. Later in the conversation, she told me about a talk she had had with a friend. Sometime after the talk, her friend told her that she had had a tremendous impact on her, that the talk had helped her in making certain basic decisions about her life. The woman told me, "I was really stunned. I always consider conversations with friends just talk. It never occurs to me that anyone really listens to me, or that what I say has any effect on anyone."

This is not to say that for every aspect of a relationship with a child we can find a substitute, and women who decide not to have children can somehow "make up for it" by looking elsewhere. I believe a relationship with a child is as unique as a relationship with a friend or lover. Each has its own special qualities. But myths about having children do prevent women from seeing just what it is they want from having a child and from participating in such an intimate way in another life. It is something which needs closer examination, so that when a woman decides not to have children she knows what she is giving up—both the negative and positive aspects of being a mother—knows it in a real, concrete way, and not in the foggy, idealized, sticky-sentimentalized version with which we are all so familiar.

3. The Consequences

Myths and private fantasies are not the only obstacles in the way of women coming to terms with their childlessness. There are also the very real, often harsh, circumstances of living in a society where a woman who does not marry and, above all, does not have a child, is stigmatized, characterized as cold, as unwomanly and unfeminine, as unnatural in some essential way. I wince when I recall how throughout my twenties, when I was certain that I was destined to marry and to have children, I would assume with total confidence that a married woman who did not have children must either have physical problems or deep psychological ones. And I remember with some shame the freedom with which I would mouth these opinions.

Today many of us know better. But although we may understand that a woman has a right to choose to remain childless, the society in which we live still does not, and most of the time it is extremely difficult to be a woman who is deliberately not a mother. On the most immediate level, a childless woman must deal with the painful confrontations and equally painful silences between her family and herself. Let me use myself as an example. I am an only child, a survivor of World War II. My father was killed during the war, as was his whole family; my mother is the only family I have. Most of her friends are, like us, surviving members of families which were wiped out. It was an unstated aim of the individuals of this circle to regenerate the traditional family, thereby making themselves "whole." And over the years, most of them were quite successful. Some remarried; those who did not had the satisfaction of watching their children grow up and of knowing that they would take the "normal" route. Soon there were in-laws, then grandchildren. The nuclear family seemed to reassert itself.

It has been extremely difficult as well as painful for me to live with the knowledge that I deliberately never produced the child who could have continued "my father's line," that I never provided my mother with the new family and the grandchildren she was sure would appear, which she thought were her right to expect. I know that other women, coming out of different circumstances, have experienced similar difficulties and pain—women who were raised as only children, who were given the burden of providing their parents with the stereotypical props of old age. These women have complained bitterly about how their parents' disappointment in them (as if they had failed at something) has affected them. The "you're-the-last-of-the-line" argument always makes the woman who chooses not to have children appear perverse, stubborn, ungiving, selfish. Equally painful can be the excitement of parents when they inform the childless daughter of the birth of a friend's grandchild. I have heard this kind of excitement in my mother's voice, and have often resented the fact that nothing that I could achieve could elicit that tone of voice, that kind of lasting, enduring satisfaction. Her envy of her friend is clear; and underneath it, I know, lies a silent, unstated criticism of me: I have held back.

A woman who is not an only child is often relieved of this kind of burden and pressure when one of her siblings marries and gives birth. But this, too, creates its own problems; often the childless woman feels resentment and jealousy because the parents seem so pleased with the other sibling for making them grandparents. A woman once told me how her sister, who had recently given birth, said to her that she was glad she had been able to provide their mother with the pleasure of seeing her first grandchild. The mother was dying. The woman felt deeply hurt, not only because of her sister's insensitivity to her feelings, but also because she felt she had nothing comparable to offer her mother.

At moments like these, women often yearn for the perfect excuse which will relieve them of the burden of having chosen to remain childless, which will convert them back into "warm, loving women." The choice seems too great a responsibility, seems too much against the values of our society. I remember a few years ago, when I had to have surgery on my uterus, how frightened I was at the prospect of having a hysterectomy. I told the doctor that, if at all possible, I wanted to keep my ability to have children. What I did not express to anyone, and barely to myself, was that a part of me wished that in fact a hysterectomy would be necessary. By becoming sterile, I would be relieved of having to make an agonizing decision. Remaining childless would no longer be a result of my "perverseness." I would be childless because I could not bear children. What could anyone possibly say to me after I had had my hysterectomy? I have heard other women reluctantly confess similar secret thoughts, women with raised, feminist consciousness, who nevertheless find it difficult to make the decision not to have children, and also to take full responsibility for it without feeling defensive and to some degree unjustified.

In the end, I did not have a hysterectomy, and my childlessness is a result of my own decision. The process by which that decision was made is in large measure difficult for me to reconstruct. To a certain degree, I think I made it over a long period of years, during many of which, on the surface at least, I was not consciously thinking about the issue. Certainly, for a long time I thought there was no decision to be made; I was sure that I would marry and have a family. Furthermore, I never doubted my intense desire to have a large family, never stopped to question whether I really wanted this, or whether it was something I thought I should want. Looking back, I find that often, in order to appear normal to myself, I adapted attitudes and values which were clearly not my own. In this particular case the unconscious argument went as follows: A normal woman wants children; I am a normal woman; I want children. This kind of short-circuiting of real feelings is quite common with many women, women who cling to fantasies created by others. These fantasies, many women think, will keep them in the mainstream, will prevent them from appearing different or conspicuous.

I fantasized about my future family for a long, long time, though in my actual life there was nothing to indicate that I was moving in that direction, that the fantasy would become a reality. I never married, never became pregnant. Yet I continued to assume that it was simply a question of time, that of course *it* would happen. *It* did not.

At the age of thirty, I was finally able to admit to myself that I did not want to marry. That realization, however, did not resolve the question of whether or not I should have children, and so I began to think about the issue in more real, more concrete terms. Two years later I became involved with a woman, and a year later I had to have my operation. At that point I was already thirty-three, was beginning to realize that I had to make a clear decision. And I made it by doing nothing about it. I thought a good deal about children, my need for them, my intense longing for them, my fears about being without them. But I did nothing.

The long years during which I was making my decision were extremely diffi-cult. Most of the time I felt inadequate and incomplete. I was conscious that many people around me thought it was peculiar that I was not being swept away by "a normal woman's instinct" to bear and rear children, an instinct that should have overridden any of my qualms about marriage. The message communicated to me was that I—a woman alone, without a partner, without children—was enigmatic at best, superfluous at worst. In those years, I was unable to articulate to myself or to others that I was following other instincts. The best defense that I could muster was to say, "I'm too *selfish* for that life." Nevertheless, I evolved my deci-sion and stuck to it.

4. Conclusion

This past April I became thirty-six and I think it is not accidental that it was about that time I began thinking about writing this article. Though most of the time I really do not know what to make of my age, it is around the issue of having a child that my age becomes real to me. For if I do not feel thirty-six (whatever feel-ing that is supposed to be), I certainly know that biologically my body is thirty-six, that the time for bearing children is almost over for me, and that once I pass a certain point, the decision not to bear a child is irrevocable. That the decision has already been made is very clear to me, though I cannot pinpoint the exact moment when I made it. No matter what my age, the issue is closed.

Often, of course, I wish I had done *it,* done it in those unconscious years when so many women I knew were doing it. They are now mothers whose children are almost adults—eight, ten, twelve years of age. Frequently I find myself envying those mothers for having gotten it over with in those early years. That certainly seems to be the perfect solution: have the child in the past so you can have it now. Fantasizing in this way, I can easily skip over all the hardships and frustrations that many of these women have experienced in the past ten or twelve years of rais-ing their children under extremely difficult circumstances, hardships which they continue to experience, and which I can only partly understand.

Still there are moments when I can actually assert a certain amount of pride in the way I have chosen to lead my life, when I can feel extremely good about the fact that I did not succumb and did not keep myself in line. I am pleased that I withstood the pressures, that I kept my independence, that I did not give in to the myths that surrounded me. I know, of course, that there are various reasons why I did not and others did, which include conditions over which none of us had very much control. Nevertheless, I do experience momentary delight in the fact that I escaped and did what I wanted to do (even when that was somewhat unclear), that I did not give in to the temptation to please my mother, did not give in to the pleas of my father's ghost to keep him alive, did not conform with the rest of my friends, but instead kept myself apart and independent in some essen-tial way. In moments like these, I can easily take responsibility for my life and say it is the life that I have chosen.

None of this is ever very simple. There are pleasures that one gives up when one decides not to have children. But as I keep telling myself: you can't have everything. Choices have to be made, and consequences have to be lived with. The act of choosing inevitably brings loss. It is a difficult lesson to understand and accept. I keep trying to relearn it.

While writing this article I visited my mother, who had just discovered, stuck away somewhere in a closet, my favorite doll. I was surprised by my instant sadness at seeing and then holding it. The sweetness of the face, the smallness of the head against the palm of my hand. I felt as if I wanted to cry. But in touching it, it was not a baby I envisioned, but rather myself, five or six years old, cradling the doll in her arms and rocking it gently to sleep.

This Is a Question I Do Not Answer

MARY MACKEY

"You don't have children, señora? Your blood, then, is it poisoned?"

"You have no hijos? *A woman so old! Is there something wrong with your husband? Is he less than a man? When he tries to make love to you, does his chile wilt?"*

*I*t began in 1966, the summer my husband and I drove from Ann Arbor, Michigan, to Cierro de la Muerte in our old battered Plymouth Valiant so he could study hummingbird mites in the jungles of Costa Rica. We had been married less than a year and I was only twenty-one, but nearly every woman I met along the inter-American highway that summer had a baby in her arms and two small children pulling at her skirts, and all of them wanted to know where my children were.

"This is a question I do not answer," I repeated politely in Spanish. The mothers looked at me dumbstruck, as if no woman who had been given the chance would refuse to explain her childless state. Many of them threw me a look of pity and changed the subject, but one stared at me darkly and muttered: "This is not God's plan. A woman must give her husband children. You must be a bad woman. Very bad."

For the next thirty years, until I looked too old to be presumed fertile, the questions continued. The pressure on me not only to bear children and—that failing—to account for why I hadn't, never let up. And when I went on stubbornly refusing to offer an excuse (on the grounds that I was not obliged to share my private life), more than one person turned nasty.

"You," a rather well-known female poet once angrily wrote me in the early 1970s, "are obviously the abortion type, not the mother type."

"You're obviously one of those selfish, self-centered feminists," a man I had just met at a party snarled at me when I admitted I had no children.

Well-meaning mothers warned me that I was foolishly missing out on the best thing in life; friends urged me not to wait too long; distant acquaintances swore I

29

would live to regret what they assumed to be my voluntary childlessness. I even had one man describe to me in great detail the lonely old age I was going to lead without any children to care for me. According to him, after a long life of thoughtless narcissism, I would end up in a nursing home, drooling and babbling, with bed sores all over my body. "How," he asked grimly, "would I like that!" Never mind that he had walked out on his own son and daughter, never saw them, and never sent them any child support. He was absolutely certain his kids would be there for him when he was no longer able to spoon his granola into his mouth.

During the three decades when I asserted my right to remain silent, I was constantly struck by the question, "Do you have children and if not, why not?" This was a question that only women were obliged to answer under pain of being suspected of immorality and selfishness. No doubt cultures exist where the majority of people believe that a man who has not fathered a child is less than a man, but I have never seen a man backed up against a wall and lectured like someone who is suspected of harboring a secret lust to kill puppies.

I think my most insensitive interrogator was an old boyfriend I reencountered at a high school reunion. It had been nearly thirty years since we had briefly dated, grappling a bit in the back of his Chevy but never having sex. In the interim he had prospered, girthed, and fathered two children. At the reunion we nodded to each other politely, but three days after I flew back to California I received a long, bombastic letter from him in which he upbraided me for not having had children and informed me that he should have gotten me pregnant when I was seventeen. Not married me, mind you; not helped me raise these phantom children he regretted not fathering; just impregnated me like a stray tomcat so I—who had clearly put my perverse desire to be a novelist before my desire to be a mother—wouldn't have missed out on what it meant to Really Be a Woman.

For a while I toyed with sticking his letter in an envelope, slapping a stamp on it, and sending it to his wife, but I decided that, cruel as I found it, she would find it even crueler, and I had no desire to shatter any illusions she might still have about him after twenty years of marriage.

From Rita Will

RITA MAE BROWN

*N*oel Coward said of Christmas, "That terrible pall of goodwill is about to descend upon us again." I agree with this fellow Sagittarian.

New York City during Christmas jolts memory out of your pocket better than an earthquake. When I lived there the constant advertising, spectacular window displays and over-the-top decorations at Rockefeller Center inspired nausea, since I couldn't buy a damned thing.

When I could, I'd volunteer to drive a car to a southern city during Christmas. There were a lot of drive-away companies then. Someone would fly to Miami and need their car delivered. This was the only way I could go home. Baby Jesus and I would crawl down those parts of I-95 that were finished until we reached the Pink Palace, the Ixora Express, the home of skinks, parrots, palmetto bugs, and Mom.

Perhaps the monochromatic tones of Manhattan dulled my senses, but each time I visited the maternal unit that house became pinker. Finally I told Mother to tone it down—or grow bougainvillea over it.

Aunt Mimi's houses changed color like chameleons. Her first color was lemon, reflecting her tart years. Her next color was charcoal with white trim, reflecting her sophisticated years. Lastly she opted for white with aqua trim, reflecting her prudent years, since white needed repainting far less often than the other colors.

Mother complained that Sis was losing her nerve, settling for a white house. Too boring. The world should be in pink, like her, of course, or deep yellow. Then again, a pale lavender brightened up the subtropical neighborhood, and there was always that standby, lime green.

Aunt Mimi had carted her cotton-wrapped Christmas tree to Florida, horrifying Mother, who declared it a health hazard. This further provoked Aunt Mimi, who retaliated by rising above her little sister's childish pranks.

That would never do.

Perhaps they indulged in this animosity due to the welcome news that Wade was in Okinawa and not, so far, in Vietnam. What an irony that Wade should wind up on the island where his father had been pinned in a foxhole occupied by three dead Japanese soldiers. Uncle Kenny said the worst moment was when his boots smashed through the rib cage of one of the dead men. He was not one to dine out on war stories. As an adult I was beginning to understand why.

Now that neither sister could be drained by genuine worry, life could return to normal, their version.

Since Mother couldn't get a rise out of Sis over the allegedly bug-infested tree, she whipped out to the Sunrise Shopping Center to buy a new pair of glasses— wire-rimmed spectacles, the counter-culture look then in vogue among the young. Afterward she buzzed over to Aunt Mimi's to show off her purchase.

"You look like a teenager. You're too old for that," said Aunt Mimi, who favored pointy glasses with rhinestones in the corners.

"Jealous."

"Act your age."

"You know, Sis, you haven't been the same since seeing Mary Pickford in *Pollyana.*"

"What's that got to do with the price of beans?"

"You were overly influenced by the wicked aunt."

"Juts, you're soft as a grape. Now act your age and take those ridiculous glasses off."

"Pea brain." Mother twirled her purse. Since it was big enough to flatten an elephant, this was no mean feat.

I helped myself to a Coca-Cola in the refrigerator since they were warming up and Mother did not yet need my strong, silent support. As I had just arrived the night before, I figured that once they wore themselves out, Aunt Mimi might remember to ask me how I was, how my studies were progressing. I was staying at NYU for graduate school and since they were taking only one in sixty applicants, I felt grateful to be there.

No such luck.

I hadn't paid attention to exactly what they were saying so I don't know how they quickly leapfrogged from low-level sniping to all-out war. By the time I reached the living room Mother defiantly stood in the middle of the room and Aunt Mimi had retired to her favorite chair as though to a queen's throne.

"You're full of shit."

"See, that's what got Rita in trouble in the first place, your vulgar language and your refusal to take the child to the One True Church. God as my witness, I tried. I even took her to mass when you were busy."

"I didn't appreciate your giving her rosary beads." Mother dredged up an incident from when I was six.

They never forgot a damned thing.

"Why am I in trouble?" I asked like a stupid ox. I should have kept my mouth shut.

"I know of your cross to bear."

"Huh?" I squinted at Aunt Mimi.

"Shut up, Sis. You don't know jackshit."

"That is twice you have used that nasty word under my roof and during the high holy days. Juts, Juts." Sis shook her head, delighting in her moral superiority.

"You're both nuts." I sat in Uncle Mearl's chair. He was out painting houses and making a good living at it, too.

"Don't sit down," Mother commanded. "We're going home."

"I know all about it." Aunt Mimi gazed out the jalousie window as though communing with a higher power. All she needed was backlighting.

"You're all hat and no cattle," Mother bluffed.

Aunt Mimi leveled her pretty gray eyes at my brown ones. "You're a homosexual. I know everything."

"I am?"

"See?" Mother shot me one her dagger looks.

"You don't lie any better than she does." Mimi indicated her precious baby sister.

"I'm not lying. I'm not a homosexual. I have a whimsical disregard for gender." I thought that was a refined way to put it.

"That's worse. Make up your mind." Aunt Mimi pointed to a knitting needle that she had pulled out of her basket, which always sat next to her chair.

"Aunt Mimi, I'm trying to get my Ph.D."

"That doesn't prevent you from sleeping with women."

In fact, it had not, but those moments had been so few and far between and of such short duration that I hardly thought they defined my entire personality.

"You don't know anything." Mother warily moved toward me.

"Tell me the truth," Aunt Mimi demanded. "I'm the one who held you in my arms all the way back from Pittsburgh in the blizzard. You owe me the truth."

If there is one phrase I despise, it is "You owe me." However, Aunt Mimi had a point. I did owe her. You can't participate in any group of people, much less a family, if you aren't truthful. Nor can you be part of a community without incurring obligations.

"Oh, little Mary Sunshine, saving the world." Mother grimaced, edging for the door. "Come on."

I stood up. "Bye, Aunt Mimi."

"Well?"

I echoed Popeye. "I am what I am."

She took this as confirmation. "I knew it! I'll pray for you. I'll light a candle for you—"

"I'd rather you lit your hair."

Mom snatched my wrist and hauled me out of there with astonishing force for a woman past sixty.

As we rolled over the little bridge leading from Aunt Mimi's subdivision, she grumbled, "This will be a hell of a Christmas."

"Can't be any worse than the Christmas after Daddy died."

"That's the truth."

She pulled into the parking lot of the drugstore out on Route 1. "I wonder who's been running their mouth."

"Wade," I said.

"What'd you tell him?"

"I didn't tell him anything, Mom, but he visited me in New York. He's not stupid. Anyway, people have been saying that about me for years. I guess I look gay, I don't know."

"You don't look gay. Athletic, yes. I wish you'd marry and go about your business."

"I know."

"I'm going to have to live with this."

"It's better out in the open."

"No, it's not. She'll trumpet this to the whole world. Both her girls married beneath them. This is her revenge. I was determined you'd do better than Virginia and Julia Ellen."

"Mom, keep your voice down."

She purchased eyedrops then harangued me as we walked to the car.

"You don't have to tell."

"If you are that ashamed of me, I'm not coming home anymore."

She let it drop. When we walked through the door the phone rang.

"Hello." Mother listened, then stuck her tongue out. "I take it back, then. You're not a pea brain. You're a pissant."

The rest of the vacation involved various family members checking in to see if what they'd heard was true.

Meanwhile I washed the windows, reorganized the storage space in the carport, put down fertilizer for a Eureka palm Mom said she had to have, and played with Baby Jesus.

Aunt Mimi, unable to stay away, drove up the day I left to say goodbye and breathe a sigh of relief. She worried that I'd slept with Russell when I was in high school. Now she knew that wasn't true.

I was insulted. Mother laughed. Thanks, Mom.

"I know this breaks your mother's heart but in some ways it's good. There won't be any unwanted children," Aunt Mimi piously intoned.

"I didn't say it broke my heart." Mother swung her leg over the arm of her favorite upholstered rocker, the one with swan heads carved on the armrests.

"Julia, it has to. No grandchildren. No son-in-law to help every now and then."

"Help with what?"

"It's so nice to have a man around the house," Aunt Mimi sang.

"Men are a lot of work," Mother said. "Anyway, Sis, who knows what the future will bring?"

"I'll have grandchildren and great grandchildren and you'll be left all alone."

"She's got me," I said.

"What good are you in New York? You'd never walk away from your real mother," Aunt Mimi said.

Here it was again: I wasn't "one of them." Under the circumstances, it seemed a blessing. I shrugged, which irritated Mimi even more. Miffed, she declared I'd come home one day with my tail between my legs, I'd never amount to a thing. My real mother had never amounted to a thing, either, and my real father had had a great athletic career, which he had proceeded to drink away.

From *Rita Will*

Another slip of the tongue.

"Shut up, Sis."

"Alcoholism gallops in her—" She stopped. "You don't drink?"

"No, but if I lived around you I would," I said.

"That is impertinent."

"Well, honey, safe journey." Mother propelled me to the car.

They both knew who my natural father was. I had been sure of that from the moment of Aunt Mimi's slip before we left for Florida. I didn't dwell on it, though. I chose to focus on what was in front of me, not what was behind me. Whoever he was, he didn't give a fig for me, so I didn't see why I should give a fig for him.

What bothered me was their lying, that and the fact that once again Aunt Mimi had given me a slip for Christmas, something I never wore. Mother gave me freeze-dried cashews, which I loved, a pair of Levi's 505s, 28 waist, 31 leg, and socks. Since she lived in Florida, she couldn't get me a heavy sweater, which was what I needed.

And Aunt Mimi always left the price tag on the slip. You'd open the present, she'd see the dangling tag (which she had altered to make the slip seem more expensive), then she'd jump out of her chair with a "Silly me." After a great show of embarrassment, she'd remove the tag.

That bothered me.

As I ate a pickled egg Mom had packed for me and fed Baby Jesus some of her fried chicken—Mom cooked the best fried chicken in the world—I cruised along. Somewhere between Brunswick and Riceboro, Georgia, it occurred to me that those two were a novel, or a series of novels. I wanted to call it *Looney Tunes* but Warner Brothers might not like the idea.

I figured in time I'd find out what to call the book.

Old Maids

SANDRA CISNEROS

My cousins and I,
we don't marry.
We're *too old*
by Mexican standards.

And the relatives
have long suspected
we can't anymore
in white.

My cousins and I,
we're all old
maids at thirty.

Who won't
dress children,
and *never*
saints—
though
we undress them.

The aunts,
they've given up on us.
No longer nudge—*You're next.*

Instead—
What happened in your childhood?
What left you all mean teens?
Who hurt you, honey?

But we've studied
marriages too long—

Aunt Ariadne,
Tia Vashti,
Comadre Penelope,
querida Malintzín,
Señora Pumpkin Shell—

lessons that served us well.

The daughter of fur

MARGE PIERCY

Malkah my orange and lily white cat
was called the apricot shadow
the first weeks she lived under the bed.

Now sometimes I wake in the downy
armpit of night, and she is kneading
my hip and purring, purring.

She comes when I call to her.
She lets me touch her anyplace,
her belly of white peonies

her bannering tail, her sharp ears,
the tender pink roses of her pads.
Mama, she says, kneading me, Mama.

I never trusted my mother, not past
age nine or ten. I loved her with a fine
orange and blue flame, but trust?

A wry joke. Looking into her eyes,
I was schooled in lying. I graduated
cum laude. Sometimes even yet

I lie when I need not, out of habit.
Where have you been? Noplace.
Who did you speak to? No one.

She had to monitor my breasts,
she had to police my hair and lips,
my cunt hatched snapping turtles nightly.

The daughter of fur

Mother cats don't worry if kittens
are pretty or docile. They teach
them to hunt and cover their shit.

I learned to do that, rather well.
I am a suitable mother to orange cats
as I would never be to a human child.

We all come dragging flotillas
of tin cans, bones and old clothes,
but I never dream of passing them on.

The Vow

Elissa Raffa

I can point to the exact moment I decided to never have children. It is in the spring of sixth grade, the end of my second year in public school, and Mrs. Dolan is nothing like any nun or lay teacher I've ever known. She has broad shoulders and wiry black hair that leaps from her high forehead. She uses the daily newspaper as a text for our reading and writing lessons, and she listens to her students like our lives are worth something.

Mrs. Dolan never tells me I'm wrong about anything. She's the kind of woman I want to be some day: solid and smart and apparently not attached to a man. She never talks about her husband, and it takes me until April of that school year, when she finally drops some mention of him, to figure out that she is married. I am heartbroken, but I scold myself about how I should have known what "Mrs." meant. Still, she hasn't mentioned any children. That, in itself, is interesting.

It is the end of a long, hot, uneventful Friday, just minutes before the bell will send us spilling out to the line of yellow buses. For now they wait with their motors idling. The exhaust drifts in through open windows. Mrs. Dolan sits on the front edge of her desk, where she can be closer to her students. Her green cotton skirt is hiked up a little, and I can almost reach out from my first row seat to touch her knee, which is covered in nylon. She is telling us about an article that she has clipped from the *New York Times*. I feel too sleepy to listen well, so I lean back and watch the words form on her lips.

"Sociological," she says, and it looks like she is blowing smoke rings. "Report on research results."

And then in a flash I am alert to the significance of what she is saying.

"People who were abused as children grow up to abuse their own children."

She does not say "more likely" or "unless they go to therapy, unless they work very hard to do it differently." She says unequivocally "they do" and "they" means me.

Maybe Mrs. Dolan hasn't noticed the black-and-blue bruises that peek out from the cuff of my short-sleeved madras shirt. Maybe she isn't speaking directly to me. Even so, the knowledge rings through my body: *I am never having children.* I look around to make sure I haven't spoken this vow out loud.

It isn't a new thought, only a confirmation of the danger I have always felt, the dread that tightens in my twelve-year-old chest at the sight of infants in strollers.

I begrudge them their neediness. I do not want anyone dependent on me. I have always feared this makes me selfish.

Of all the adult women in my family, on both my mother's and father's side, only one, my Aunt Bea, has no children—and it's not that she *doesn't* have children, it's that she *can't*. It is a tragedy, not a choice. It is 1971 and I have never heard of abortion, yet my instinct is to refuse motherhood. Now, thanks to Mrs. Dolan, I can recast this instinct as a righteously selfless choice: No injustice will be transported beyond this point. I will use my own body as a road block.

Mrs. Dolan sets the clipping down on her desk. "Questions?" she asks. "Comments?" My classmates and I sit, suspended in awful silence, until the bell rings. "Have a good weekend," she calls after us, as if nothing has changed. But I have made a vow.

A week later, my first period comes while I am wearing white shorts and playing after school at Marcy Goldberg's house. Marcy's basement is outfitted as her very own art studio. We are making horses out of modeling clay when I feel the sticky warmth spreading through my shorts.

"I have to go," I tell Marcy. She wants to know if she should bake my horse in the kiln, but I am up the stairs and out into the blasting afternoon sun. I run the quarter mile home, strip off my blood-stained shorts and underpants, and help myself to a Modess pad and elastic belt from the box my sisters keep in the hall closet.

It is unusual that no one is home. My sister Angela, back from college for the summer, has taken my mother out shopping. I pace the house, trying to adjust to the strange lump between my legs. My mother and sister come in with shopping bags and lay out their purchases on my mother's bed. I watch them from the doorway to her room.

"I got my period," I announce.

"How did you know about that?" my mother asks, as if the fact that she has never bothered to tell me anything could stem the tide of my sexual development.

I run into the bathroom and slam the door. I open it and slam it, open it and slam it, so that the mirrors rattle on the wall. I hate my mother. I hate her.

"Open up," Angela says.

I open the door a crack. She pushes her way in, and slams the door behind her. Then she hoists herself onto the long pink Formica counter and grabs hold of my shoulders.

"Don't listen to Mommy," she says. "She's crazy. She's too freaked out to talk about body stuff. Talk to me."

My sister shows me how to rinse my bloody clothes in cold water. She gives me her own copy of *Our Bodies, Ourselves*. She intends for me to read about pregnancy and birth control, but every night in bed, before I fall asleep, I read the chapter, "In Amerika They Call Us Dykes." My mother and I never discuss my period again. She never tells me that now I can be a mother. She has borne four daughters, and it is not a job she would recommend.

This is my body. The words from the Mass become my mantra. They separate me from the blows that fall on me, and from the huge man named Daddy who delivers the blows. *This is my body. Mine.* At six, I improvise a hunger strike. For days, maybe weeks, I refuse to eat anything but white grapes and saltine crackers. My father's fury grows, but I have found new power: I can control what goes into my body. *This is my body, not his. And I am never having children.*

My mother is sick with multiple sclerosis, and I am the youngest daughter. At fourteen, I am old enough to cook and clean, but not old enough to escape like my sisters did to college, a job, or an efficiency apartment. Every afternoon, I come straight home from school so my mother won't be alone when her attendant leaves at two o'clock. Every night I cook for my parents: rigatoni with meatballs, or meatloaf, or lamb chops and escarole. Always a mixed green salad with olive oil and wine vinegar. Everything seasoned with a large dose of resentment.

I think my mother should be cooking. Not because I am an ungrateful troublemaker as my father would have it, but because she can. I want her to stay engaged, to hold on to the abilities she has, to fight isolation and not give up. But she has my father talking in her other ear, telling her that she is already useless. He orders her physical therapist and occupational therapist out of our house, even though insurance will pay for their weekly visits. He doesn't want these women, these strangers, meddling in how he runs his home.

My mother is depressed as well as disabled. She has withdrawn from her life; she has no opinions about anything, not even what she eats or watches on TV. I set two ultimatums: First, I will cook, but I will not think about what to cook. She will have to create the menus. Second, I am a vegetarian. I will cook meat; I will squeeze fatty ground beef between my fingers, mixing in the right condiments and molding it into meatballs or American-style meatloaf, but I will not sit down with them and eat it. I exaggerate my role as a servant, putting dinner on the table, and then retreating into my bedroom with a provolone sandwich. On nights when my father works late, I eat my cheese sandwich at the table with my mother, and leave his dinner in covered pots on the stove.

On nights that he is home, when I slam his plate down in front of him, my father says, "You'll make somebody a good wife some day."

"I'm not getting married." My answer never varies.

"Sure you will, some day, after college."

"Never," I contradict him. "I'm never getting married."

"Don't say that." He frowns with exaggerated sadness. "A woman needs to get married and have children." A common enough belief among Italian men, but he speaks with the added authority of his medical school training. "A woman is not a woman until she has brought forth a child from her womb. It is a woman's highest duty to bear children. It is her biological function. That is why she has a uterus."

"What is *your* biological function," I ask him, "To get women pregnant?"

My mother begs me to stop talking like this. So disrespectful. But I know his answer. His highest duty is to use his superior brain. Mine is to pass his superior intellect on to a male child.

•

I want to use my own brain. I want to think and write, talk and laugh, argue about politics. I want to be generous and have many friends. But I want no one to need me: no husband, child, or parent. I fantasize about living alone in a small house at the edge of a small town. There are fields and woods nearby, and I can write at home and walk every day to the post office. I imagine living with dogs and cats, and many friends coming and going at all hours of the day and night. But I can always say goodbye, lock the door, and be alone.

At thirty-three, my life in Minneapolis fits fairly well with my teenage fantasy. My little white house looks like a farmhouse, in spite of the cheap asbestos siding. I live alone on the first floor; a friend rents the upstairs apartment. We don't live in the country, but the kitchen is outfitted with 1940s farmhouse appliances and the empty lot next door has become a community garden for the neighbors on the block. I can walk to the post office, to a beautiful urban park, to my lover's house, or to visit my friends. In the morning, I go to work as a teacher; in the evening, I do my writing at home. Many people do come and go, and many political meetings happen around my kitchen table. I am happy to cook rigatoni with mushroom sauce for my friends; to welcome my lover into my bed; to say goodbye, lock the door, and be alone sometimes. I am happy that no one—not even a dog or cat—depends on me for dinner every night. Most of the time, I remember to water the plants.

Once every year or two, on my visits to New York, my father corners me with unsound, unsolicited medical advice.

"Get your hormones rebalanced," he tells me, "You don't have to be a lesbian forever."

"You don't know what the fuck you're talking about." I yell at him for my own sake but also for the sake of the lesbian patients he might have burdened with such a suggestion. Has he actually prescribed hormone treatments as a cure for lesbianism? I am too afraid to ask.

When he sees I mean business, he changes his tune. "You should look into artificial insemination," he says. "You don't have to be childless forever." In his book, it is worse for a woman to have no children than to raise a child without a father.

Since the early 1980s I have witnessed every possible method of lesbians achieving pregnancy: with frozen and fresh sperm; from known and unknown donors; delivered by doctors, midwives, friends who are go-betweens, or sometimes by the donor himself, in a jar wrapped in a brown paper bag, or even by fucking. I sat in on the early discussions about lesbians seizing our reproductive capacity as a revolutionary act, and on more recent discussions about lesbian motherhood as an antirevolutionary waste of time. I have watched lesbians who have been out to their parents for ten or fifteen years agonize over how to break the news that now they are pregnant.

Even my friend Barbara, whose parents are pro-choice activists, must prepare herself for a fight: a child needs a father; how can you choose to burden a child like this; you're being selfish; you can't have it both ways. After a while her parents will adjust to the idea, come to visit, and bounce a happy grandson on their knee.

No one but me has a father who actually pushes artificial insemination. "Many single women are choosing AI," he instructs me.

"I'm sure they are, but I'm not interested in motherhood. And it's my uterus." *Mine.*

"Of course it's your uterus. Who said it wasn't?"

"I'm saying it's none of your business how I use it."

I never tell him that I have already offered to have AI and give the baby to my sister Angela.

It's a deal that never comes through, but it is one I am willing to make out of love for my sister. Angela had cancer when she was twenty-eight, a vaginal tumor caused by my mother taking DES, and all the radiation and surgery has messed up her reproductive system.

At twenty-three, I fly to New York for my grandmother's ninety-fifth birthday party.

"Come here," Angela says and pulls me into the bathroom, still our refuge in our parents' house. We used to spend hours together in this pink and brown tiled room. She'd comfort me when I cried. I'd hang out to watch her straighten her hair around beer can curlers and put on white eye shadow. Today her hair and eye makeup are fine; she has dragged me in here to proposition me.

She wants kids really bad and she's checking out her options. She doesn't want to bullshit about her ability to raise a kid of color; she wants a white kid, and adoptions take forever. She's looking into direct adoption, and she's approaching both me and our cousin who already has kids about having a baby for her. Would I?

"Sure," I say on the spur of the moment. Although I have never wanted to raise a child, my first response to the idea of pregnancy is pretty neutral. I do feel squeamish at the thought of Angela's husband Ron being the sperm donor, at her whole emphasis on making a baby as genetically like them as possible. I don't challenge her on the white baby issue: at least she can admit what a cultural vacuum she lives in. This is before Baby M and the media debates about surrogacy. We don't talk details. We don't talk about what if I went through the pregnancy and couldn't bear to part with the child, probably because neither of us can imagine me acting that way. We also don't talk about how will we tell the child. Or what might happen if we differ about whether to tell the child.

Our conversation in the bathroom is the closest I ever come to getting pregnant. Within a few months, Angela and Ron have arranged a direct adoption. They have a daughter, and I am off the hook.

Which doesn't mean that my uterus ceases to be a topic of conversation. I visit New York less and less frequently, but I hear reports from my old best friend, Jacob.

Jacob and I were inseparable throughout junior high and high school and, ever since I moved to the Midwest, his social life has revolved around two of my sisters.

He's Jewish, always available on Catholic holidays, always invited to holiday dinners at my parents' house. My mother's fifth daughter, we call him. Or my replacement.

Everyone knows that Jacob is gay, everyone acts like they've never heard of HIV, and they've all picked him out as my sperm donor.

"You should have heard them," he tells me after Easter dinner one year. "Your father, your sisters. All about how you should have a baby and how I should provide the sperm."

The older my sisters get, the more curious they become about my reproductive capacity—something they wouldn't think twice about if theirs were working well. But all three of them have struggled with different reproductive health problems and I, being the youngest, am the most likely to have escaped exposure to DES. My mother's obstetrician closed his office years ago and shredded the files. We can't prove that she didn't take the drug while she carried me. But everyone assumes that I could get pregnant on the first try. They imagine that I am letting a precious resource go to waste.

I don't tell Jacob that they're probably wrong. While he was out learning about gay sex, and before I even knew how to find lesbians, I was experimenting with hetero sex in the cramped backseats of cars. Three or four times a week for all of eleventh grade I took the risk of fucking with no birth control, and although I worried a lot, I never got pregnant.

I do tell Jacob to quit repeating my family's comments to me. "I purposely don't visit," I remind him. "Why would I want to hear their crap through you? Besides, you should have told them your sperm is promised elsewhere."

It is promised to Barbara, my best friend in Minneapolis.

"He's cute," she whispers the first time she meets him, "And Jewish. Do you think he would be a sperm donor?"

"Ask him," I encourage her.

The weather is sweltering, and we seek relief by going to the longest movies we can find. We watch *Fannie and Alexander* and *Gandhi* in air-conditioned comfort, in the middle of the day, when they're cheap. When we run out of movies, we hang out at the science museum in the hands-on technology exhibit. We play with the robot arm, and the whisper dishes—two parabolic reflectors that make it possible to hear someone speaking in hushed tones from all the way across the museum.

In the whisper dishes, Barbara propositions Jacob. He says he'll think about it.

The next time he visits Minneapolis is three years later. Barbara has a lover, a house, a job. She is ready to have a baby.

"Do you think he's still willing?" she wants to know.

"Ask him," I say.

He is willing, even to be HIV tested—something he has resisted all along on political grounds. They get together to talk schedules and contracts. She'll buy him an airline ticket for the two or three days around her September ovulation. He'll be unemployed and free to travel by then. They negotiate his level of involvement with the child: how many visits per year, how long each visit can be.

I think maybe I have made a mistake. What if Jacob takes Barbara to court for custody and it's my fault for introducing them? Not likely. I know these friends; I know they can both be counted on. Then what if I change my mind about not having children? What if I am letting a precious resource swim away? Maybe I should be negotiating these things with Jacob.

It isn't that I want children, it's just that every once in a while I reconsider my vow. In the years since I left my parents' house, I have learned to stop panicking at the sight of infants. When Barbara's son Ben is born, I practice holding him close to my chest. I learn to appreciate his helplessness and how he changes by leaps and bounds, to believe that it is possible to interpret and satisfy his needs. I have gone from saying never to probably not to maybe. After all, this is my body. My choice. Will I ever decide yes? Probably not.

What would have to be true before you would be ready to have a baby—or another baby, if you are already a mother? It is a writing assignment I give my high school women's studies class every year. Some of my students are mothers; some already have their second child. Most of them are thousands of times more likely to get pregnant than I am. Still, I always do the assignment.

I would have to be willing to spend one-third of my income on day care. I would have to be willing to raise a son. I would have to be willing to put my writing and political activism on hold for a few years. I would have to change my habit of doing a million things in one day from six A.M. to midnight. I would lose the freedom to say yes to anything that comes my way. At thirty-three, I amend my vow.

I vow to never have children, not out of fear, but in freedom. I have enough time to be a good auntie to Ben, and to my sister's two girls—although it is harder from a distance of twelve hundred miles. I have enough time to offer my phone as the referral number for a Young Lesbians and Friends group, to take calls from sixteen- and seventeen-year-old women who have never talked to a "gay woman" before. I have enough time to use my brain and my big mouth, to make trouble as a teacher, in local politics, wherever I can. I have a spare room in my house, which I can offer to friends in crisis who need a temporary place to stay. And I have enough money to keep the room empty and unheated when the crisis is past and I really want to be alone.

"You'll be lonely when you're old, if you don't have children," my father warns me.

He is frail now, and fifty pounds thinner since a stroke ripped through his left side. His thick black hair has all turned to white. He is still cruel to my mother, but I refrain from being cruel to him. I don't say: *Look at you. You had four children, and not one of us will be taking care of you.* But it is true. We all do our best to avoid him.

As far as I know, he has never had a friend in his life, except maybe the man who owned the Italian pastry shop around the corner from his office. Except for his daily cup of espresso with the other old men there, I never saw him socialize with anyone. Except for his accountant and lawyer, he never invited anyone to our house. When he was my age, a young father, he was lonely. But he worries about me becoming a barren old maid.

"Listen," I tell him, "I'm never having children. And that's not the end of what's interesting about my life; it's the beginning."

He doesn't ask me what I mean.

Tie Me Up, Tie Me Off

Jodi Sh. Doff

*B*iologically speaking, I'm a breeder. That's what the gynecologist said. Except he phrased it a little differently. I believe his exact words were, "You're a lucky one. With those hips, you can drop one a year." I was fifteen years old and dropping one a year wasn't part of the five-year plan. In fact, it wasn't part of the any-year plan. I got myself on the Pill—and quick.

Unfortunately, Doctor Demento was right. I am a breeder. Over the next fifteen years, I was pregnant five times. In those days there was no such thing as the mini-Pill—they packed you so full of hormones that your breasts plumped up like Ball Park Franks just to make room for all that extra estrogen. A nice consolation prize, but all those synthetic hormones were no match for my own. I got pregnant twice. All the Pill did for me was save me the expense of a clinical abortion. I held on to them each only up a month or so, and then literally tossed the baby out with the bath water. Still, it was too close for comfort for me. I needed to find something safer and more effective.

Doctors had a policy about IUDs at the time. They wouldn't give you one unless you'd already had a baby or an abortion. Sort of closing the barn door after the baby's already in the bassinet isn't it? But, I'm a good talker and I had those lovely wide hips and all, so . . . I tried two different styles of that tiny piece of plastic, my favorite being the one shaped like the astrological symbol for Aries. Not my sign, but I was young and it felt sorta spiritual. It was, and the spirits declared me a breeder. I got pregnant two more times. Once for each style of IUD. Again, I held on to each for about a month and then spontaneously aborted (an innocuous, clinical term meant to sound simpler and less painful—emotionally, physically, and psychically—than the word miscarriage: it's not).

Back to the Pill, the New Improved version, which seemed to work (or maybe I just wasn't getting it as often). I had those fabulous big plump boobs back and was a happy little bedhopper until they came out with all those damned studies. The ones that said the Pill caused cancer (which runs in my family). That it's worse if you're a smoker (which I was). That you had to get off it every coupla years or when you finally had a baby, it would be born with three heads. You remember those studies.

So once again I found myself looking for an answer and wishing I could just fall for guys who were sterile. Anyway, two weeks after getting off the hybrid

48

hormone train, I wind up pregnant again. Did I forget to mention that the Pill acts as a fertility drug for the first few weeks after you go off of it? Where do you think all those quadruplets came from? So I'm pregnant, and this one doesn't look like it's going to leave quietly and of it's own accord like the other four, even though I gave it every reason to want to leave. Not wanting to get an abortion (and that was a strictly financial decision), I headed downtown and copped a blood-thinning brew, illegal in the States, but this was Chinatown, where nothing is impossible if you know the right pharmacist. Within a week the blood was flowing like, well, like blood. Unfortunately, it was coming from every orifice other than the right one. My nose, mouth, rectum, everything but my pootie. I'm a breeder, remember? My body didn't want to give this one up.

Well, biologically I may have been a breeder and psychically I was (and still am) a caretaker, but emotionally and spiritually I was a mess. There was no way I could take care of a baby. I couldn't even take care of myself. For Chrissakes, the next morning I couldn't even remember the name of the guy who got me pregnant, where he lived, or where we met. I debated the possibilities for about an hour and then it was off to see the Wizard. But I had so much Chinese Hot Sauce in me, the Wizard sent me home for two weeks to detoxify, afraid I'd bleed to death on his table. Probably right; at that point, every time I sneezed, I sneezed blood. So I had two more weeks to decide if I was doing the right thing.

I keep hearing women talk about the agonizing decision to abort. Not for me. I love kids. I really do. I used to be a kid. And I think they deserve the best the world has to offer—every chance, every opportunity, a house full of love, toys, curiosity, and patience. My house (and I mean this in the most esoteric sense) was full of shit. And hypodermic needles, coke spoons, faceless guys crashed out on the couch, violence, and empty bottles of whatever wine happened to be on sale. I don't think kids deserve that. And that's not the kind of stuff you can change overnight just because you find out you're pregnant—again. Sure, you can clean up the stuff and toss the guy out into the street and swear you'll never get high again and maybe you won't, but probably you will, and if you can't even remember where you slept last night how're you gonna remember to feed and clothe and care for a tiny baby?

I opted for the abortion. As much for the baby's sake as for my own. I dragged my mother along with me. She cried a little, over the grandchild she wasn't going to get to love and spoil, but in the end she agreed with me. I wasn't fit to be a mother. I was barely fit to be a daughter!

I needed to make sure this situation never came up again. What if next time the decision wasn't so clear? Time marched on and I found myself looking at mothers and babies in a different way than when I was younger, something more tender and maternal. Maybe next time—and ya know with these hips there was definitely going to be a next time—I wouldn't be thinking so clearly and I'd keep it. What then? Then I'd have beautiful baby of my own, right? Probably not.

Probably, if it was born alive at all, it would have fetal alcohol syndrome. Probably it'd be way underweight, early, and sickly. Probably retarded. It's one thing to pump all this booze, drugs, and nicotine into an adult body, but babies and especially fetuses, they need gentler care to have a fighting chance. And I knew, deep in my heart, in the place where the truth resides and can't be denied, I knew that I was capable of losing my temper and hurting a baby. As horrifying as it was, I knew I could pick up a crying child, on a day when I was hungover or sleep-deprived or just generally miserable with myself, I knew I could pick that baby up and send it flying against the wall.

And that was the clincher. I wanted to make sure I was never given the opportunity to hurt a child. So for my thirtieth birthday I got a tubal ligation. My doctor fought me—I was too young, he said. I fought back—my money, my body, my future, my decision, I said. This time, both my parents came and waited downstairs. This time my mom cried a lot for the all grandchildren she would never have. Upstairs, waiting to go in and have my fallopian tubes permanently sealed and cauterized, I ranted, raved, and cried. Screaming at my parents over the courtesy phone for having the audacity to call upstairs and see how I was, screaming at my doctor face to face for even answering the phone and daring to give them any information at all. He must've thought I was insane, and I probably was at the moment. But after a few minutes in a small room with me and my temper, he stopped fighting and began to see the truth. I wasn't fit to be a mother.

My oldest friend at the time wouldn't come with me. She didn't talk to me for months afterwards. I'd betrayed her. She wanted children. She loved kids and was horrified that I had closed off that avenue of possibility for myself forever. She didn't understand then, I don't know if she even gets it now, I did it *because* I love children, *because* I knew that I was capable of hurting a child. I couldn't control my temper, but I could control my ovaries, so I made the only possible decision. Not out of selfishness, but out of love. For all children. No one deserves to come into a violent household, and since I didn't know how to stop the violence, I did the next best thing. I stopped the babies.

It's been nine years since the operation. Ten or twelve since the abortion. I don't drink or do drugs anymore. I know where I slept last night and with whom. I never think about how old my son or daughter would have been if I had had him or her. I never think about the others, the ones that slipped away quietly like thieves in the night. I don't think about adopting a child someday. I don't think about being a mother at all.

I get a little jealous when I see my friends with their new babies, or strangers on the street with happy little kids. I stop and lecture strangers who let their kids run around —wandering this way and that—so anybody could just come by and scoop the kid away. And I generally prefer the company of kids to that of grownups.

I get a little sad sometimes, too. For what I won't ever have, for the things I'll never know about loving a child. And I still know that I made the right decision. I'm sorry my life led me to the point of degradation and misery that it had to be made, but I'm never sorry I made it.

Minor Surgery

HETTIE JONES

*M*rs. Thompson had hold of her middle daughter's feet, which were cold. She moved closer, hugging them to her side, and managed to tuck one under her left arm. But when she put her two warm hands around the other it felt so familiar she was momentarily suprised, as though having unexpectedly come upon another, naked limb of her own. Even the texture of the skin was so like. She turned and stared as if to corroborate what touch had told her, but looking at it then, encountered his foot, saw once more the shape and arch of the father of the child.

Briefly but as always she gave in to memory, and her mind leapt with images that would put him at this event. Mrs. Thompson saw them all in an instant and made them fade just as fast. She went back to rubbing the feet she loved—which became once again themselves, as the child was inevitably not either parent but her own self—and turned her attention once more to Mrs. Weinberg, the pleasant-faced, fiftyish nurse at the front of the room.

"Look, we're all human," Mrs. Weinberg was saying matter-of-factly, in the middle of her lecture on birth control. "But we're also all different, and it's up to you to find the method you can live with, and stick to that."

The girl in the next bed was staring in a bored way at the ceiling. Her boyfriend reclined beside her, caressing her thigh. She raised a hand.

"Yes?" said Mrs. Weinberg.

"How long before I can get another IUD?"

Mrs. Thompson resisted the sympathetic, bitter laugh that rose in her throat. If the one the girl already had hadn't prevented her pregnancy, perhaps a different one might. It had happened before. But clearly she was sticking to the one method she could live with, even if it hadn't worked.

"How many other people here got pregnant through birth control?" Mrs. Weinberg asked without preamble.

Mrs. Thompson's daughter raised her hand. "Diaphragm," she said with a rueful little smile, then lay back, looking tired and only half avoiding her mother's worried frown. Several weeks before, when they had first discussed the problem, and Mrs. Thompson's company had been requested for this trip, she had said, offhandedly, "When people get pregnant with a diaphragm it's usually from not using it." But her middle daughter's eyes had turned angry and she had scoffed, "Are you kidding? I'm not *like* that." And Mrs. Thompson had dropped the subject with another offhand response, a shrug, because she knew that she herself had been, at one time, like that, incautious, hating it so.

Another of her daughters had admitted to it. Said, self-deprecating and disgusted, "But I only fucked up *once.*"

"Once is all it takes." But she had been reminded, not accused, and thinking of it Mrs. Thompson bit her lip in rage and sorrow now, recalling that one collapsed asleep in a public park, waiting, waiting for it to be over and done with.

But this one was to be fast. Except the doctor—who else?—was late. Mrs. Weinberg was using the time to run a group, Mrs. Thompson could see, and she was good at it. Exuding good humor and reassurance, she had produced a cup of coffee for Mrs. Thompson, and had her patients undressed and in bed in a matter of minutes. They were all now drinking orange juice, and on a first-name basis.

"Yuriko, were you using any birth control when you got pregnant?" Mrs. Weinberg asked, speaking slowly and raising her voice a bit in the hope of making herself understood. The Japanese woman to whom the question had been addressed sat up in bed saying "Pardon? Pardon? I don't understand," but smiling pleasantly. A mother of two, in her thirties, she was apparently unworried. After a few more tries Mrs. Weinberg gave up the question, as she had several others, and made a note to ask this also of Yuriko's husband, who spoke English but had declined to sit in the hospital room where now four patients lay, in a row in their snap-at-the-back gowns, awaiting, on this bright May Thursday, that which was called, in what Mrs. Thompson saw as a typically ironic euphemism, "Minor Surgery."

Mrs. Thompson's middle daughter's feet were, she knew, too cold for comfort. At last it occurred to her that she could remove her own socks and place them on the feet of her daughter. She bent to untie her sneaker, disgusted with herself for not having thought of this sooner, and thinking again, "Minor Surgery."

Her daughter had used the term earlier when Mrs. Weinberg approached them in the waiting room, where they sat huddled together sleepily, the first arrivals. The patient was supposed to have a light breakfast, so after rising at dawn and driving to the hospital they had gone to a local store and then eaten in the car, and then, not quite sure of where they were supposed to be, had come up ahead of time. Mrs. Weinberg had looked from one to the other and Mrs. Thompson's daughter had spoken first. "Thompson, for minor surgery," she had said.

But the authority in the young woman's tone (which was all Mrs. Thompson really heard as it gave her such pleasure), did not take away the remaining question from Mrs. Weinberg's gaze, which returned to Mrs. Thompson and rested there. "And this is my mother," her daughter said, seeing, and on top of, the problem.

Mrs. Weinberg's welcoming smile broadened. "Oh, I was wondering, I didn't—" Mrs. Thompson interrupted her with a patient cold smile that she had learned how to use to deal with other people's confusion when confronted with herself plus child or children, who were all different shades.

But Mrs. Weinberg, to Mrs. Thompson's interest and relief, didn't like some, succumb to embarrassment and fumble around to cover it up. "I can't tell you how much it means to me to see a mother here with her daughter," she said, showing them into the then empty room.

Now her words, as she repeated this sentiment, caught Mrs. Thompson with a sock in her hand. "It's still uncommon, even though everything's legal, to see a mother with her child. Here anyway," Mrs. Weinberg said, this time for the benefit of the other three patients and to extend the range of the discussion, which was floundering.

Mrs. Thompson looked up to find all eyes on her, expectantly. But she thought seeming unusual or heroic might divert too much attention to herself, and she suspected this might embarrass her middle daughter, of whom she was exceedingly fond. So she said, with a smile, "Well, thank goodness things are different than they used to be, we're at least *here*," and turned to her daughter's bare foot.

There was then a sudden and prolonged rapping at the door and Mrs. Thompson watched the patients all relax into their pillows, relieved to be resting silently and ignored for a moment, as plump and efficient Mrs. Weinberg bustled to deal with the interruption, which proved to be a young couple for whom there was no bed. Again Mrs. Thompson had a chance to admire not only Mrs. Weinberg's intelligent and calm cheerfulness, but her resourcefulness as well, for she soon had the new arrival gowned and ensconced in a large overstuffed chair. Crowded in with this girl was her lover. They snuggled down, making an easy adjustment, wriggling and giggling until they had it all right, whence they appeared, to Mrs. Thompson's concern, like a pair of pretty doll babies put out for display. "I know that girl," her daughter said sotto voce, and as she raised her other foot to be clad she wiggled her toes at her mother. Well, misery loves company, Mrs. Thompson thought, and then chastised herself mentally for the sarcasm when after all that was nothing but true. And in this instance particularly, the usual words of comfort consisted in naming who else it had happened to.

Mrs. Weinberg obviously had similar thoughts and still intended to discourse on them after the arrival of the new couple, whom she was now introducing. "And this is *Mrs.* Thompson," she said beaming, and then not quite repeating herself, said: "It's a wonderful thing to see a mother here with her daughter. That's hardly ever so, and I hope it's a trend."

Mrs. Thompson looked up. "I like seeing the men," she said, and then half regretted the remark because she wasn't sure she actually did. This hadn't anything to do with her daughter's friend, who though not with them was aware and concerned. But she had wanted in some way to include the two present, who seemed at once loving and attentive as well as embarrassed and uncomfortable and guilty and still vaguely extraneous despite everything, which of course made each one defensively sexy. She felt unexpected pity for them, and generosity, and pleasure when both smiled at her remark.

Still the presence or absence of a man among all those here increased some ambivalence Mrs. Thompson could not help feeling. She looked at the lone young woman in the bed near the window, who had a book she read from time to time. At the foot of her bed was the chair with the beautiful children entwined in it. Mrs. Thompson saw the set of the lone girl's face, and thought of herself. Had she too appeared that way once, that first time, so quietly unwavering, so outwardly unaffected and calm? But no, that couldn't have been, for though it was only the sight of his face she could remember, the pull and taste of tears came back to her, as still in her mind he sat, young, thin, and forlorn, his familiar cropped head bent, in the bus terminal, occasionally lifting his eyes to the window, as if hoping that at the last minute she'd get off.

Mrs. Thompson rested her cheek against her daughter's feet, dispelling the image. Mrs. Weinberg was looking at her. "It's a question of choice and timing," the nurse said, and by thus hovering on the edge of rhetoric brought Mrs. Thompson squarely to the present. "Too often we don't see the long run," she said. "The decision to *have* a baby will also probably come up." She nodded toward Yuriko, to Mrs. Thompson, and then informed them in a satisfied—though not smug—way, that although she firmly believed in abortion she'd had four children herself. One was a nurse at this very hospital, she revealed, adding happily, " And I expect my ninth grandchild next week."

There was a murmur of appreciation around the room—nine!—as if this albeit casual association with such fecundity alleviated the negativism in the air. Mrs. Thompson, who was not thinking of grandchildren, grinned.

"This is not to say you're not making an important decision," Mrs. Weinberg cautioned. "Or that you may not experience certain feelings of loss. But of course part of that is physical. . . ." She went on, explaining.

Mrs. Thompson stared at the floor between her now bare ankles and tried to focus on a square of linoleum tile. But only he was there again, outside the dirty bus, and they were twenty-two years old. And then with great tenderness, as though touching the petal of a rose long pressed, she remembered how he had taken her home, to his family doctor, for the swollen, leaking breasts, the bloated belly had taken her by surprise.

And then she had gone to Pennsylvania, because the freedom so recently gained she could not relinquish, though he thought only that she would not have his child. She glanced across at the lone girl, who lay reserved and patient, her fingers holding her place in the book. In Pennsylvania, Mrs. Thompson remembered, there had been shock and concern on the part of whoever had asked the questions. "No one with you? You've come alone?" Some part of the willfulness that others took for courage now rose up in her and flew across the room. She wanted to seize the lone girl by the shoulders, hold her in her arms. But others have done that, Mrs. Thompson thought, lapsing into her own rhetoric, think of all the women who marched, and testified, and died. The Pennsylvania doctor's daughter had died, she remembered. Or so the story went. Suddenly every event of that time came flooding like a river from her memory: the night-before pills, the hotel with its Gideon Bible, a phone call—what had they said?—panic before the needle, gutfire, drugged sleep, grief.

"Marmie!" Mrs. Thompson's middle daughter suddenly whispered. "Mami! Dame jugo! Ah mant chuice!" It was a joke between them.

Mrs. Thompson patted her daughter's leg and reached for the container on the Formica bed table. Mrs. Weinberg had gone to the doorway and was conferring there with someone unseen in the corridor.

"Did you ever have an abortion?" the girl in the next bed demanded suddenly, addressing Mrs. Thompson in an accusing, petulant way. Her boyfriend stared, interested and hostile. Demanding acknowledgment of the sins of the fathers, Mrs. Thompson thought briefly and inaccurately, with a quick, hesitant glance at her middle daughter, as if for permission to speak. But that one's eyes were also amused and waiting. *I know* you didn't abort *me,* she seemed to be saying.

"Well, yes," said Mrs. Thompson, and then searched her mind for some story they could appreciate. "I went once to this famous doctor," she said. "He was kind and charged very little, twenty-five dollars I think, but he had to practice way out in rural Pennsylvania where the authorities wouldn't find him. Or maybe that was the only place where he could afford to pay them off sometimes," she added, speculating, "because he spent a lot of time in jail."

"But anyway, it was a small town with only one main street, and right behind that the mountains, sharp and sudden and dark." Mrs. Thompson, gesturing, drew the mountains in the air. A lonely, forbidding place, she thought. Why was I not frightened? "But as I was waiting for the bus to go home," she continued the story, "a car drove toward me, and slowed down, and it was full of guys—" Mrs. Thompson flashed an amused glance at the young man. "—and one of them leaned out the window and yelled at me, he yelled, 'Oh you must have been a BAAAADDDDDDDD GIRL!'"

So when Mrs. Weinberg rejoined them they were all laughing. As though she had told them a tale of the gold rush, Mrs. Thompson thought. As though it had been that long ago. And why should they not think those times distant, she reflected, as Mrs. Weinberg repeated a few points about the "procedure" they would soon undergo. Why should they not think barbaric and untenable such moral hypocrisy and the danger in it. To say nothing of the pain, of course, she reminded herself, that void surrounded by circumstance. The core of it somehow, yet also, and mercifully, unrecollectible.

She was still thinking of this when a few moments later Mrs. Weinberg's daughter poked her head in the door, and after graciously acknowledging her mother's introductions, informed them that the doctor had at last arrived. He would be with them shortly, she said, so the first patient could now come in and get ready.

"Your companion may come with you, if you wish," Mrs. Weinberg announced to the room, while looking straight at the Thompsons.

Mrs. Thompson, unprepared, turned to her middle daughter with the question. For answer she got a wrinkled nose and an almost apologetic, negative shake of the head. And so it was settled. Mrs. Thompson preferred to let children lead their lives. She would go down to check the car, she told her daughter, since the meter where they'd parked was broken, and get the rest of the breakfast they had left. So she watched as Mrs. Weinberg and Mrs. Weinberg's daughter led away her daughter, the red and green striped socks jaunty and incongruous below the hospital gown. And then after some difficulty finding the elevator, she got to the street.

The sun had warmed the car and the food in its paper bag looked soggy, but Mrs. Thompson took it anyway and was about to go back inside when she noticed a traffic cop and went to explain about the meter. They had a friendly conversation, though not a long one, and so she was taken aback when she reached the hospital room and found her daughter already returned to bed. Mrs. Thompson threw down the paper bag and bent to embrace her, and only then, stepping back, saw the pain.

"Oh it wasn't bad," her daughter said mildly from the middle of a bloodless, disillusioned face. "It was over quicker than I expected and I thought it would hurt much worse." Then she closed her eyes.

Mrs. Thompson's heart contracted and she tried to put what she felt into the squeeze she gave he middle daughter's hand. But though the pressure was returned, she knew her sympathy wouldn't lessen anything.

Meanwhile the next girl had had her turn and was carefully helped back to bed. Her boyfriend had been with her, but now he too went to see about his car. "You said it didn't hurt you?" the girl asked of Mrs. Thompson's daughter. "It hurt me a lot."

Her voice was small, as though all the arrogance had been sucked out of her. Along with her uterine lining, Mrs. Thompson thought, and her IUD. Sitting amid all this pain she tried not to move much, and spoke quietly to the girl of home remedies, herbal teas, and the like, that might relax her when she got home.

"It was worse than I expected," the girl said reproachfully, with some of the tense anger that seemed to be part of her nature. "It really hurt," she said, and turned away.

"Well, yes," said Mrs. Thompson, who heard the hollow sound of her own voice accepting another generation's blame. She too looked away, but only to see Yuriko being brought in, accompanied by her cheerful, apple-cheeked husband, who stayed to see her in bed and then left again. Yuriko's arms lay like long pale columns outside the covering sheet, and she was staring at the wall.

The lone girl was out in surgery, the couple in their chair were silently and fearfully embraced. Mrs. Thompson couldn't bear to look at any of them, and not knowing where to put her eyes, could not prevent their turning inward to the comparisons. How much better that they are lying here, even if they have to be in pain, she thought, and then could not keep from thinking of the subway platform.

Her friend had taken her to Brooklyn, to the nurse. They had with them one of the children, perhaps the middle daughter now lying here. In the dark, low-ceilinged apartment the procedure was done on a large double bed, its dust ruffle and satin coverlet not quite hidden underneath the rubber sheet. There was no anesthetic, just true grit, a metal probe, and a rubber tube. But there was also the warm, silent room and a sympathetic woman, risking her freedom and her future for fifty dollars. Pain was beside the point, yet to be expected. They did not speak of it, or of the trembling of her elevated legs. But on the subway platform, when the cramping began in earnest, as the still-inserted tube leaked air to bring about miscarriage, Mrs. Thompson had leaned against her friend. "You okay?" her friend said in a low, worried voice, with an answering pressure of her arm. "I'll be okay," said Mrs. Thompson, who was not thinking, amid the dirt and noise of the old elevated station, under the pale spring sun, that this time she might be one of the ones to die.

Because she had had her children and there was no choice. Yet she could not die either, could only do what she had done. Mrs. Thompson looked once more at Yuriko and imagined the children for whom she was lying there. Yuriko still had not moved.

By now the girl in the next bed had directed her hurt and angry gaze out the window. Her own daughter lay silent and limp. Overriding the sunny room, images of pain crowded Mrs. Thompson's mind. Images of fear. Of hemorrhaging on street corners, of the time the nurse's tube had taken two weeks to do its job.

And before the Supreme Court decision, the doctor's mill in the suburbs of the legal state, where the waiting and recovery room had only a few beds, so most of those recovering had to lie on the floor, while those waiting who could not find space to sit, stood. Their clothing had been taken except for dresses or blouses, and so those who had worn pants were naked below the waist. There must have been twenty-five of them at least, but the one Mrs. Thompson remembered was a Southern girl, a young belle as hairless as a ten-year-old, and exhibitionistic about it. She had stood naked but for a skimpy sweater, displaying her shockingly virginal pubes.

But she had been far along, too far for this procedure perhaps, though not too far for the doctor's money, at one hundred dollars a pull. Mrs. Thompson, after the familiar unbearable pain complicated by the new, terrifying noise and vibration of the machine, had recovered quickly. But on her way out she had encountered la belle, on a toilet. A nurse stood nearby but still the child seemed alone, mascara streaking her cheeks and a pool of terrible memory in her eyes. Mrs. Thompson had stopped to stroke the pretty blond head. "You'll be all right soon," she had murmured, but as the girl nodded, and two large tears welled out of her eyes, Mrs. Thompson could see that the source remained, that memory would hold it, dark and unfathomed amid circumstance, like her own. And she had left the place angry and bitter that even legality could assume the price was pain.

And who is responsible, she thought now, angry again and tired of being always indignant about foams that didn't work and were despicable (like diving into a bowl of whipped cream he had said) and the tasty jelly and rubber baby buggy bumpers that for some women spoiled all pleasure, every ability to work that thing. She went on, raving in her mind, at the pill with its fake pregnancy followed hard by embolism, the IUD of babies and untreatable infection. And still—*still*—two of the five in this room, she thought furiously, and no one even knew about Yuriko.

But Yuriko was married, maybe she made three. Or maybe she and her handsome husband had seized each other one morning between the kitchen and the bathroom, after the children had left for school. And of the others—the remaining two—it had been known, even back then, that there were some who could not deal. "You'll be back," the Pennsylvania doctor's nurse had said to a friend of Mrs. Thompson's some twenty years before. "You'll come back, because there are some who do, and I know them, I know who."

But of what use is sagacity if only to condemn and condemn? Mrs. Thompson remembered the Fox woman, who had told her story to the anthropologists around 1910. She was married young to an older man. We didn't want children, so a woman gave me something to drink, she had said. Some years later, after this husband's death, she married another, drank a different potion, and bore five children before she drank something else. It was all written in plain Indian, opposite the English translation, and it had seemed to Mrs. Thompson that there could have been no reason on earth for her to lie.

But now the arrival of the lone girl interrupted her thoughts again and she watched the nurses put the girl in bed. A ruddy, freckled brunette, her face now was drawn; she seemed older, and dazed. In shock of course, Mrs. Thompson thought, they're all in shock. The girl sat unmoving at first on the edge of the bed, until Mrs. Weinberg's daughter helped her to lie down.

And here came Mrs. Weinberg herself, puffing a little and with her curly gray hair frizzed some, to check whether Mrs. Thompson's daughter felt well enough to get up, since in the large, world-renowned medical center they had given over only this small room and this one good woman, and this busy morning they were even minus a bed that the doll children would soon need.

"I'm okay really," said Mrs. Thompson's daughter, and disappeared swiftly into the bathroom with her clothes. After one worried glance at the closed door, Mrs. Thompson began getting herself together. Until suddenly Mrs. Weinberg was there, leaning close across the bed table.

"I wanted to ask you—" and she leaned even closer. "Your daughter's—isn't she—black?"

Mrs. Thompson reared back, jolted from the broader direction of her thoughts. "Why, yes," she said, with her customary vague hostility, for liking Mrs. Weinberg's work didn't mean she had to accept all her opinions.

But Mrs. Weinberg seemed relieved. "Well, I thought maybe—" She hesitated, then stammered, "I—I just wanted to say—" And then it came out: "My ninth grandchild will be black," she said.

The first thing that came to Mrs. Thompson's mind was, "Well, I expect *all* of mine will be." But right in front of her was Mrs. Weinberg's round, kindly face, and there was her good work, and at least she had not said "half-black."

"My son has married a Haitian girl," Mrs. Weinberg explained, before Mrs. Thompson had quite come up with an answer.

"Well then, give them all your love," Mrs. Thompson replied.

"Oh, well, *that* goes without saying!" Mrs. Weinberg said a little louder, as if tired at last of Mrs. Thompson's suspicions.

So that Mrs. Thompson herself felt, finally, ashamed, having again underestimated this woman, all the while entrusting her middle daughter to her anyway. "Look, the world—" she said by way of apology, with a dismissive gesture, and then laying her hand on Mrs. Weinberg's warm, competent arm, "Let's hope the world will catch up, somehow, eventually. . . ." Yet she wanted to add, harshly, would you have aborted this one, for that reason, would you? She saw once more his face at the bus station, thought of him thinking that. And then, a vision she had long forgotten, the contorted face of her father, weeping, begging her to abort, not what as a woman she had not been ready to have, which was long gone, but the first real baby, the child made, carried, birthed, loved. "Just love them," she said again to Mrs. Weinberg. "There is nothing else you need do."

Unconvinced, with a half smile, Mrs. Weinberg shook her head, but Mrs. Thompson knew that she would learn the lesson easily and soon. And at that moment the bathroom door opened, and out marched her middle daughter, sophisticated, bemused, and still quite gray beneath her brown. She held the brightly striped socks on high.

"Don't forget to call me if you need me," Mrs. Weinberg said, giving her a hug. "Don't forget your instructions, don't forget your pills."

Then, smiling, they said their goodbyes, and Mrs. Thompson and her middle daughter spied another elevator down the hall. There they stood, waiting, as the pretty children came from surgery to claim the bed.

Outside, in the brilliant summer morning, someone down the block was cutting grass. They didn't speak but walked slowly, arms around each other's waists. Just that way Mrs. Thompson had also walked with another daughter: silent, supportive, and relieved. But now she was wearier than ever of the problem, warier of failed preventives, and angrily, endlessly aware that their lives, like the lives of all women, still depended on a house of cards that could any day come tumbling, tumbling down.

How long must we wait for what must be done for us! Mrs. Thompson cried in her mind, and though unspoken the words seemed broadcast into the pleasant, warming air.

And whatever her middle daughter picked up of them, her reply, the statement she made, was in any case a testament for those with the only right to life, those already born. She said, in a language they had now perfected, "Thank you for being my mom."

From The Joy Luck Club

AMY TAN

I learned to love Tyan-yu, but it is not how you think. From the beginning, I would always become sick thinking he would someday climb on top of me and do his business. Every time I went into our bedroom, my hair would already be standing up. But during the first months, he never touched me. He slept in his bed, I slept on my sofa.

In front of his parents, I was an obedient wife, just as they taught me. I instructed the cook to kill a fresh young chicken every morning and cook it until pure juice came out. I would strain this juice myself into a bowl, never adding any water. I gave this to him for breakfast, murmuring good wishes about his health. And every night I would cook a special tonic soup called *tounau*, which was not only very delicious but has eight ingredients that guarantee long life for mothers. This pleased my mother-in-law very much.

But it was not enough to keep her happy. One morning, Huang Taitai and I were sitting in the same room, working on our embroidery. I was dreaming about my childhood, about a pet frog I once kept named Big Wind. Huang Taitai seemed restless, as if she had an itch in the bottom of her shoe. I heard her huffing and then all of a sudden she stood up from her chair, walked over to me, and slapped my face.

"Bad wife!" she cried. "If you refuse to sleep with my son, I refuse to feed you or clothe you." So that's how I knew what my husband had said to avoid his mother's anger. I was also boiling with anger, but I said nothing, remembering my promise to my parents to be an obedient wife.

That night I sat on Tyan-yu's bed and waited for him to touch me. But he didn't. I was relieved. The next night, I lay straight down on the bed next to him. And still he didn't touch me. So the next night, I took off my gown.

That's when I could see what was underneath Tyan-yu. He was scared and turned his face. He had no desire for me, but it was his fear that made me think he had no desire for any woman. He was like a little boy who had never grown up. After a while I was no longer afraid. I even began to think differently toward Tyan-yu. It was not like the way a wife loves a husband, but more like the way a sister protects a younger brother. I put my gown back on and lay down next to him and rubbed his back. I knew I no longer had to be afraid. I was sleeping with Tyan-yu. He would never touch me and I had a comfortable bed to sleep on.

After more months had passed and my stomach and breasts remained small and flat, Huang Taitai flew into another kind of rage. "My son says he's planted enough seeds for thousands of grandchildren. Where are they? It must be you are doing something wrong." And after that she confined me to the bed so that her grandchildren's seeds would not spill out so easily.

Oh, you think it is so much fun to lie in bed all day, never getting up. But I tell you it was worse than a prison. I think Huang Taitai became a little crazy.

She told the servants to take all sharp things out of the room, thinking scissors and knifes were cutting off her next generation. She forbade me from sewing. She said I must concentrate and think of nothing but having babies. And four times a day, a very nice servant girl would come into my room, apologizing the whole time while making me drink a terrible-tasting medicine.

I envied this girl, the way she could walk out the door. Sometimes as I watched her from my window, I would imagine I was that girl, standing in the courtyard, bargaining with the traveling shoe mender, gossiping with other servant girls, scolding a handsome delivery man in her high teasing voice.

One day, after two months had gone by without any results, Huang Taitai called the old matchmaker to the house. The matchmaker examined me closely, looked up my birthdate and the hour of my birth, and then asked Huang Taitai about my nature. Finally, the matchmaker gave her conclusions: "It's clear what has happened. A woman can have sons only if she is deficient in one of the elements. Your daughter-in-law was born with enough wood, fire, water, and earth, and she was deficient in metal, which was a good sign. But when she was married, you loaded her down with gold bracelets and decorations and now she has all the elements, including metal. She's too balanced to have babies."

This turned out to be joyous news for Huang Taitai, for she liked nothing better than to reclaim all her gold and jewelry to help me become fertile. And it was good news for me too. Because after the gold was removed from my body, I felt lighter, more free. They say this is what happens if you lack metal. You begin to think as an independent person. That day I started to think about how I would escape this marriage without breaking my promise to my family.

It was really quite simple. I made the Huangs think it was their idea to get rid of me, that they would be the ones to say the marriage contract was not valid.

I thought about my plan for many days. I observed everyone around me, the thoughts they showed in their faces, and then I was ready. I chose an auspicious day, the third day of the third month. That's the day of the Festival of Pure Brightness. On this day, your thoughts must be clear as you prepare to think about your ancestors. That's the day when everyone goes to the family graves. They bring hoes to clear the weeds and brooms to sweep the stones and they offer dumplings and oranges as spiritual food. Oh, it's not a somber day, more like a picnic, but it has special meaning to someone looking for grandsons.

On the morning of that day, I woke up Tyan-yu and the entire house with my wailing. It took Huang Taitai a long time to come into my room. "What's wrong with her now," she cried from her room. "Go make her be quiet." But finally, after my wailing didn't stop, she rushed into my room, scolding me at the top of her voice.

I was clutching my mouth with one hand and my eyes with another. My body was writhing as if I were seized by a terrible pain. I was quite convincing, because Huang Taitai drew back and grew small like a scared animal.

"What's wrong, little daughter? Tell me quickly," she cried.

"Oh, it's too terrible to think, too terrible to say," I said between gasps and more wailing.

After enough wailing, I said what was so unthinkable. "I had a dream," I reported. "Our ancestors came to me and said they wanted to see our wedding. So Tyan-yu and I held the same ceremony for our ancestors. We saw the matchmaker light the candle and give it to the servant to watch. Our ancestors were so pleased, so pleased. . . ."

Huang Taitai looked impatient as I began to cry softly again. "But then the servant left the room with our candle and a big wind came and blew the candle out. And our ancestors became very angry. They shouted that the marriage was doomed! They said that Tyan-yu's end of the candle had blown out! Our ancestors said that Tyan-yu would die if he stayed in this marriage!"

Tyan-yu's face turned white. But Huang Taitai only frowned. "What a stupid girl to have such bad dreams!" And then she scolded everybody to go back to bed.

"Mother," I called to her in a hoarse whisper. "Please don't leave me! I am afraid! Our ancestors said if the matter is not settled, they would begin the cycle of destruction."

"What is this nonsense!" cried Huang Taitai, turning back toward me. Tyan-yu followed her, wearing his mother's same frowning face. And I knew they were almost caught, two ducks leaning into the pot.

"They knew you would not believe me," I said in a remorseful tone, "because they know I do not want to leave the comforts of my marriage. So our ancestors said they would plant the signs, to show our marriage is now rotting."

"What nonsense from your stupid head," said Huang Taitai, sighing. But she could not resist. "What signs?"

"In my dream, I saw a man with a long beard and a mole on his cheek."

"Tyan-yu's grandfather?" asked Haung Taitai. I nodded, remembering the painting I had observed on the wall.

"He said there are three signs. First, he has drawn a black spot on Tyan-yu's back, and this spot will grow and eat away Tyan-yu's flesh just as it ate away our ancestor's face before he died."

Huang Taitai quickly turned to Tyan-yu and pulled his shirt up. "Ai-ya!" she cried, because there it was, the same black mole, the size of a fingertip, just as I had always seen it these past five months of sleeping as sister and brother.

"And then our ancestor touched my mouth," and I patted my cheek as if it already hurt. "He said my teeth would start to fall out one by one, until I could no longer protest leaving this marriage."

Huang Taitai pried open my mouth and gasped upon seeing the open spot in the back of my mouth where a rotted tooth fell out four years ago.

"And finally, I saw him plant a seed in a servant girl's womb. He said this girl only pretends to come from a bad family. But she is really from imperial blood, and . . ."

I lay my head down on the pillow as if too tired to go on. Huang Taitai pushed my shoulder, "What does he say?"

"He said the servant girl is Tyan-yu's true spiritual wife. And the seed he has planted will grow into Tyan-yu's child."

By mid-morning they had dragged the matchmaker's servant over to our house and extracted her terrible confession.

And after much searching they found the servant girl I liked so much, the one I had watched from my window every day. I had seen her eyes grow bigger and her teasing voice become smaller whenever the handsome delivery man arrived. And later, I had watched her stomach grow rounder and her face become longer with fear and worry.

So you can imagine how happy she was when they forced her to tell the truth about her imperial ancestry. I heard later she was so struck with this miracle of marrying Tyan-yu she became a very religious person who ordered servants to sweep the ancestors' graves not just once a year, but once a day.

Antisocial Baby Notes

SUZANNE OSTRO

Evolutionary biology keeps reminding us that we are animals, designed by natural selection, not for discovering deep truths of nature, but for breeding.

—*John Horgan*

*E*verybody makes such a big deal about it. If I ever thought about having children, it was like the weather. It might rain or it might not, but I wasn't going to waste my time obsessing about it. Of course, I didn't go out of my way to get pregnant. I used contraceptives most of the time—except occasionally, when I thought I was madly in love with someone completely unsuitable. The responsible types never crossed my mind.

Once, when I was married and in Paris, my in-laws tried bribery and told my husband that if we'd have a child, they'd make us an allowance. (God knows, they could afford it, but why they wanted to reproduce my husband was beyond me.) I said if they could guarantee the baby would be born with a live-in governess, I'd consider it. Then, for a couple of months I thought well, I'll get pregnant. But I never did, and then it seems to have slipped my mind.

I suppose in somebody else's terms I wasn't properly "socialized." Evolutionary biology seems to have made a wrong turn here; nobody ever propagandized me to be fruitful and multiply. The only pressure I ever really got was to go to medical school. My father was a doctor, as was his older sister, Sophie, her husband, and various other relatives. It was what you did in my family.

Sophie was my role model. She'd come from Russia at twenty-three, studied English with a tutor for a year and a half, and then had gone on to medical school. She graduated in 1912, the only woman in her class. She never had children; it certainly would never have occurred to me to ask why.

When I finally told my father at seventeen that I really didn't want to be a doctor, he said something that was pretty amazing for the 1940s, when the ideal young woman aimed for a husband early on, had 2.5 children (I imagine they divided the halves among themselves so they'd come out even), wore aprons, smiled cheerily, and used pressure cookers. He said, "Well, you better decide what you want to do with your life, or you'll spend it washing some man's floors."

It was a generation where most of my female friends spent their teens talking about getting married like they were competitors in a race. Which I suppose they were—I know every one of them was married before they were twenty, many disastrously, and had children right away to nail themselves in place. I was surrounded by perky housewives with shinier than shiny floors, whiter than white laundry, Norman Rockwell children, always smiling, smiling. Much later I thought wistfully what a pleasure it would have been to grow up instead with Cagney and Lacey. I probably would have been a cop.

Once I was actually sorry I wasn't pregnant. I was having a long affair with someone I thought I was in love with. He couldn't deal with any kind of commitment, so he spent most of his time out of town, and I spent that time living with a warm, nice man with whom I was good friends. Both of them knew about each other, since I didn't waste any energy lying about it.

I'd spend Monday through Friday with the one who lived in, and then he'd split for a friend's apartment while the other came in for the weekend. On Sunday night I'd ride the subway down to Penn Station to see him off and then keep going downtown to pick up the one who spent the week. I must say they were both very good about not asking questions about each other.

One month I was about two weeks late with my period. I was convinced I was pregnant and told them both. The nice guy I was living with was delighted, said he'd always wanted a kid, and that he'd marry me but he wouldn't get a job and support me (us). This was the Beat Generation and he'd never had a job. The one who couldn't commit announced frostily that he certainly wouldn't marry me but that he'd pay 50 percent child support since those were the odds of his being the father. When I finally got my period, I confess to being disappointed—the situation was so intriguing. A child with two half-fathers making a whole (well, let's not go that far)—think of the possibilities!

When I was much older—going through menopause, as a matter of fact—I asked my very smart gynecologist why he thought I'd never gotten pregnant when I hadn't used contraceptives. He said that since I'd had fibroid tumors all my life, I'd probably been pregnant any number of times but that the fetus had had trouble attaching and had miscarried. Like mother, like child. . . .

Once or twice I wondered what it was like to be pregnant, and I thought it must be an enormous strangeness and probably pretty awful to have your body so deformed, blowing up like a balloon, and even worse, to have a parasite growing inside.

•

My mother was too self-absorbed to be a model for anything, except she was a good cook and she played the piano well. All the information I received from her about having children was that she'd gotten pregnant three weeks after getting married "because I was stupid enough to think douches worked." Family legend had it that she didn't talk to my father for another three weeks after she found out about the fallacy of douches.

There's this myth that all normal women want children, but nobody tells you what they mean by "normal." What it means is having been socialized to breed. To continue the species. To ensure the survival of the race. The problem I see is that we have no real predators. I get cold chills when I think of us, having wrecked one planet, blasting off into space to spread like a virus through the universe.

In my early twenties I had a very sharp analyst who made two comments that stayed with me. One was that if everyone had children for the right reasons, the population would drop by 80 percent. The second was the day I said halfheartedly, "Maybe I should have a baby," and he responded solicitously, "Why don't you go home and write a poem."

Once I went to Greece with a man who had left his wife and six—count 'em, six—children. Every time we went to see another member of his family, he was always asked ritually, "How many children do you have?" And when he answered proudly: "Six. All sons!" everybody would stand up and applaud. It didn't seem to matter that he was there with his girlfriend; nobody asked what exactly was happening with his wife and the six children. The simple reason for applause was that he had spawned six male children.

The truth of the matter was that every time the marriage got worse, his wife got pregnant. When he finally walked out for the penultimate time, she said "But I thought this child (number 5? 6?) would keep you." I imagine this does not come under the heading of Children for the Right Reasons.

Relax, dear Reader, he went back to them after his family convinced him that if you're going to have that many, you'd better stay put and help with the shopping.

My Russian paternal grandfather, twice widowed, was married three times and had six children. Cyril died at sixteen of some childhood disease. Boris went mad in his late teens and was hospitalized. Emmanuel was gassed in WWI. Sophie, as I said, became a doctor. Sara got married in her late forties to a widower with four children, whom she left after a year and a half. Then there was Marcus, my father. And I'm the only descendent—that family ends with me, which is a strange thought. Like Greek fate. Or, more likely, a Russian novel.

Pretty Story

AMY HEMPEL

$\mathcal{N}$o one has ever told me that I am good with children. A short time ago, I went to a dinner party. The hostess was setting the table—there were eight of us that night—when her daughter, a barefoot seven-year-old, demanded we play the game.

I had not played the game before. You had to build a tower out of narrow cross-placed pieces of wood, then pull away the pieces one at a time without making the tower collapse.

I am not good at games, and the girl was sure of her moves. Yet somehow I was good at this, and when the girl removed the piece that made the tower fall, she ran to her mother screaming, "I didn't lose!"

A psychic has told me I will have two children. This makes me shake my head. Picture it: I know you are not supposed to leave a baby alone. Not even for a minute. But after a while I would think, What could happen to a baby in the time it would take for me to run to the corner for a cappuccino to go? So I do it, I run to the corner and get the cappuccino. And then think how close the store is that is having the sale on leather gloves. Really, I think, it is only a couple of blocks. So I go to the store and I buy the gloves. And it hits me—how long it has been since I have gone to a movie. A matinee! So I do that too. I go to a movie. And when I come out of the theater, it occurs to me that it has been years since I have been to Paris. Years. So I go to Paris and come back three months later and find a skeleton in the crib.

The appetite of a baby is a frightening thing to me. I watch a mother spoon food into her baby's mouth, then spoon back in what the baby spits out; to me, it is the job of spackling. If I had a baby, I would change overnight from a woman who worries about the calories in the glue of an envelope to someone who goes to the corner for coffee, a nightgown showing beneath my coat, the hem of that gown clawed to shreds by a cat.

A friend of mine tried to get pregnant and found out she could not. I said, "The world doesn't need more babies," and she said she wasn't going to do it for the world.

I brave shower after shower in which the stacks of gifts divide clearly into gifts from moms and gifts from non-moms. The moms give practical items with safety as a theme: a net to keep a crawling child from slipping through the railing of a deck, a mirror that affixes to the dashboard of a car so the driver can see the infant in the car seat behind, a dozen earnest gadgets to "baby-proof" a house. Whereas I will have chosen a mobile to hang above the crib, baby animals painted on china disks—a breath sends them swinging against one another with a sound to wake a baby down the block.

Here's a good baby story: It happened in the Caribbean Sea. A woman went into labor after her husband's small fishing boat sank, and the current pulled them apart. He would later be rescued and reunited with his wife, but there was no sign of him yet when the woman's life preserver was not enough to hold her above water. She panicked, scanning the horizon where she thought she saw a squall, the water churning with storm. It moved toward her, closing in till she could make out leaping forms; it looked to her like hundreds of leaping fish. She bobbed in the waves, enduring contractions, and the school of dolphins moved into formation around her. Later she would learn that they can locate a BB with their sonar, so it was no trouble for them to detect her daughter, about to be born.

The woman screamed when a phalanx of dolphins dove and then surfaced beneath her, lifting her above the level of the sea. But as she pushed her baby out, she saw that they were there to help her, and because the dolphins were there, her daughter didn't drown.

The dolphins held their position, a buoyant grid beneath her, and kept the mother and daughter safe until human help arrived. Had help not come so soon, might the nursing mother dolphin have offered her richly fatted milk to the baby?

"They were sent to me by the Holy Father," the woman would tell her husband. "He wanted our baby to live."

"The dolphins chattered like little children," the woman said. "When my baby was born, the dolphins went wild. They bobbed up and down; their smiles were so beautiful!"

In gratitude, the woman named her daughter Dolphina Maria. The dolphins slipped away through the waves, intercessors supporting humankind on the sea, allowing them to return to land cleansed of sin. Deep inside their bodies float the few bones left from the hind legs they once had on land.

It is such a pretty story told to me by a Cuban woman I met in a bar at the beach. She left the bar before I did; a drunken man took her place. He leaned into me and said, "I see in your dark eyes that you have suffered, and you have compassion, and I have suffered, and I have compassion, and I see in your eyes that I can *say* things to you—"

"My eyes are blue," I said.

The only time the word *baby* doesn't scare me is the time that it should, when it is what a man calls me.

Something I Forgot to Tell You

DEBORAH BOE

There is something I forgot to tell you
about me. It's along the lines of
you don't know really
who it is you're dealing with.
For instance, I bleach my hair.
Right away you're disappointed.
I don't like babies.
You put the little box from the jeweler's
back in your pocket.
I never notice whether the house is clean
until the belt I wear every day
gets lost in the things I haven't worn
in weeks.
Now you're looking at your watch.

It's not that I was hiding things,
but that you never looked close.
You thought I was like,
or not like, your mother maybe.
You made up habits for me to have.
clean, natural, maternal instincts
for me to wear under those
French lace items you love in black.

Well, I'm telling you it's not like that.
I'm telling you I sleep till noon,
won't help out with the rent
ever, stay up all night writing
stanzas you can't make heads
or tails of. And it doesn't bother me
that I'm probably going to be alone
for a long time. After all,
that's the way I planned it.

Meditations on Childlessness

Vicki Lindner

1

I am in the mauve waiting room of the women's clinic a few months before my fiftieth birthday. I plan to ask my gynecologist to prescribe estrogen. Before I put my feet in the stirrups, however, I supply this progressive clinic with an overview of my marital and reproductive history on a standard form, which means answering the same personal questions I am asked every time. As if, I think, at forty-nine-and-a-half my answers are likely to change. Once again I check *Single, No live births, One abortion,* then move on to today's pressing issues of menopause: *Hot flashes, Sleeplessness, Headaches, Mood swings. . . .*

2

I should have decided not to have children for ecological reasons (the world population doubled during my fertile years), or to manifest a liberated woman's protest, more meaningful than burning a bra. Like my sister-in-law, who helped end our line by tying her tubes, I might have declared, "I just don't like children," exercising my right to cranky, personal choice. I could have said I remained child-free in order to have more time to write. In fact, I never decided to finesse the act that comes as naturally to most women as song to a bird. My desire not to have children was much like their desire to have them—so instinctive, so visceral, so unnaturally natural—that I rarely thought about the issue at all.

3

I now believe that I didn't have children because of a family story—a tale my mother told for the first time when I was a very young girl. The story is about the night her own mother died in her ninth month of pregnancy at age forty-four. My mother, fourteen, awoke to a commotion; my grandmother gasped, taut abdomen ballooning, on the kitchen floor. "Hurry! Call the doctor!" her father cried, and my mother was so frightened that she ran outside in her nightgown without any shoes. When the doctor finally arrived, drunk, after the patient was dead, he offered to carve the child out of my grandmother's womb with a butcher knife. My grandfather, a steel worker, and member of the Wobblies as well as the Ku Klux Klan, suggested he'd use the knife on the doctor before he'd stand by for that.

As I grew older, and this story took on the power of myth, it became easy to imagine my mother, tall, gaunt as a milkweed stalk, destined to endure two nauseous, severely anemic pregnancies herself, stumbling barefoot into the Illinois snow on a night so cold it turned her moonlit exhalations to shards of ice, unable to feel her frozen feet strike the ground, running, as one runs in a dream, not moving forward, her flannel nightgown binding her thin flanks, to crank a wealthier neighbor's telephone.

After my mother's death in 1989, I learned that she had been obliged to quit high school to cook and keep house for her widowed father and younger brother. Intelligent, curious, a fine amateur botanist who grew the only yellow primrose New Jersey has produced, she couldn't claim a degree most hat check girls possess. So ashamed was she of this embarrassing secret that she took it with her to the funeral urn. Once I asked how her mother's death had made her feel about having children. "I was afraid . . ." she murmured, a wary vagueness shielding her eyes.

I don't know the medical cause of my grandmother's death; she may have suffered an aneurysm, or a heart attack. But I never doubted—until right now—that she died of pregnancy.

4

The only time I found myself pregnant, at twenty-eight, while teaching English and working as a nightclub hostess in Kyoto, Japan, I succumbed to a terror that surpassed all those I had previously known. This dismaying physiological betrayal could not possibly be true! Wasn't I a modern woman who had up to now controlled her destiny, including ovaries? Never mind that I had run out of birth control pills while traveling through Asia and had trusted a whispered instruction to an inexperienced lover, who spoke little English, to protect me from fertilization. Although I had taken advantage of improvements in birth control technology, perhaps I believed that my fervent desire to avoid getting pregnant had kept me not so. When I tasted the first dizzy nausea, then woozed into a faint as I exited the public bath's boiling *ofuro*, I was sure that I hovered in the shadow of death— my inherited fate of utero-inspired physical destruction, plus ego-annihilating loss of control. What was happening to my body did not seem natural: the fish smells floating from the English conversation school's kitchen through my unheated *tatami* room nauseated; bloat made me notice my breasts; I lusted with covetous appetites. My metamorphosis into an unconscious gene-copying species, a jackdaw or silk moth, felt like the onset of a fatal illness.

Roe v. Wade was not law in America then; when I learned that abortion had been cheap and legal in Japan since World War II, after many fathers of unborn children were killed, I experienced a relief so intense it felt like ecstasy. My freedom, the potentiality for an undefined female existence, would be saved! When the lover, a short, delicate man, himself the illegitimate son of an Osaka industrialist, captured my icy hand in a Zen temple garden of concentric raked sand and asked with hesitant wonderment, "Don't you want to have child?" I was astounded, almost insulted by the question. "No, I barely know you—No, *no!*" I protested.

After the procedure I indulged a mild curiosity about the fetus, which seemed as much part of my body as a malignant tumor: "*Oki Desta ka?*" I asked the doctor in rudimentary Japanese. *Was it big?*

"No," she replied. "*Chisai desu.*" *It is small.*

Later that day I bowed to the postmaster and collected my mail; in it was a photograph of a New York friend's fuzzy-headed newborn with a note that described her lengthy, heroic labor and exclaimed, "I'm ready to do the whole thing again!" I realized, then, with irritating confusion, that I had aborted a child. I also sensed, for the first time, that there was a psychic gulf, as wide as the Pacific, between myself and most of the world's women. Then I donned my green satin jeans and, hemorrhaging, taxied to my part time job as a nightclub hostess in Hanamikoji Shinbashi. I never wrote to that friend again.

5

A friend who has a baby does change. She can't host late, drunken parties or samba at Sounds of Brazil any more. She won't meet you for coffee in an hour. She only pretends interest in your love affairs. Her fierce, protective ray zaps interlopers. She paws the forest turf: back off or I'll charge. Wrapped through, in, around infant succulence, oblivious to her pale aprons of flesh, split nails, she throbs like a wasp in a bowl of milk. You can smell her intensity, a pheromone-scented hank of coarse hair. Kneeling in her fervent Medicine Wheel, she defends her blood unit's social interests—in middle-class America, garnering property, one's share of the wealth. On the phone her voice is remote as Isis's, directing her fertile buzz toward the moon. A whimper sends her winging cribside: Bye, got to go now. And *you*, crooning lethargically, you don't understand.

Once I asked a single mother, an artist, who had a child in her late thirties as she was getting a divorce, to tell me, a curious childless woman, what IT was really like. We were walking in a pine forest at the onset of spring; the little boy was at his dad's. This was, I knew, an unusual occasion for her, now strapped for cash, working a straight job, to have an hour of free time to spend alone with a friend. She turned and faced me on the gum-muddy trail; "I never believed I could love anybody so much."

6

Few women's lives can be lived without regret, as every choice seems to preclude another. I don't regret not having a child, but sometimes I regret not wanting to have one. I regret drifting far from the stream of shared female concern; I regret not ever loving anybody *so much*. I regret my ongoing delight in solitude and freedom, because a "normal" woman does not want to be free or alone. I regret my lack of connection to young children, savvy, silver-tongued creatures, who sensibly like primary caregivers most. Because I opted for an adventurous, open-ended life, I wish I had been much more adventurous, braver, reckless even, more joyfully and indiscriminately promiscuous, physically more tough. Why couldn't *I* have shaved my head and hitchhiked around the world, or bicycled across Siberia?

I wish I had understood who I was sooner, so I could have been more defiantly myself. Because I didn't produce children, I regret not producing towers of books.

7

At thirty-three I attended a Manhattan party to celebrate the birthday of a friend's one-year-old son. Each tiny guest had a goo-gooing adult posted behind it, puffing enthusiastically at the cake candle. Every one of these former swingers, I realized, had reproduced. A tipsy red-haired lawyer approached, leered, "Don't *you* want one, too?" My philandering T'ai Chi master offered to donate his Tantric sperm so I could have one too, advising, "Better hurry, you're thirty-four!" Around me, women I'd never thought would have one were quickening, burgeoning like loaves, breathing at Lamaze, or trying to. My relatives, wisely not questioning my wayward desires, pointedly did not ask if I wanted one too.

So at thirty-six I visited the New York Coliseum's adoption fair. The prospects were displayed in loose-leafed notebooks supplied by their orphanages. Beneath the blurred images, taken by photographers who failed to stop down the lens when shooting a dark face, the children's names, vital statistics, mental and physical health problems were inscribed. I learned that New York State would pay me to adopt an older black or handicapped child. I believed then, as I do now, that in a fragile global ecology, endangered by population growth, it makes more sense to recycle a starving, unwell, or unwanted child than to create another. I believed, and still do, that most Americans reproduce their own genes because their culture has made them so narcissistic they are convinced that they could love only a clone. Yet, then, as now, I knew I didn't want to adopt; I only wanted to want to adopt. I wanted to write another novel on quiet Sunday mornings; I wanted to go to Honduras in May; above all, I wanted to not know what I'd be doing after that.

Nevertheless, I returned to my rent-stabilized tenement and appraised it with adoption in mind: the nine-by-six bedroom with thin futon I unrolled at night; the plant-filled living room, too small for a couch; the closet-sized studio where I eked out a living as a freelance writer. Where, exactly, would the handicapped child fit? Although Italian immigrants had raised families of six in this cramped space, I could see no room for an extra being in it now.

8

Instead of adopting, I began to teach, a career that nurtures more children, if not as profoundly, than parenting does. Between stints of writing and traveling, I taught in libraries, settlement houses, a private high school, a prison, a detention home. For a while I taught truant children of drug-addicted parents—a volunteer gig. For years I have taught middle-class college students at the University of Wyoming.

As a professor of writing—a discipline that cracks secrets open like eggs—I have learned that many children are abused by parents who would have no more dreamed of not having children than a rabbit would. Although a surprising number of my university students unveil stories of physical or sexual abuse, more, I gather from what they don't confess, were sabotaged by material indulgence and benign neglect. Their parents, often divorced, overburdened, struggling emotionally, battling guilt, loved their children *so much*, but lacked the time, skill, and persistent energy to teach them to imagine, or the ethic their children would need to produce imaginative work. Stuck in front of TVs, expensive stereos, and computer games, sent to play sports, to indifferent classrooms, to church, they are fettered by a dearth of personal recognition. They can't construct the words to a dream. Yet, with self-protective wisdom, they realize that art can bulk out inner lives, which is why, I am sure, so many nonreaders sign up for writing courses.

It is no accident that teaching was once deemed a proper career for spinsters. At first my students respond angrily, then with touching, submissive gratitude to the childless professor, who doesn't love them, but has the emotional space to pay attention, insist that they fulfill her demands—and their real desires—for creative energy and discipline. My offerings have few personal expectations attached; the students take what they want, but because I am paid by an institution, they owe me not. I nurture these deprived strangers in the only way I can, then watch them pass on, leaving me behind like a stone washed clean in the riverbed, to be replaced by others, perhaps more able to carry away what I know.

9

I am sitting in a cafeteria in the John F. Kennedy International Airport in New York City, waiting for my flight back to Wyoming. A woman enters with an infant daughter, diapers bulging beneath blue coveralls, determined to toddle forth into the surging path of passengers. The young mother, greasy hair scraped into a pony tail, is lugging the equipage that burdens women who have transmitted their genes in a civilized world—insulated cooler case, folding metal stroller, quilted diaper bag, totes stuffed with bottles, pacifiers, and toys composed of nonrenewable petroleum resources. She must, as she awkwardly juggles these costly American infant supplies from one hand to her armpit, catch the speedy toddler trying to break free. I see the mother frown, frustrated. Then the daughter abruptly ceases her flight, and the two settle down at a nearby table, the child standing on her mother's lap. Faces a few inches apart, they are absorbed, like Narcissus in his image, in each others' mouths and eyes. They kiss. "Ahhh," says the mother as the little girl explores her red lips with her fingers. For an instant she becomes aware that she is being watched by a chic, middle-aged woman, wearing a vintage brown velvet hat, taking this photographic note, then turns back to her poetic simile, her reflecting pond. And that, I think, is in some way the point, the benefit of my torqued family mythology: standing apart on my lonely airport pinnacle, I am free to observe.

10

Floating above the human plain, I read that ninety-eight percent of the animal species that inherited our planet have gone extinct. Demographers of the pessimistic school warn that the combination of increasing population, environmental degradation, food shortages, and unequal distribution of wealth could result in mass starvation, disease epidemics, multitudes crossing national borders, warfare for resources, and the simultaneous breakdown of the planet's ecosystems.

Americans, who don't take this alarming scenario personally, blame poor nations for overpopulation and point to their own country's low birth rate. (Not in Alaska or Utah!) Unfortunately, a low birth rate alone offers no reason to rejoice. According to Paul and Anne Ehrlich, a baby born in the resource-greedy United States represents twice the destructive impact on the environment as 3 born in Italy, 35 born in India, 140 born in Kenya, and 280 born in Chad, Haiti, or Nepal.

Resources must be conserved and redistributed through political acts. Whatever the future holds, people are unlikely to stop having children; no animal sacrifices its reproductive interests to prevent its species from dying out. Although *Homo sapiens* are the only creatures capable of thinking into the future, they copy their genes with the same indifference to collective survival as animals with less evolved brains. Like elephants who mate, oblivious to thinning grass on the savannah, they maximize individual fitness with reproductive success.

Americans, believing themselves superior to poorer humans, sentimentalize and politicize their reproductive acts as well as their children's wanton consumption of resources. Women opting out of childbearing are not rewarded or praised for their ecologically responsible genetic sacrifice; instead, the culture isolates them with subtle moral pressure and fines them with higher taxes. *Selfish* is the term (implied more than spoken) for the childless, when it is childbearers, firing nerve cells in their thoracic ganglia to produce mating songs, who are so selfish they are killing us off.

11

As a fifty-year-old woman who did not reproduce, I hover on the verge of genetic extinction. The traits that make me tall, green-eyed, street smart, and unusually healthy, along with the complexities of my Polish, Austrian, French, and English forebears, will be sprinkled in the form of ashes from a barren, Rocky Mountain peak, assuming there is someone sufficiently mournful around to do the sprinkling—a former student perhaps. Although remaining child-free did not represent a politically conscious choice (What did I know in my fevered fertile days about exponential population growth?), in retrospect I can say, with a lonely human's sorrow, "I did the right thing about that." The idea of my total death, moreover, offers a satisfying image of closure: my life is my life, and only I am responsible for its legacy.

12

Who will inherit my jewelry collection? This is the question that focuses my regret. For years I've collected other cultures' heavy silver—Navajo pawn bracelets, Algerian filigree and coral, Ethiopian crosses—as well as gaudy junk—Mount Rushmore earrings. I hide the treasures inherited from my mother: a string of real pearls; a lion stickpin, diamond in mouth; a gold Buddha with a wise ivory face. Yesterday I put a deposit on an antique Mexican silver and jade bracelet, thinking that unless I bypass life expectancy, I have only twenty-six years left to wear it.

Because my brother, both favorite cousins, and I have produced no heirs, I planned to leave this finery to friends and instruct them to pass it, along with my globe-trotting style, on to their daughters. Then it occurred to me that my friends' offspring might not appreciate this inheritance; weighty, eccentric, ethnic jewelry could encumber lithe girls surfing the internet in 2022. What if they despised it? Or pawned it? Should I bestow it on other childless women, allies in nonconformity, instead? Meanwhile, I store my holographic will, legal in Wyoming, in the glove compartment of my Subaru; it lists each ornament beside the heiress apparent. When I am angry with a friend, I cross her name off. Later I realize there is adornment—and friends—I've failed to include. I may instruct my estate to sell these old baubles in a flea market and donate the proceeds to Planned Parenthood.

13

I am lying on the gynecologist's table, naked beneath a paper gown. Although this progressive doctor asked me to wear street clothes during our first interview, we have dispensed with time-consuming formalities since. "I don't want to waste any more of my days on fatigue and hot flashes," I tell him. We discuss the long term effects of unopposed estrogen. My mother died of breast cancer and she didn't take hormones! "In the polluted world we live in," I state, "I am likely to die of some kind of cancer, estrogen or not."

The doctor nods sagely. "None of us is getting out of this alive," he admits.

The author would like to acknowledge the contributions of animal behaviorist Dr. Gordon Schuett, Arizona State University; *The Population Explosion* by Paul R. Ehrlich & Anne H. Ehrlich, Simon & Schuster, 1990; *Animal Behavior: An Evolutionary Approach* by John Alcock, Arizona State University, 1979; *State of the World*, A Worldwatch Institute Report on Progress Toward a Sustainable Society, W.W. Norton & Co., 1994 and 1995; and Diane Raptosh for the poems "The Quickening," "Lullaby for the Unborn," and "Labor Song."

The Case Against Babies

Joy Williams

*B*abies, babies, babies. There's a plague of babies. Too many rabbits or elephants or mustangs or swans brings out the myxomatosis, the culling guns, the sterility drugs, the scientific brigade of egg smashers. Other species can "strain their environments" or "overrun their range" or clash with their human "neighbors," but human babies are always welcome at life's banquet. Welcome, welcome, welcome—live long and consume! You can't draw the line when it comes to babies because . . . where are you going to draw the line? *Consider having none or one and be sure to stop after two,* the organization Zero Population Growth suggests politely. Can barely hear them what with all the babies squalling. Hundreds of them popping out every minute. Ninety-seven million of them each year. While legions of other biological life forms go extinct (or, in the creepy phrase of ecologists, "wink out"), human life bustles self-importantly on. Those babies just keep coming! They've gone way beyond being "God's gift"; they've become entitlements. Everyone's having babies, even women who can't have babies, *particularly* women who can't have babies—they're the ones who sweep fashionably along the corridors of consumerism with their double-wide strollers, stuffed with twins and triplets. (Women push those things with the effrontery of someone piloting a bulldozer, which strollers uncannily bring to mind.) When you see twins or triplets do you think *awahhh* or *owhoo* or *that's sort of cool, that's unusual,* or do you think *that woman dropped a wad on in vitro fertilization, twenty-five, thirty thousand dollars at least* . . . ?

The human race hardly needs to be more fertile, but fertility clinics are booming. The new millionaires are the hot-shot fertility doctors who serve anxious got-tahavababy women, techno-shamans who have become the most important aspect of the baby process, giving women what they want: babies. (It used to be a mystery what women wanted, but no more. Nietzsche was right. . . .) Ironically—although it is far from being the only irony in this baby craze—women think of themselves as being *successful, personally fulfilled* when they have a baby, even if it takes a battery of men in white smocks and lots of hormones and drugs and needles and dishes and mixing and inserting and implanting to make it so. Having a baby means *individual completion* for a woman.

While much effort has been expended in Third World countries educating women into a range of options which do not limit their role merely to bearing children, well-off, educated and indulged American women are clamoring for babies, babies, BABIES to complete their status. They've had it all and now they want a baby. And women over thirty-five want them NOW. They're the ones who opt for the aggressive fertility route; they're impatient, they're sick of being laissez-faire about this. Sex seems such a laborious way to go about it. At this point they don't want to endure all that intercourse over and over and maybe get no baby. What a waste of time! And time's a-wasting. *A life with no child would be a life perfecting hedonism,* a forty-something infertile woman said, now the proud owner of pricey twins. Even women who have the grace to submit to fate can sound wistful. *It's not so much that I wish that I had children now,* a travel writer said, *but that I wish I had had them. I hate to fail at anything.* Women are supposed to wish and want and not fail.

The eighties were a decade when it was kind of unusual to have a baby. Oh, the lower classes still had them with more or less gusto, but professionals did not. Having a baby was indeed so quaintly rebellious and remarkable that a publishing niche was developed for men writing about babies, *their* baby, their baby's first year in which every single day was recorded (he slept through the night . . . he didn't sleep through the night . . .). The writers would marvel over the size of their infant's scrotum; give advice on how to tip the obstetrician (not a case of booze, a clock from Tiffany's is nicer); and bemusedly admit that their baby exhibited intelligent behavior like rolling over, laughing, and showing fascination with the TV screen far earlier than normal children. Aside from the talk about the poopie and the rashes and the cat's psychological decline, these books frequently contained a passage, an overheard bit of mommy-to-baby monologue along these lines: *I love you so much I don't ever want you to have teeth or stand up or walk or go on dates or get married. I want you to stay right here with me and be my baby. . . .* Babies are one thing. Human beings are another. We have way too many human beings. Almost everyone knows this.

Adoption was an eighties thing. People flying to Chile, all over the globe, God knows where, returning triumphantly with their baby. It was difficult, adventurous, expensive and generous. It was trendy. People were into adopting bunches of babies in all different flavors and colors (Korean, Chinese, part-Indian—part-Indian was very popular, Guatemalan). Adoption was a fad, just like the Cabbage Patch dolls which fed the fad to tens of thousands of prepubescent girl consumers.

Now it is absolutely necessary to digress for a moment and provide an account of this marketing phenomenon. These fatuous-faced soft-sculpture dolls were immensely popular in the 1980s. The gimmick was that these dolls were "born"; you couldn't just buy the damn things—if you wanted one you had to "adopt" it. Today they are still being born and adopted, although at a slower rate, in Babyland General Hospital, a former medical clinic right on the fast-food and car-dealership strip in the otherwise unexceptional North Georgia town of Cleveland. There are several rooms at Babyland General. One of them is devoted to the premies (all snug in their little gowns, each in its own spiffy incubator) and another is devoted to the cabbage patch itself, a suggestive mound with a fake tree on it from which several times a day comes the announcement CABBAGE IN LABOR! A few demented moments later, a woman in full nurse regalia appears from a door in the tree holding a brand-new Cabbage Patch Kid by the feet and giving it a little whack on the bottom. All around her in the fertile patch are happy little soft heads among the cabbages. Each one of these things costs $175, and you have to sign papers promising to care for it and treasure it forever. There are some cheesy dolls in boxes that you wouldn't have to adopt, but children don't want those—they want to sign on the line, the documentation, the papers. The dolls are all supposed to be different but they certainly look identical. They've got tiny ears, big eyes, a pinched rictus of a mouth and lumpy little arms and legs. The colors of the cloth vary for racial verisimilitude, but their expressions are the same. They're glad to be here and they expect everything.

But these are just dolls, of course. The real adopted babies who rode the wave of fashion into many hiply caring homes are children now, an entirely different kettle of fish, and although they may be providing (just as they were supposed to) great joy, they are not darling babies anymore. A baby is not really a child; a baby is a baby, a cuddleball, representative of virility, wombrismo, and humankind's unquenchable wish to outfox death.

Adoptive parents must feel a little out of it these days, so dreadfully dated in the nineties. Adoption—how foolishly sweet. It's so Benetton, so kind of naïve. With adopted babies, you just don't know, it's too much of a crap shoot. Oh, they *told* you that the father was an English major at Yale and that the mother was a brilliant mathematician and harpsichordist who was just not quite ready to juggle career and child, but what are you going to think when the baby turns into a kid who rather than showing any talent whatsoever is trying to drown the dog and set national parks on fire? Adoptive parents do their best, of course, at least as far as their liberal genes allow; they look into the baby's background, they don't want just any old baby (even going to the dog and cat pound you'd want to pick and choose, right?); they want a pleasant, healthy one, someone who will appreciate the benefits of a nice environment and respond to a nurturing and attentive home. They steer away (I mean, one has to be realistic, one can't save the world) from the crack and smack babies, the physically and mentally handicapped babies, the HIV and fetal alcohol syndrome babies.

Genes matter, more and more, and adoption is just too . . . where's the connection? Not a single DNA strand to call your own. Adoption signifies you didn't do everything you could; you were too cheap or shy or lacked the imagination to go the energetic fertility route which, when successful, would come with the assurance that some part of the baby or babies would be a continuation of you, or at the very least your companion, loved one, partner, whatever.

I once prevented a waitress from taking away my martini glass, which had a tiny bit of martini remaining in it, and she snarled, *Oh, the precious liquid*, before slamming it back down on the table. It's true that I probably imagined that there was more martini in the glass than there actually was (what on earth could have happened to it all?), but the precious liquid remark brings unpleasantly to mind the reverent regard in which so many people hold themselves. Those eggs, that sperm, oh precious, precious stuff! There was a terrible fright among humankind recently when some scientists suggested that an abundance of synthetic chemicals was causing lower sperm counts in human males, but this proves not to be the case; sperm counts are holding steady and are even on the rise in New York. Synthetic chemicals *do* adversely affect the reproductive capabilities of non-human animals (fish, birds), but this is considered relatively unimportant. It's human sperm that's held in high regard, and in this overpopulated age it's become more valuable—good sperm that is, from intelligent, athletic men who don't smoke, drink, do drugs, have AIDS or a history of homicide —because this overpopulated age is also the donor age. Donor sperm, donor womb, donor eggs. Think of all the eggs that are lost to menstruation every month. The mind boggles. Those precious, precious eggs, lost. (Many egg donors say they got into the business because they didn't like the idea of their eggs "going to waste.") They can be harvested instead and frozen for a rainy day or sold nice and fresh. One woman interviewed in the *New York Times* early this year has made it something of a career. *I'm not going to just sit home and bake cookies for my kids, I can accomplish things,* she says. No dreary nine-to-five desk job for her. She was a surrogate mother for one couple, dishing up a single baby; then she donated some eggs to another couple who had a baby; now she's pregnant with twins for yet another couple. *I feel like a good soldier, as if God said to me, "Hey girl, I've done a lot for you and now I want you to do something for Me,"* this entrepreneurial breeder says. Egg donors are regular Jenny Appleseeds, spreading joy, doing the Lord's work and earning a few bucks all at once as well as attaining an odd sense of empowerment (I've got a bunch of kids out there, damned if I know who they all are . . .).

One of the most successful calendars of 1996 was Anne Geddes's Babies. Each month shows the darling little things on cabbage leaves, cupped in a tulip, as little bees in a honeycomb and so on—solemn, bright-eyed babies. They look a little bewildered though, and why shouldn't they? How did they get here? They were probably mixed up in a dish. Donor eggs (vacuumed up carefully through long needles); Daddy's sperm (maybe . . . or maybe just some high-powered New York dude's); gestational carrier; the "real" mommy waiting anxiously, restlessly on the sidelines (want to get those babies home, start buying them stuff!). Baby's lineage can be a little complicated in this one big worldwide-webby family. With the help of drugs like Clomid and Perganol there are an awful lot of eggs out there these days—all being harvested by those rich and clever, clever doctors in a "simple procedure" and nailed with bull's-eye accuracy by a spermatozoon. One then gets to choose among the resulting cell clumps (or the doctor gets to choose, he's the one who knows about these things), and a number of them (for optimum success) are inserted into the womb, sometimes the mother's womb and sometimes not. These fertilized eggs, unsurprisingly, often result in multiple possibilities, which can be decreased by "selective reduction." They're not calendar babies yet, they're embryos, and it is at this point, the multiple possibility point, that the mother-to-be often gets a little overly ecstatic, even greedy, thinking ahead perhaps to the day when they're not babies any longer, the day when they'll be able to amuse themselves by themselves like a litter of kittens or something: if there's a bunch of them all at once there'll be no need to go through that harrowing process of finding appropriate playmates for them. She starts to think *Nannies probably don't charge that much more for three than for two* or *heaven knows we've got enough money or we wouldn't have gotten into all this in the first place.* And many women at the multiple-possibility point, after having gone through pretty much all the meddling and hubris that biomedical technology has come up with, say demurely, *I don't want to play God* (I DON'T WANT TO PLAY GOD?) or *It would be grotesque to snuff one out to improve the odds for the others* or *Whatever will be will be.*

So triplets happen, and even quads and quints (network television is still interested in quints). And as soon as the multiples, or even the less prestigious single baby, are old enough to toddle into day care, they're responsibly taught the importance of their one and only Earth, taught the three Rs—Reduce, Reuse, Recycle. Too many people (which is frequently considered undesirable) is caused by too many people (it's only logical) but it's mean to blame the babies, you can't blame the babies, they're innocent. Those poor bean counters at the United Nations Population Fund say that at current growth rates, the world will double its population in forty years. Overpopulation poses the greatest threat to all life on earth, but most organizations concerned with this problem don't like to limit their suggestions to the most obvious one—don't have a baby!—because it sounds so negative. Instead, they provide additional, more positive tips for easing the pressures on our reeling environment such as car pooling or tree planting. (A portion of the proceeds from that adorable bestselling babies calendar goes to the Arbor Day Foundation for the planting of trees.)

Some would have it that not having a baby is disallowing a human life, horribly inappropriate in this world of rights. Everyone has rights; the unborn have rights; it follows that the unconceived have rights. Women have the right to have babies, and women who can't have babies have an even bigger right to have them. These rights should be independent of marital or economic status, or age. (Fifty- and sixty-something moms tend to name their babies after the gynecologist.) The reproduction industry wants fertility treatments to be available to anyone and says that it wouldn't all be so expensive if those recalcitrant insurance companies and government agencies like Medicare and Medicaid weren't so cost-conscious and discriminatory and would just cough up the money. It's not as though you have to take out a permit to have a baby, be licensed or anything. What about the rights of a poor, elderly, feminist cancer patient who is disabled in some way, who wants to assert her right to independent motherhood and feels entitled to both artificial insemination into a gestational "hostess" and the right to sex selection as a basis for abortion should the fetus turn out to be male when she wants a female? Huh? What about her? Or what about the fifteen-year-old of the near future who kind of wants to have her baby even though it means she'll be stuck with a kid all through high school and won't be able to go out with her friends anymore, but who discovers through the wonders of amniocentesis and DNA analysis that the baby is going to turn out fat, and the fifteen-year-old just can't deal with fat and shouldn't have to . . . ? Out goes the baby with the bathwater.

But these scenarios are involved merely with messy political or ethical issues, the problematical, somewhat gross by-products of technological and marketing advances. Let the philosophers and professional ethicists drone on and let the baby business boom. Let the courts figure it out. Each day brings another more pressing problem. Implanted with their weak-cervixed daughter's eggs and their son-in-law's sperm, women become pregnant with their own grandchildren; frozen embryos are inadvertently thawed; eggs are pirated; eggs are harvested from aborted fetuses; divorced couples battle over the fate of cryopreserved material. "We have to have better regulation of the genetic product—eggs, sperm and embryos—so we can legally determine who owns what," a professor of law and medicine at a California university says plaintively. (Physicians tend to oppose more regulation however, claiming that it would impede research.)

While high-tech nations are refining their options eugenically and quibbling litigiously, the inhabitants of low-tech countries are just having babies. The fastest growth in human numbers in all history is going to take place in a single generation, an increase of almost five billion people (all of whom started out as babies). Ninety-seven percent of the surge is going to take place in developing countries, with Africa alone accounting for 35 percent of it (the poorer the country, the higher the birth rate, that's just the way it is). These babies are begotten in more traditional, doubtless less desperate ways, and although they are not considered as fashion statements, they're probably loved just as much as upper-class Western babies (or that singular one-per-family Chinese boy baby) and are even considered productive assets when they get a little older and can labor for the common good of their large families by exploiting more and more, scarcer and scarcer resources.

The argument that Western countries with their wealth and relatively low birth rate do not fuel the population crisis is, of course, fallacious. France, as national policy, urges its citizens to procreate, giving lots of subsidies and perks to those French who make more French. The U.S. population is growing faster than that of eighteen other industrialized nations and, in terms of energy consumption, when an American couple stops spawning at two babies, it's the same as an average East Indian couple stopping at sixty-six, or an Ethiopian couple drawing the line at one thousand.

Yet we burble along, procreating, and in the process suffocating thousands of other species with our selfishness. We're in a baby glut, yet it's as if we've just discovered babies, or invented them. Reproduction is sexy. Assisted reproduction is cool. The announcement that a movie star is going to have a baby is met with breathless wonder. A baby! Old men on their third marriage regard their new babies with "awe" and crow about the "ultimate experience" of parenting. Bruce Springsteen found "salvation" with the birth of his son. When in doubt, have a baby. When you've tried it all—champagne, cocaine—try a baby. Pop icons who trudged through a decade of adulation and high living confess that motherhood "saved my life." Bill Gates, zillionaire founder of Microsoft, is going to have (this is so wonderful) a baby. News commentators are already speculating: Will fatherhood take away his edge, his drive; will it diminish his will to succeed, succeed, succeed?

It's as though, all together, in the waning years of this dying century, we collectively opened the door of our home and instead of seeing a friend standing there in some sweet spring twilight, someone we had invited over for drinks and dinner and a lovely civilized chat, there was death, with those creepy little black seeds of his for planting in the garden. And along with death we got a glimpse of ecological collapse and the coming anarchy of an over-peopled planet. And we all, in denial of this unwelcome vision, decided to slam the door and retreat to our toys and make babies—those heirs, those hopes, those products of our species's selfishness, sentimentality, and global death wish.

The Arm Baby

LYNDA SCHOR

*T*he waiting room is already crowded at eleven A.M. Institutional looking, but not depressingly ugly. We look for two seats together.

"I'd better show this at the desk," I say, letting go of Phil's hand for a moment. He remains beside me instead of leaving me to find seats—he seems to always know how I feel, my needs.

"I wonder how long I'll have to wait?" I whisper, as if in some holy place, or at a concert. I'm of two minds: I'd like to get this operation over with as quickly as possible, yet I'd like to not have it at all. The thought that anyone involved with administering this outpatient surgery could possibly leave us waiting here, given how natural it is to be nervous, if not terrified, nearly brings tears to my eyes. Phil leads me to a seat, sits next to me on eggshell naugahyde. As often happens, my anxiety transmutes into heightened perception, so that everything in the waiting room, and all the people, are clear, the colors bright. Two babies stand on a couch near their mother. They look exactly alike. Each has one wall-eye. Across from us is another couple. The woman has straw-colored, frizz-permed hair, and rests an entire arm over the enormous rotundity of her belly. But what can be wrong with her? This is outpatient surgery, not a maternity ward. I become conscious of my arm lying over the back of Phil's seat, the large lump that's to be removed very much like the pregnant woman's belly. Though it's covered with a loose shirt sleeve, I self-consciously remove the arm from the backrest and clasp my hands in my lap. My mind races while Phil reads magazines, his way, I guess, of relieving his tension—by not being here. But one of his hands, square and large, with what I call "substantial" fingers, rests passively, yet protectively, on my thigh.

The lump in my upper arm, called a lipoma, is, as a few doctors have told me, nothing to worry about. Not life-threatening, or malignant, it's some fatty tissue that's pulled itself together into a unit and taken on a life of its own, continuing to grow. Maybe because I have asthma, I'm afraid that if I'm fully unconscious and suddenly can't breathe, no one will notice; maybe it has something to do with completely giving up control, but I'm terrified of anesthesia. So I've been given the option of having an intravenous tranquilizer, and, of course, localized Novocain. Although nervous about an operation anyway, I'll be glad to get rid of this lump, which I like to think of as having developed from the constant swelling

84

of weekly allergy injections, probably because I feel comfortable if I can pinpoint a cause. It's bad enough that I feel colonized by the lump, uncontrollably taken over; it's worse if I can't think of any reason for its developing. For some reason I'm ashamed of it. Aside from its being ugly, my sleeves can hardly surround it, and I won't buy any clothing, however appealing to me, that has sleeves that end above the lump, or that will reveal its unusual and freakish swelling.

The invasive protrusion symbolizes and accentuates, to me at least, the general growing looseness and lumpishness of the rest of my body, which has to do with aging.

My empty stomach roars and whines in outrage, in spite of my not having any appetite, because I wasn't allowed anything to eat or drink, not even a glass of water, since midnight. It screamed and groaned like that all during Phil's breakfast at the Village Den, where I watched him demolish orange juice, two eggs over easy, hash browns, sausages (all in spite of cholesterol restrictions), toast, and three and a half cups of coffee. He'd offered to forego breakfast just for me, but I didn't mind watching him eat. Usually he loves our meals together. He likes to watch me eat with my hands, pick up slices of bacon, whole pork chops with my fingers. He enjoys feeding me, running the spoon under my bottom lip to catch any drips. "Isn't she cute?" he asks anyone and everyone.

It's not just watching Phil eat breakfast, I know I'm set apart, alone in this. Though he's come with me, this lump is only mine—there's no illusion that we are somehow in this together. It reminds me of when I went off to the hospital to have my kids. Although their father (a former husband) came with me, we were both aware that the pain and the physical danger were mine alone. And this lump is worse than a pregnancy. It isn't alive, made of both our DNA, or nurtured by Phil and me together. It will just be placed in some container, tested for malignancy, and thrown away.

"Let's tell them to save the arm-baby for us in a jar, so we can take it home," Phil joked, spearing a piece of sausage he'd already cut with his knife. Aside from his devilish talk, he's mature and civilized in his table manners.

"You're only saying that," I said. I know he doesn't and never did want a child, which is one reason he never had any (aside from his being somewhat sterile), and I fear that if this wasn't simply empty joking about an arm-baby to cheer me before an operation, he wouldn't be eating with such relish.

I remember one of our first dinners together. While we shared *mariscada con salsa verde* and *paella a la Valenciana*, while he put an entire scallop embellished with grains of saffron-yellowed rice into my mouth, bade me eat my salad with its bright cadmium orange dressing for my health and digestion, I accused him, one piece of rice embarrassing me by shooting from my mouth onto the pristine white table cloth.

"I think men (people, I corrected) who never have kids, who don't want to, always remain immature. And selfish. They're selfish to begin with. For that reason I never go out with men who don't have children. They always want to be the baby. They're jealous of my children and fight them for my attention. Also, they're usually too controlling. For me, I mean," I qualified. "I have nothing in common with people who direct every aspect of their lives," I said, full already, but mashing my yellow rice into the dark green sauce. An entire open clamshell stood up bizarrely in the center of my plate. "I'm attracted to people who have a give-and-take relationship with their karma, who don't eliminate the positive possibilities of unplanned events."

Was I thinking then of my three children of an early marriage, all unplanned, one of the three born, in fact, before the marriage? Moreover, this tirade was cruel, given that, due to a varicocele, it wouldn't be that easy for Phil to get anyone pregnant, and because he told me about his past in a sharing way, making himself vulnerable so that we might get to know each other better, each of us hoping for the other's nonjudgmental empathy. But he seemed too pleased, too happy with that blow of fate, that throw of the dice. Two former wives had moved on to have children with other men—one because Phil definitely wasn't ready when she was, the other because he wasn't willing to have the operation he needed for fertility, or become obsessed with desire for children as she was. That he let go so easily after ten years of marriage makes me angry. It also frightens me. How loyal is he? Is he more loyal to a way of life, his freedom, his permanent immaturity, than to a person? Is he ready to go on to the next woman who happens to possess the dark hair and adventurous spirit he's so attracted to?

How different is he from Alain, who said he was in love me, but who left me, a concrete person, to look for a hypothetical lover young enough and willing enough to bear his child? And right before I met Phil there were other men I dated who were seemingly seeking a woman for a relationship, but really looking for a walking uterus.

My second husband and I broke up because of our disagreement about having a baby. Supposedly we were madly in love. But even though he was a lousy stepfather to my children and remained a combination child/lover to me, two years ago, when I was forty-two, and had just gotten over my last biological-clock anxiety urge to give birth to one last infant, he decided he couldn't live without a child of his own.

Phil didn't reassure about how loyal he could be, or make any kind of pledge. He didn't tell me what I wanted to hear—that with me everything will be different. He hung his head over his *paella*, his shock of white hair dipping into it, and smacked himself across his own cheek, a shocking gesture that made further vituperation redundant.

"Don't you dare do that," I said.

A woman wearing a pale green duster over her regular clothes, her short hair like pecan icing slathered over her head with a pastry knife, holds a clipboard and looks around the waiting room. I shrink into Phil, whose hand tightens its grip on my thigh. It's the pregnant woman she wants. I try to overhear something, but can't. Without looking back at the man she came with, the woman, holding her stomach as if it's a package, her luggage perhaps, allows herself to be led from the room. My heart starts pounding. I inhale deeply.

"Do you want me to read to you?" asks Phil, putting his arm around me. I touch the lump in my arm. It's usually soft, like my body, only more so—like gaining too much weight in the wrong spot. But now it feels harder. I caress it, trying to feel its edges, its boundaries, where it ends and I begin.

"Uh huh." I nod, mouth dropping open like a sleepy child settling in to be soothed.

He reads from an article he was reading about new types of electronic speaker. I'm not the least bit interested, but it doesn't matter—I couldn't concentrate anyway—I just allow myself to be wrapped in his voice, in rhythms and comforting cadences.

When I met Phil, I didn't think any man who didn't have children could understand women, could be nurturing. Maybe I thought that having had children might enable a man to relate to me and to my choices better. Even more, to my non-choices. I think of myself as a person who is not defeated by fate, but who uses chance. Just the way you can't plan a short story or a novel exactly. It grows with you, strange things creeping in, revealing unexplored and dangerous paths. I feel relieved, for instance, that my children were accidents, that I got pregnant when abortion was illegal. There was no way I could have chosen to have them, yet I can't picture a life without them. Well, maybe I would have traveled a lot, like Phil. Maybe I'd have been able to have a lucrative career. Maybe I'd have written four or five more books. Maybe I'd be married to one of the many guys I dated once or twice, but who left because they couldn't stand my kids, or didn't want to become instant dads.

"Do you want me to read more?" Phil asks.

"Uh huh," I say in a high-pitched voice. I hear myself, and then look around, embarrassed. I look at Phil. Once when my grown daughter Theodora spent a weekend with us, by the time we took her to Penn Station Phil was morose and totally uncommunicative. Very unlike him. "What's wrong?" I asked, after Theodora left. "Are you tired?"

"It's just that she acts like a child when she's with you," he said.

I thought a minute. "What do you mean?"

"She acts and talks like a baby."

"I talk like a baby sometimes," I said.

"It's different," said Phil, putting his large arms around me, melting.

Is it also fate that my second husband, Harry, had an undescended testicle? That my lover Stefan had his testicles shot off by the Nazis? That Eric had had a vasectomy? How could I know that probably the IUD I got after my third child was born, and which caused all those infections, amounted to a form of permanent birth control. At this point, that's a tragedy I'm thankful for.

Right now I can't deny there are advantages to Phil's not having any children: I don't have to help take care of them when they visit him, I don't have to watch him bring them up in ways that I don't approve of, we don't have to spend the money that we need for computers, or for a trip, on a bike or a railroad set, or a bribe, or child support, and I don't have to be the foil for intermittent rage at his child's mother, a person he'd have to be involved with for at least twenty years. I laugh with him when I point out a cute baby on the street, or in a store, and he makes a face and says uucchhh. Still, I wonder about that. How he can be so nurturing to me, and seem so totally uninterested in children.

I run my fingers back and forth along the soft fabric of Phil's shirt, rest my head on his arm. I like being nurtured for a change. We're good parents to each other—better than our real ones ever were.

He and I are more alike than I realized in the beginning, when I was sure our relationship wouldn't work.

Feeding me the flan he said was good for me, in between spoonfuls of brownish gold junket-like pudding, with sudden bursts of crisp maple flavor, Phil spoke about one's relationship with choice, chance, Karma, as well as one's relationship with one's past.

"What about your former husbands, my former wives?" he asked.

Your former wives were all mistakes, mine were part of a learning process, I wanted to say. "Is my interpretation of my past a myth I create in order to justify, be able to live with, my own sheer stupidity? I like to think there was just as much positive stuff as negative in all my choices. That it's impossible to keep reevaluating one's past with the vision one gets from moving on. To go even further," he says, his own lips parting sympathetically under his bushy mustache as he aims a spoon, overflowing with flan, at my mouth, "whether thinking about one's past from a negative point of view is truer, or thinking about it positively is truer (and I doubt one could reach truth, whatever that is, that way) looking at your past positively makes you feel better—makes you do better, makes one act better—it's all interconnected—see what I mean?"

He looked at me, but his eyes were glazed like the flan. He was still thinking. "If you can't learn to look for all the wonderful results of extreme and what others might call destructive acts, choices, non-choices—if you can't be on good terms with your past, then your entire life is poisoned."

I was absorbed in what he was saying. His face in front of me was the universe; the restaurant had disappeared. He seemed finished, yet looked distracted, like he was hunting for an example, which might turn out to be his former wife, Laura, who, according to Phil, always sees the negative, so in order to avert what to me was someone he used as an example far too often, I smiled coquettishly. Then, raising my hand, I stuck my forefinger into his mouth.

"Remember last night, when I screamed in my sleep? And I told you I was dreaming that we were asleep on our futon, and I had this funny feeling, and I woke up to see, standing above us, this huge guy? And because he was so close, like not downstairs or anything, where we could use some tricky strategy to save ourselves, and you were still asleep, we were completely defenseless? Even though I screamed for you to wake up, I knew this was it for us? I see now," I hurry to explain, as a man in a pale green duster searches for someone I'm sure is me, "that that dream was related to this operation. I realized," I say, "that, no matter how much you wanted to, you couldn't save me."

Phil stands up when I do, wipes his hand nervously along his thigh, and gives me a kiss. "How long will it be?" he asks the young redheaded guy who's come for me.

"About three hours, including the recovery room," he says. "You don't have to wait here. You have plenty of time to go eat or something." He turns to me. "Do you want to leave your coat here with your husband?"

"I'll take it," I say, now knowing why—as if there's a possibility Phil will leave, go to a bookstore, some record store, and somehow never come back.

It's awkward waiting with a total stranger, among vast hordes of white-smocked nurses, for an elevator that takes forever to arrive, following him to my doom. He's nice, makes conversation about the slowness of antiquated elevators. Finally he says, "Come," takes my hand, and sprints with me through the crowd to the stairs. "You don't mind, do you?" His freckles stand out on his skin, white in the pale stairwell. There's nothing wrong with me, I think, running up the stairs after the youngster, giggling a bit. I follow him through winding corridors. He opens a swinging door marked SURGERY. A large male nurse, dressed in loose green pants, a loose green shirt, and what looks like a green chef's hat, hands me, folded on one large black hand, similar greens. The haven't left me unescorted for a minute. Perhaps they think there's a danger of patients running away.

He shows me to a small locker room. "Like mine," he says, pointing to his cotton shirt. "Top ties in back," he says. "Robe in front. What size shoes do you wear?"

Once locked in the tiny room, totally naked, even my wedding ring and wrist watch off, outfitting myself in this strange loose clothing, its easy-access style only a pretense at cover, by the time I bend to pull on the size-medium slippers, I watch some small tears drop onto the rubber.

I have to force myself to leave the closet in my borrowed greens, and what resembles a shower cap on my head. The nurse, who was waiting for me, introduces me to my doctor. When I'm this nervous my sharpened perceptions seem to go along with, or cause, an attenuated awareness of the humor in a situation, so seeing my doctor wearing a hat that looks like a combination of the Dalai Lama's and the Pope's, a green robe something like mine, and a different style rubber shoe, then looking at the three of us sitting on benches in our fantastic outfits, hearing once again reassurances about the lump in my arm, how many people have them, though usually they don't grown as rapidly as mine, and how they're never (that doesn't meant they won't test it) malignant, I have to make an effort not to make the jokes I can't help thinking of.

"Are we ready?" the doctor asks.

Once in the OR, everything seems speeded up. I show the doctor my asthma inhaler. "I want to keep this with me, just in case," I say.

"Sure," he says, like a parent humoring a child, allowing it to carry some favorite toy. He hands both the inhaler and my eyeglasses to the nurse, who put them both into a plastic bag, then lays them on a table.

I do everything they tell me, climbing onto a stretcher, holding my arm out for the IV.

"How are you?" asks the anesthesiologist.

They tell me to turn onto my stomach, a better position for access to the upper arm. I begin to feel very relaxed; this is all happening so fast. "Mmmm," I mumble.

"How are you?" shouts the anesthesiologist. If I don't answer, he repeats the question. He wants to see if I'm conscious. Soon I'm so relaxed I resent the constant questions. The work going on alongside me on my arm, stings once in a while, but mostly feels far away. I just want, want desperately, to fall into a deep, complete sleep.

"Here it is," I hear.

"How are you?" asks the anesthesiologist.

"Fine," I say, enraged, but it comes out groggy.

Then there are cheers, and the sound of applause.

Have I fallen asleep for a moment? When I'm thrown onto another stretcher by three or four people, onto my back, my small breasts heave into view, having only been covered with a sheet. At the same time, gauze is being wrapped around and around my arm.

In the recovery room, I'm propped to a near-sitting position, and an IV stand with a fluid bag is attached to the needle already in my arm from the tranquilizer transfusion. My wrapped arm lies on the other side, beside me. I feel no pain (it's probably still full of Novocain), but treat it tenderly nevertheless, while I wonder what they will do with the lump, what it looked like, how big it was. While my blood pressure is being taken, I breathe a long sigh of relief.

"You'll stay here for at least an hour," says the recovery room nurse. "You can't leave until you void in that bathroom over there, and can walk without feeling dizzy."

I notice the woman from the waiting room on another bed, also with an IV. Obviously she's still pregnant; her belly rises to the level of her head, even though her bed is raised.

There's a slight commotion as my doctor, the male nurse, and two other nurses push their way through the beds. They are all smiling and chattering. One of them is carrying a small bundle wrapped in white flannel.

"Put your arm like this," the doctor says, creating a rounded well with my good arm. He places the bundle inside, near my face, then pries the flannel blanket open. I see a tiny tiny baby, asleep, one miniature fist, the size of a grape, near its minuscule, nearly invisible nose. It wriggles and grunts without opening its eyes. In a glance I see that, though tiny, it's perfect; all its parts are there including fingernails like microscopic fish scales. Like Phil, its skin is so light it's transparent pink, and, like Phil when he was a baby, its hair is a faint orange fuzz on its minuscule head.

I look at the doctor questioningly, then at my arm. He shakes his head up and down, grinning, obviously pleased.

"It's a boy," he says. "What a surprise."

Now what, I wonder, inhaling the baby smell, involuntarily running my lips along its infinitesimal peach-fuzz head. What a joke! The last thing I want is a baby. I've been loving my life now, our lives, the feeling of freedom the childless people have, for the first time. Then I think about Phil. How will he react?

A nurse accompanies me downstairs, this time in an elevator. She holds the baby, wrapped and bonneted, and a huge bag of stuff for him—bottles, blankets, I don't know what, while I carry my coat and purse. My shoelaces flap—I'm still in a daze, spaced out from the tranquilizer. Phil rushes over to me, hugs me, and smiles, holding up a red and yellow bag from Tower Records.

"Are you okay?" he asks. "Let's see the arm."

Before I can show him, the nurse comes close with the baby.

"What's this?" he asks. No one answers. The nurse smiles and opens the blanket so Phil can see. He looks at the baby for what seems like a long time, then looks at me. His face nearly covered by his shock of pale hair as he once again studies the infant, I just see, on his chin and cheeks, a sudden flush of red, as if he's weeping. Whether it's with joy, surprise or horror, I can't tell. After another long moment, he shakes his head slowly, sniffles, then takes the baby carefully from the nurse, who makes sure he's holding it properly. He opens the flannel cover more, to further expose the walnut-sized pink face, then gently rearranges the blanket so the baby will be well protected from the cold outside. Somewhat surprised, though maybe not really, I flush with pleasure. No questions asked, Phil's accepting this totally unexpected event. My arm is beginning to sting from the stitches, and to throb hotly. Phil's large nose is buried in the baby blanket, sucking in pheromones, bonding, as I struggle to get my arm with its large bandage into the sleeve of my coat. Phil begins walking toward the exit, then, almost as an afterthought, nods for me to follow. Still very weak, and slightly dizzy, I must make a huge effort to balance. I automatically reach out to Phil, but he's carrying our tiny baby in one arm, and all its stuff in the other, and I realize he's got no hand left for me.

Outside the Hive

A Meditation on Childlessness

PATRICIA FOSTER

*R*ecently, I took a walk with a
friend who had had cervical cancer in her early thirties. As we walked beneath the
live oaks surrounding my house, admiring the swags of Spanish moss and the
blooming dogwoods, my friend, to my surprise, began to talk about her regret at
not having children. "It's probably unseemly at my age, but I still want them," she
said. "Oh, I know I shouldn't get pregnant, but I admit I've toyed with the idea.
You see, I can already imagine the baby."

I nodded as if in agreement, though my own mind went dumb with a different anxiety. Although I was also childless, my imagination dug in its heels at the
thought of having children. I had no nightmares or dreams about children, as if
I'd wandered witlessly into female adulthood without any thought to biology. I
felt suddenly uneasy, as if there were something wrong with me, some failure of
the imagination, some narrative block. And I say imagination, not body, because
having a child is surely as much an act of the imagination as it is of the body. And
yet with me, no scenarios spun out their fine threads of possibility. When I tried
to see the swirling dot that is a beginning cell, it metamorphosed into a period,
that all-too-familiar symbol of punctuation.

After we had finished our walk and my friend left to meet her husband, I sat
alone in my living room, saying softly to myself, *You've got to think about this, you've
really got to think.* I realized I'd never come to terms with this fact of childlessness,
had never articulated my own private response to it. It seemed to me that I didn't
so much make a decision to remain childless as that I woke up at age forty-five and
noticed it. Yet I knew this couldn't be true, and I was suddenly curious about the
underpinnings of my choice, one unacknowledged by me for a long time.

It began, I think, in history. Not just the history of my family but the history of a
region, of a period of American life, the fifties and sixties where men and women
conformed to roles that separated them into neatly ordered camps. For white
middle-class people, this period was a romanticized version of Eden, where families were generally intact and the economy was bursting at the seams. Every day,
men went out in the world to make a living while their wives stayed home and

raised the family, cooking, cleaning, and running errands, reading to children and helping them with their homework. On the surface, it seemed quite clear which group I should align myself with. And yet I might as well confess: for most of my life I haven't wanted to be a woman. Or, perhaps, what I feel is much more subversive: I haven't thought of myself as a woman, though goodness knows I've certainly tried all the masks of femininity the market produces. Instead, growing up, I thought of myself as an "it," a neuter, neither phallic nor fecund, neither girl-child nor boy-child. As a teenager, I dreamed about becoming a woman the way American writers dream of the pastoral. I felt both the need to return to the feminine and the impossibility of the act.

Of course, my gender ambiguity is probably quite natural, given that in my family, my sister and I were brought up as honorary sons, ambitious boys hiding out in dresses, our long hair a mere frill of affectation. "The girls," we were always called, and I thought this a sly, preposterous trick. We lived our entire childhood and adolescence in a small Southern town, a traditional town in which young girls went off to college, got married, had children, and then settled down to a scheduled domesticity: making costumes for dance recitals, hosting fish-fries for the church, attending Little League ballgames, sometimes even catching a foul ball. All of this seemed proper and right for the women in our town, and yet my sister and I knew that we were not meant to repeat such lives.

On Sundays, when my dad sat with my sister and me at the kitchen table after Sunday dinner, he often talked about the possibilities of "life" with a capital *L*. "It's easy to be a big fish in a *small* pond," he'd begin theatrically, raising his eyebrows as he looked at us over his black frame glasses. "The difficult thing is to be a big fish in a big pond."

"In a city," my mother would add, turning from the dishes she was rinsing in the sink. "I've never wanted to live in a small town," she'd continue, "but your father . . ." and she'd start the dishwasher, letting us draw the necessary conclusion.

Thus the big pond was where my sister and I focused our attention, and in our minds this was an idealized image, a romanticized place of glory and applause. It meant living in a dream city with skyscrapers and bright lights, doing something noteworthy, something that made the hustle and bustle come to a sudden, surprising halt. *The big pond.* It sounded so heady. My sister and I felt harnessed to ambition as if it were an engine carried buglike on our backs, its motor always running. "Compete, compete, compete," the motor hummed, little hammers beating against our skulls. Miraculously, we were also expected to present ourselves as girls, to be polite, pretty, and accommodating in the social world while the engine revved privately, internally, gearing up for school and competition. . . . I often felt caught like a fish on a hook, wiggling against an inevitable paradox: how to pursue ambition while retaining feminine beauty and charm. It all made me very tired.

Even as early as age six, I understood that babies changed a woman's life forever. In first grade I remember overhearing my mother say casually to a friend about a pregnant girl in our town, "Now her life is over!" which made me think that the young girl and her baby would live the rest of their lives tucked inside a closet or consigned to a cellar with rotting apples, belching furnaces, and old clothes, never to come out for homemade ice cream or for the Lineville Christmas play at the First Methodist Church.

At this time I was enthralled by the lives of older girls, high school girls—particularly those whom my parents indicated would "go somewhere in the world"—hoping, I suppose, to follow the arc of their lives. One of my father's friends, Ronnie Flanagan, had such a daughter, Margaret, who pranced before us with the sassiness of a woman on the cusp of the world. When we visited their house, I loved to go into Margaret's room and watch her sitting at her vanity, rolling her hair on twisted plastic rollers, part of a home permanent kit, pictures of Elvis Presley and Teddy Roosevelt pasted side by side on her vanity mirror. I admired everything about her, from her sharp bossiness with her parents—she argued constantly for an extended curfew, for the right to go to the dances in Pell City, for the right to stay up late and read—to the articulate symmetry of her room, the vanity, the desk, the bookcase, and especially the bed with the crocheted doll dead center, its skirt spread out in a perfect circle. Margaret, who was robust and athletic, who made As on all her quizzes, who carried the C-D encyclopedia with her to the bathroom, had a tall, handsome boyfriend, Mitchell, who was as shy as she was talkative. When he came to pick her up, even his beauty seemed to fade a little before the force of her personality, and yet Margaret always touched his shirt affectionately and beamed back her trigger-happy smile into his face. Mitchell had a younger brother who was in my class, a boy named Peter who did swashbuckling tricks with a stick to impress the girls. The only unfortunate thing about Peter were his ears, which stuck out like paper tabs from the side of his crew-cut head. . . .

It happened that in the fall of my first-grade year I became enamored with Peter, and it was agreed between us in our carefully worded notes that we would be boyfriend and girlfriend for the year, with occasional heated hand-holding in the cloakroom. It pleased me to be chosen, and especially to be chosen by someone who was connected, even incidentally, to Margaret. Peter said she ate dinner with his family every week, that one time he caught her smoking a cigarette in the back yard and when she saw him, she pitched the cigarette across the street into the ditch and asked him if he could throw that far. He said of course he could and threw his mother's garden trowel into the next field.

Near Thanksgiving, the weather turned slightly cooler so that we had to wear jackets over our dresses and knee socks instead of the short, folded-down kind we'd been wearing. I loved the cool weather, the way the heat came up from vents in the floor, ballooning my dress, the red-gold leaves falling suddenly from the trees at each gust, and the delicate patterns of frost on the windows where I could spell out my name. I looked forward to Thanksgiving, not only because I'd be out of school for four days, but also because I'd have two big dinners that day with extra desserts: one at noon with our family—chocolate cake with fudge icing—and the second in the evening with the Flanagans, who always had homemade apple pie.

And yet Thanksgiving morning we woke to a shock: we would *not* be going to the Flanagans after all. Sixteen-year-old Margaret had eloped the night before with the silent, handsome Mitchell! My mother, talking on the phone to Mrs. Flanagan, was distraught, as if Margaret were her very own daughter. Her voice conveyed all the horror and shame of someone dying, someone getting killed in an automobile accident right before your eyes. As she poured coffee for herself and my father, she said sadly, "Well, there goes Margaret's life!"

Somehow in the midst of the conversations that followed about Margaret, I assumed that she would have a baby. I don't remember if she actually did have the baby that year, but I remember the edge of concern over the possibility, which women talked about in lowered voices when my sister and I came near. Of course, we heard all the undertones, the worried phrases—"She couldn't be!" and "It would be a tragedy"—even in the hushed voices of the women who played bridge with my mother. And we knew that women often had babies once they were married. Mostly I felt mad at Margaret, who still wore pleated skirts and mohair sweaters, who probably continued to give herself home permanents and tack up pictures of heroes on her vanity, because she'd disappointed me, and would now have a life of closets and cellars, or some tawdry equivalent. The arc of her life had suddenly gone flat.

When I went back to school after Thanksgiving, I met Peter in the cloakroom. He smiled at me and held out the candy he'd brought me wrapped up in aluminum foil with an orange ribbon on the top. I took the candy cautiously, not sure if this meant we were tied to each other, and if so exactly what that entailed. It was my earliest concern about relationships, one where gifts often implied more than their surface pleasure. I worried suddenly that he might ask me to elope as his brother Mitchell had done with Margaret, and before we left the cloakroom, I turned to him and said peremptorily, "I'm not having any babies!" and walked briskly out into the room, relieved to have said my piece.

During elementary school, when my sister and I played dolls, we never let them have babies. Perhaps the stories of young girls in trouble, girls like Margaret who would no longer go anywhere in the world, had struck home, making us queasy about letting our young dolls become mothers. We loved grown-up Madame Alexander dolls instead of Betsy Wetsys and demanded that they do absurd but interesting things in the world: sing loud, shmaltzy songs in nightclubs, have a house with the roof open to the stars, or best of all, live in Greenwich Village and work as a window designer at Bloomingdale's. Of course, we combed and washed our dolls' hair, dressed them for exotic dates, but our imaginations never took us into the heated interior of family life. Often we gave our dolls lessons, dancing lessons, clarinet lessons, baton lessons, swimming lessons, mimicking the way we spent most of our time. We'd put them on the end of the couch and say strictly, "Now you have to swim under water the length of the pool," then nurse them along the long green couch, mechanically kicking their legs . . .

We knew that my father had always wanted five boys and one girl and must have been surprised at the odds of two girls and one boy. *What? Only one boy?*

Though my sister and I became "honorary sons," these actual words were never spoken. Instead the idea was intuited in the hallways of our imaginations, in the public life demanded by its applause. And it was applause we wanted, great rolling rounds of applause, like putting a seashell to your ear and hearing only clapping. Standing ovations would be even better! The point of life, I decided, was figuring out just how to get your due. And in some sense how to turn girlhood into boyhood, into the kind of approval that shouted its good news. Almost every week we saw my father's picture in the local newspaper, and this acknowledgment of status and worth became one of our requirements. "Don't come home until you get your picture in the paper," he said to me once when I was in my twenties. My friends thought he was teasing, that this was mere rhetoric, but I knew he meant it. Hadn't this been the legacy of my childhood?

Although my mother often lived both roles—having a career as a biology teacher and taking care of house and children—she never taught my sister and me any homemaking skills. "What's this?" I asked, holding up a sieved bowl. "A colander," she answered, taking it from me and draining the spaghetti. That was it. End of lesson. We never learned how to cook, sew, or clean house—"This is a dustmop," my mother-in-law said when I got married, "This is Windex"—and yet despite these absences in our education, our daily lives were intimately connected to the feminine. We knew, for instance, that the female world was divided into mothers and nonmothers, and like many children who easily hold a contradictory idea in their heads, we saw there was something eccentric, sad, even peculiar about the childless women who occasionally surrounded us. In my mind, these women were failures not because they didn't have children, but because they hadn't gotten out of town, hadn't done something fabulous.

We often heard hushed conversations in the kitchen between such women and our mother about some aspect of their "difficulty." Nobody mentioned the word infertility. That would be indelicate, impolite. I imagined my second-grade teacher, Mrs. Peak, leaving school with our stack of spelling words and printing exercises, driving home to a lonely, dark house in Bon Secour where she spent three hours in solitude waiting for her husband to get home from work. Solitude seemed the enemy in a region defined by gregariousness. In my own yard playing on the jungle gym with my friends, I tried to imagine what Mrs. Peak would do with those idle hours. Maybe she soaked her feet in Epsom salts, as Mother occasionally did when she'd had a long day, or perhaps she made curtains and bedspreads, as Mrs. McTeague sometimes did when her kids were at the swimming pool. She certainly would be relieved of the many tasks of chauffeuring kids around to dentists and Cub Scouts. Sometimes while I climbed crablike across the bars, I imagined Mrs. Peak sitting slumped in a chair, her hands hanging limply down the sides, her face numb with the emptiness of her life. More than anything I wondered why she had not gone to live in New York where there were crowds of people moving around at all hours. After school in New York, she could go to the Museum of Natural History and be face to face with dinosaur skeletons or Eskimo dioramas. She could visit the famous public library.

•

It wasn't until late adolescence that I saw an escape from my conflict with achievement. It was so close at hand, it was almost a joke, a quick slide into hiding. Although I didn't feel female, I began to mimic the world of the feminine, knees together, back straight, my mind a cloud of potential fashions. Spaghetti straps or strapless? Bikinis? Pedal pushers? Spike heels or square-toed flats? There was so much to assess—how to be that perfect object, sweatless, smooth, nipples never pointy, hair neatly brushed. And yet all the time I was secretly practicing for this pastel life, I felt the old ambition deep inside my bones. My sister had been racking up awards, proving herself in the masculine/feminine territory we traversed. Not only was she awarded a National Merit Scholarship and several valedictory prizes, but she was also the Speckled Trout Rodeo Queen, with her picture in the paper, a crown on her head.

I felt pale by comparison, but I didn't know the route out of envy. Instead I embedded myself in the female world and felt stuck there like jelly in a jar, my psyche taking on the shape of the container. Paradoxically, I turned my ambition to artifice, constructing beauty as my entrance into the world. More than anything, I wanted the ritual "ah-ha!," my own personal eclipse of the sun. Getting dressed for a school dance was nothing less than a theatrical production. I could have been a character in a play: the face, body, and style transformed from the ordinary to the exotic. First the face had to be contoured, the false eyelashes applied, the eyebrows drawn on, the cheeks sculpted. Then the hairpieces were fixed into place. Each night I rolled the fake bangs on an orange juice can so they would be slightly curled rather than poker straight, ready to be attached to my scalp with bobby pins. Then a headband obscured the bobby pins from the world. For certain dresses, I wore a waist cinch which gave me my Scarlett O'Hara look, the stays splicing my ribs like punishing fingers, spiky and stiff. And always, yes, the padded bra. After my disguise was complete, I stared at myself in the mirror with a furtive surprise and a hint of distrust as I reacquainted myself with the thing created. It was a slow dissolution, this losing of my real self to the charade. I breathed out my transparent, unself-conscious self and inhaled a persona. Ribs tightened. Breathing changed. Shoulders straightened. I blinked rapidly, getting used to the flutter of the lashes their thickness distorting my peripheral vision. I put myself on a cloud and ascended, arms open as if I knew what I was meant to welcome. But I didn't really know what my transformation meant. I understood only that zeal was what counted, and now I was a dark object palpitating with fierceness.

I took my fierceness like a wrapped secret to college. At age nineteen, if there was any sleeping core of longing in me, it was a desire to feel female, to make the inside and outside cohere. I didn't want to be estranged from myself, to live the metaphor of a knot. Of course, I never said a word about this to anyone, for I knew that only crazy people went to see psychiatrists. Instead, I kept my fear inside the locked box of my psyche and waited patiently, like a princess in a fairytale, for something to happen. And sure enough, this longing was awakened one night when my boyfriend Ray pulled me into the packed darkness of his closet, pressing me against the blue workshirts, soft from so many washings, hanging from several hooks. All around me I felt the clutter of clothes, the stuffiness of the closet which was long and narrow like a hallway. We had been dating for four months; love wrapped around me like a glove, protective and warm. I believed I'd found my soul mate, partner for life. Ray's lips touched me as he pushed against me, a sleeve of one of the workshirts falling over my shoulder. Through the open closet door strains of Jimi Hendrix's "Purple Haze" drifted in, the guitars whining with sexual energy. "I love you," Ray said, and I was thrilled to the bone. His lips were at my ear, nuzzling my hair, my neck. "I want you to have my babies," he whispered. I snuggled closer. I had been chosen. "Yes," I said, ecstatic, convinced. Babies were the ultimate love gift, and Ray's wanting one with me seemed to cinch my female reality.

Once I had a house and a husband, I wanted that world, the female world of lemon-pine odors and baking bread, of worry over curtain length and where to hang the oval mirror. And yet I stood in the kitchen and did not know what to do. It was a huge room, odd in its regularity, with too much linoleum and chrome, gadgets and wood. I didn't know how to work the stove, the electric can-opener, the double boiler, the meat thermometer. I had no idea what to cook, how to make a meal so that everything came together at the same time. Once, totally confused by the measurements of cooking, I stood before the butcher at Piggly Wiggly and asked for "a foot of steak." The butcher gave me a suspicious look—was I playing him for a fool?—while I waited sheepishly in front of the meat counter, fingering the pork chops, suddenly remembering *ounces*. Eventually Ray's parents sent over Loretta, their cook, to supervise my learning, to direct me in the meals of their family: chicken and dumplings, hot water cornbread, blackberry cobbler, creamed corn, stuffed tomatoes, hush puppies, sweet potato pie, and last but not least, stewed cabbage. . . .

. . . After six months of this, I gave up on domesticity, fixed hamburgers and pizza, and went back to school at Rhodes College in Memphis. My past had risen up to claim me.

And yet the tapestry of my life remains a chaos of unraveling threads. Four years later when the marriage broke up, I was greatly relieved that Ray and I didn't have children. While married and living in a small town in Tennessee, I told myself at twenty-two I was too young, still growing up, defining myself and simply not ready to be a mother to someone else. All around me women my age were having babies, but I'd quickly discovered that instead of resolving my gender fears, marriage only amplified them. Although our courtship had been a fury of desire, marriage seemed to temper even the sex drive. Once we'd settled down in Ray's hometown, he was hell-bent on losing himself to a weekend of music and partying after a sixty-hour work week at a job he despised. I know now that Ray and I were both fighting for psychic survival, that when the self is in danger, the desire for sex, and especially any thought of having children, can vanish like steam evaporating in the air. Depressed at being back in his hometown, Ray became remote, self-involved, and likewise, I held myself apart, waiting for something special to happen to me, for my talents to work along a fat vein of certainty. I spent the entire marriage watching for a sign of who to become, still waiting for rescue. Yet no sign appeared. No treasure fell from the sky. No trap door opened.

After the divorce, I still felt like a child in adult garb, a masquerade of a woman who didn't know who she was. Startled, I realized that the waiting had been for nothing, that the one positive result of the marriage had been its infertility. I was grateful I wouldn't be a single mother, a child-mother, and settled down to live alone for six years, studying art, taking classes at the university, drawing designs and portraits alone in my room. I was happy in a rebellious sort of way, like a bird gaining its wings and flying directly into a whirlwind.

In my room, I pared everything down to essentials: bed, chair, table, lamp, art supplies, camera. Here, I felt monkish, transfixed, a potential honorary son. From this perspective, my past life looked like a lull in a storm, the dead center of a hurricane. I'd wanted a protective cloak, one that would diminish the effects of the outside world and keep me young and smooth like a wrapped chocolate inside a box. Now I wanted, demanded, high winds. I immersed myself in art, working seven days a week, going to a Rothko exhibit or seeing works by Billy Al Bingston and Acconci, listening to Laurie Anderson and Philip Glass every weekend, trying to fashion a life. During this period I never thought about children, about anything that would divert me from my newly claimed world. I was in my late twenties without a boyfriend. If anyone had asked me if I wanted children, I'd have shrugged, said flippantly, "Who knows? There's still plenty of time to worry about that," and moved into the darkroom, setting up the enlarger, the trays of developer and fix, getting out my film from its plastic sheets.

And there was still time. Yet the imaginative life is a quirky life often tied to the unfinished business of childhood. For me that meant continually straddling the masculine/feminine domain, confronting my ineptitude in both spheres. Although I saw art—and then later, writing—as my salvation, the thing that made me invisible, translucent, a mind and body exploding onto cloth and film and paper, it satisfied only one part of the equation. Ritualistically, the feminine demand for seduction still reared her insistent head, and there would be days when I had a love affair with the mirror or when I lay in the couch obsessed with a recent infatuation . . .

When I met David at age thirty, I'd just finished my MFA in art. I was making collages of cloth, poems, and photographs, assembling these on a long table in the middle of my apartment. Almost immediately we began to argue, bickering like street children, shouting out our opinions about art—the typical battle of aesthetics, old code/old form vs. new code/new form and the legitimacy of all combinations in between—while sipping espresso at the Boulangerie or driving on the freeway to Torrance or Long Beach to pick up supplies. With David I didn't stop working but simply moved my supplies across the room from his in the studio where we lived. It was a huge box of a room—all concrete with eight-foot ceilings, no windows, only double garage doors that swung out like wings into a dirty alley bordered by chain link fences and signs that read: BEWARE—ATTACK DOGS. If I stood in the doorway, I could smell Mexican cooking down the alley, the greasy mixture of onions and beans. We were five miles from Venice Beach, where the roller-skaters had taken over the boardwalk and muscle builders pumped up while watching the roar of the ocean. We slept in a loft and cooked on a hotplate. With a refrigerator, a shower, workspace, and a darkroom, we considered our lives complete. We stayed up all night working, then slept until mid-afternoon. We thought of ourselves as bold and sacrificial, having nothing to do with bourgeois life. And yet the reality is we were simply poor. We were part of an underclass culture barely able to sustain our current lifestyle, sometimes trading work for rent. Of course, we didn't have health insurance. We didn't even have car insurance.

By this time my sister had finished her medical degree, had gone into practice, had borne her first child. "You'd better watch out," she told me conspiratorially over the phone, "the women in our family are exceptionally fertile. All I have to do is tell my husband I want to get pregnant, and the next month I am." I laughed with her over the phone, the very idea of me, *me*, getting pregnant. "I'm a long way from that!" I said, looking across the room at "The Raft of Medusa," my latest art piece. I wished suddenly that she could see it, the layered collage of dyed cloth, the draped netting, torn and gaping, the reedy bamboo. It would surprise her, stem the tide of her accomplishments. From a distance, her life looked like a perfect performance, one that happily combined the roles I was still trying to sort through. It seemed natural to me that her life should be jammed tight with obsession, with diversity, while I was still trying to master one straight line.

During the next three years, my sister often called and asked me when David and I were getting married, and more importantly, when we were going to have children. While she talked, I stared at the concrete slab floor, the raised scratchy surface we hosed down to clean up, the puddles of water drying near the door. There were splotches of dried paint on the tables, the one chair. We hung our clothes on a clothesline that traversed one corner of the room, their spooky shadows shifting with each gust of wind. "Ground control to Major Tooommmm," floated out the window from a neighbor's stereo above the clink of dishes, the mumble of voices. My sister had no real sense of our situation, our poverty. And I'd never felt comfortable telling her that we'd chosen this, that we'd consciously given up making money in exchange for time to make art. Of course, we had jobs, but they were simply that, incidental ways to make rent money. Never careers. By this time, my sister had had two more children, had brought a partner into her practice, had added a string of bedrooms on to her house. "My kids need some cousins," she said, pretending to tease, but I caught the serious note in her voice. "Surely, you don't want them to grow up without cousins!"

I assured her that I didn't, then went back inside the darkroom and switched on the enlarger. I knew what my sister was saying. *You can be everything.* Didn't she have three children, a full-time profession? Didn't she race from office to home to grocery store with all the impetuous haste of our childhood? This was the message of the late seventies, the women's movement in full swing, women no longer choosing between career and motherhood, but having both. It seemed miraculous, almost a demand.

Yet at night in my dreams, I was always running—in and out of doorways, through fields of weeds, alongside dirt roads, the dust kicking up in a cloud at my heels, through hospital corridors and urban streets. Usually I was running in terror, trying to escape some menace, unseen but real, in pursuit of my body, my soul. I was running, I think now, for two reasons: running *away* from the expectations of my culture to become a superwoman, with both career and children— a woman who accomplishes everything the culture demands—and running *toward* a potential future, toward a realm I could claim. In my dreams I gave the truthful answer to my sister, the answer Sula Peace gives herself in Toni Morrison's *Sula*: "I don't want to make somebody else. I want to make myself."

On some unconscious level I knew that my quest for autonomy was my only chance for survival. And I'm convinced—though others might argue the point— that children change the autonomy of a woman's life more than any other condition. From my early age, it was clear to me that I needed to live outside the "hive," as Virginia Woolf called the extended family circle. For a person overwhelmed by a crowd of three, this is important knowledge. When I began writing, I couldn't separate solitude from creativity. I hauled a desk upstairs into the loft where I could be entirely alone. It was hot and stuffy. It smelled like musty sheets and dried apples. Spiders drifted down, each hanging suspended on one silken thread. I admired them. Like me, they worked alone. I needed this atmosphere of silence, of heat, of dust motes swimming in the light. Through writing, my body taught me that my choice of solitude was not selfish but necessary, a blossoming, a way of growing up to a self I could love.

This perspective came clear to me one day recently when I was lying in bed, listening to the early morning sounds of my neighborhood—the hiss of school bus brakes, the banging of car doors, the stutter of cold engines—and I felt for the first time the strength and diversity of my needs. For so long I had felt limited by them, ashamed. But this morning, the decisions in my life were mine. Soon I would get out of bed and work on my novel. I could already feel the pen in my hand, see the cup of hot tea on the table. I thought suddenly of my own early imaginings of Mrs. Peak, about her lonely afternoons, her fearful wait for old age. I couldn't help but smile at these misperceptions. What if instead of her feet in Epsom Salts, her mind slurred by emptiness, she was home dreaming a dream like me: immersed in a manuscript, her mind making it's own convoluted web, each word drawing her closer to that internal mystery that is the self unlocking slowly from its knot, like fingers from a fist.

Part Two

KNOWING LOSS

I Get My Period, September 1964

DIANE DI PRIMA

How can I forgive you this blood?
Which was not to flow again, but to cling joyously to my womb
To grow, and become a son?

When I turn to you in the night, you sigh, and turn over
When I turn to you in the afternoon, on our bed,
Where you lie reading, you put me off, saying only
It is hot, you are tired.

You picket, you talk of violence, *you draw blood*
But only from me, unseeded & hungry blood
Which meant to be something else.

From Crossing the Moon

PAULETTE BATES ALDEN

*W*e had a conference with Dr. Kuneck and the verdict seemed to be that it was about over for us. We asked him about the GIFT program, but he had just gotten the latest national statistics for women over forty in such programs; the success rate was 9 percent. And my potential for miscarriage if I did get pregnant was 40 percent. Age was the biological wall and I had my back to it. He said my estradiol numbers were low. Some of the eggs just weren't able to do more. That made Jeff feel sorry for them—"as if we're asking them to do something they can't do," he said sadly. We could try three more rounds of Pergonal, but he thought maybe forty-two was the cut-off point.

It was difficult for me to return each time to the infertility clinic now. The realization that I was counting down to the end was tough. I couldn't imagine not going to the hospital anymore, not seeing the people there, not trying.

I was feeling so isolated that I got the idea of forming a support group of women over forty who were patients at the infertility clinic. I thought such women were different from women in their twenties and thirties. I figured that, like me, women over forty must be having to face an age-related end. We might be able to help each other along in that process.

Dr. Kuneck and Dr. Campbell were very amenable to the idea. They readily agreed to have Linda mail copies of a letter I had written to all their women patients over forty. I included my name and phone number, and told them to give me a call if they were interested in being in a support group.

I dropped off the letter the next time I went in for insemination. I had two good follicles developing, and Dr. Campbell did the insemination. He commented, concerning my effort to get a support group together, that men would never do that. "There's something about that Y chromosome," he joked.

On the way home from the insemination, I thought to myself, I'm going to get pregnant—why shouldn't I? I was surrounded by naysayers (not the least of whom was myself), but why couldn't it work? Why wouldn't it work out? I didn't see why it shouldn't. Why shouldn't I have a baby if I wanted one? Why not me? I hadn't given up hope yet. Hope couldn't be killed off. It was like a worm that someone chops up over and over with a hoe, and still pieces of it live. It couldn't be killed off, hope. It wiggled away, a tiny piece of it, to live on its own.

From *Crossing the Moon*

It was hard to imagine now what the hope was even for. A baby. A pregnancy. At a certain point it all had become a bit abstract, almost meaningless. I was just engaged in *trying*. I hated to be defeated. I hated to say uncle. I squirmed like a piece of worm meat trying to get away from the hoe.

How had having a baby, getting pregnant, become such an obsession with me? All I could think was that there must be a mechanism that clicks in once you try to get pregnant that instead of allowing you to accept that you cannot, compels you to keep trying, no matter what the odds or cost. Maybe it was actually a biological response, something built in at the deepest level to ensure the species would go on. I had never seen anything like it myself. I never would have suspected, until I tapped into it, just how powerful the desire could be.

And yet I was eventually going to have to quit. I even wanted to quit. But I didn't know how. Did I have to be dead to quit? Sometimes I felt that if allowed, I would just keep on and on, never accepting it as long as I lived. I had seen a headline in the *National Enquirer* one day in the grocery line, "101-Year-Old Woman Gives Birth." My immediate thought was that she must have been in infertility treatment and just kept on until she finally succeeded.

I had never imagined, when I was a little girl growing up in South Carolina, that one day I'd be forty-two years old, living in Minnesota, and sitting around with a group of other women over forty feeling envious because I didn't have as many follicles as someone else. There were ten women at the first meeting of the over-forty support group, and we started with our reproductive histories. Marcy, forty-five, a tall Scandinavian looking blond with bangs, had had her first baby at fifteen and given it up for adoption. She had married in her thirties and had had six pregnancies since, none of which had made it to term.

Gina, who wore her dark hair in a long braid down her back, was forty-one and recovering from a laparoscopy that had removed massive fibroids from her uterus. "I'm planning to try in vitro six times," she said. "Do you want to see my scar?" and she pulled down her slacks to show us. She had had two abortions when she was young, before she married. In addition to her fibroid problem, her husband had a low sperm count, so they were having to use frozen donor sperm.

Dede, a pert redhead who was about a size three, had tried GIFT once, and was preparing to try again. "Dr. Kuneck told me I have the ovaries of a thirty-year-old," she said proudly. Someone asked her her estradiol numbers. "I'm producing around fourteen follicles each cycle on Clomid," Dede said, "and my estradiol is right up there around fourteen hundred." I could barely produce two follicles, and my estradiol struggle to get to five hundred.

But then there was Terry, who was just forty (so young!), but who had been trying for ten years unsuccessfully. "I'm not producing any eggs, even on Pergonal," she said sadly. "Dr. Kuneck wants me to quit, but I don't want to. I'm just not ready yet."

"You don't have to," Dede said forcefully. "It's your decision. Just remain positive."

"That's easy for you to say," one of the women shot at Dede. "You've got the ovaries of a thirty-year-old!"

We all laughed, but I saw that Terry was near to tears. Several of the other women already had children, from previous or current marriages, and couldn't conceive or carry another pregnancy to term. "People don't understand about secondary infertility," Louise, the mother of an eight-year-old, said. "If you want another child, and can't have one, it's still a big loss. My own mother is always saying to me, 'You've got Kerry, why can't you just be happy.'"

The patient whom Dr. Kuneck had mentioned to me who was forty-eight was there, only now she was forty-nine. "I just didn't get the urge to have a child," she explained, "until I was forty-seven." I felt glad to be among these women, more interested than I would ever have believed in their stories.

But I woke in the middle of the night, troubled by it all. Dede, the one with the ovaries of a thirty-year-old, was a very strong, forceful personality, and she had dominated the group. The message she gave out was that any effort was worth it, that if we'd just be gung-ho, we'd succeed. Maybe it was easier to be upbeat if you were producing double-digit follicles each cycle on Pergonal. But most of those women were struggling to make one follicle. One of them was taking four thousand dollars worth of fertility drugs a month to produce one follicle and ending up ovulating early on day twenty-six. It occurred to me now, deep in the night, that some of those women were even further into denial than I was. I thought that none of them, with the possible exception of Dede, had more than a 1–10 percent chance. But they wanted, so it appeared, to keep on. I had never felt my chances were less than 20 percent, but now, after meeting the other women over forty, I felt that maybe they were actually less than that. I suspected that none of those women was going to get pregnant and have a live birth. Of course I could be wrong—that was the problem. We were always hearing success stories, of women over forty who had "miracle" births. But for most of us, I saw, that was not going to happen, and it was disturbing to me that we would all persist so.

At one point in the evening I had said, "It's got to be all right for women not to have children." They had all said of course it was all right, but it didn't seem all right for them. But maybe the more important question was, *Was it all right for me?* Maybe I should get a grip on myself. I, who had always wanted to be in control, had actually lost control of my life. Seeing those infertility patients over forty, I had the uneasy feeling that we were all seriously unbalanced. I didn't think it was unnatural to want a child. I wanted one myself. But I did question pursuing such an unlikely goal in the twilight of our fertility. Was it worth it to wreck our lives emotionally and financially? Weren't we just postponing the inevitable? Was the need for a child so powerful that it swept away rational thought? I couldn't judge the other women. But what did it say about me that I had let the desire for a child take over my life? Didn't I have enough sense of self by this time, enough maturity, really, to accept—even embrace—my life as it was? If I couldn't have a baby, was I going to become a baby myself?

Still, I understood too well how hard it was to give up. Even as I lay there calculating my own long odds, I hoped that I was pregnant. I was in the waiting state again; my period wasn't due until spring break, when we would be in Greenville.

From *Crossing the Moon*

I had made an appointment in Greenville with another infertility specialist for a second opinion. My mother had sent me a news clipping about a doctor in town who had written several articles on infertility. I called his office and told his nurse that I wanted to make an appointment for a consultation. I wanted another opinion on whether or not it was too late.

Jeff was a little skeptical of this idea. But he was willing for me to do whatever I needed to do. I knew I already had all the information and answers I needed. So it wasn't answers and information I was after. It was something else. What if Dr. Kuneck was wrong? What if he was a certain type of personality, very conservative, who himself gave up too soon? I needed to hear it from someone else, to be sure. I was looking for reassurance that it *was* too late. I felt that if I heard it again, from someone else, it would make it easier to end. But I also wanted, I realized, the possibility of some salvation, as if another doctor might say, miraculously, it's certainly not too late! You still have a good chance!

We were in Greenville and it was the thirty-first day of my cycle. Tomorrow, I'd have the appointment with the specialist to get a second opinion. I had not concerned myself too much with starting my period. I was not going to be suckered again. I usually started my period on day thirty-one on Pergonal, so I hadn't given it much thought until day thirty. Then I thought, simply, Well, I'll just start tomorrow. And that will be the end of that.

All day on the thirty-first day, I waited for my period. It was going to come. I felt bloated, crampy. Still, it didn't come and it didn't come. By evening, I was beginning to allow myself the thought that I might be pregnant. My mind seized the smallest possibility and ran with it. Soon I was actually delivering, a live birth as they say in the statistics I'd become so familiar with. All through the night, I tossed and turned, I got up to see if I had started my period and I hadn't. It was agony. Could I really be pregnant? At last? And might it not work out this time? It might . . . I imagined the irony of going to the infertility specialist tomorrow and asking for a pregnancy test. I imagined calling back to my clinic in Minneapolis, to tell them the amazing news. I burned all night long with fears and hopes, knowing I was probably not pregnant, but unable to let go of the possibility. It was a feverish, nightmarish, anguishing night. When I got up in the morning, day thirty-two, my period had arrived.

I didn't know it at the time, but it would never be like that for me again. I would never allow myself to go through another night like that one. It went too far. They had played with me enough, finally. They had made me suffer a little too much that time. I didn't even know it, but I was about to cut them off, those devils of hope and despair.

Jeff and I went to see the infertility specialist. He was a bit disorganized. When he began talking with us, I realized he had not read my files, which I had been so diligent in having sent down ahead of time. He seemed to want to figure out what was wrong with me, why I couldn't get pregnant, but I told him I had been completely checked out, it was all in my records. He seemed to want to second-guess Dr. Kuneck, and I thought I detected some male competition at work. I felt like telling him what was wrong with me was my age. As Jeff would say later, did we really have to pay a hundred and twenty-five dollars to find that out?

"It takes a woman over forty about eighteen cycles to get pregnant," he told us. He was a bald man in his fifties, in a navy blue jacket with gold nautical buttons. He reminded me of certain Southern men I had seen all my life, the country club set, the mint julep type, confident and cocky within a small local pond. "Of course, Pergonal ups those chances somewhat, but you can't stay on Pergonal forever. I'd back away from Pergonal," he said. "I'd back away from artificial insemination. There is always a chance, after all, until you hit menopause."

I was shocked. Not using artificial insemination was in direct contradiction to what Dr. Kuneck thought improved our chances. There was obviously a difference of opinion here.

"But I thought artificial insemination improved the chances of conceiving," I said.

"Nonsense," he said, rocking back in his desk chair. "In fact, it might hinder conception. Timing isn't all that important. You should just do the natural thing. You'll naturally become," he said looking at me, "the sexual aggressor a few days before ovulation." Jeff and I raised our eyebrows at each other. The guy had obviously never been in infertility treatment himself.

When we left Jeff shook his head. "What a hustler," he said animatedly. "He obviously wants you for a patient. And what was that about wanting to give you a physical? The guy gave me the creeps!"

I had to laugh. I didn't know myself if he were a hustler or a creep, and I didn't really care. I had gotten what I had come for. I was looking for some kind of loophole, some way to stop without hitting the wall. Rational thought aside, I knew I wasn't ready for The End. He had said he'd back off Pergonal; he'd back off artificial insemination. I wanted to back off all that. He had said we could still keep trying, the natural way. The message I had heard was that we could stop infertility treatment, but that we still had a chance. We had a small chance right up until menopause, and that let me off the hook, the horrible hook that it was completely over.

We enjoyed being with my parents. I was able to do things to help them out, such as take my mother to the doctor, and drive my father to the barber shop, since he couldn't drive himself anymore. At eighty-seven he was having more and more trouble with his short-term memory, but he was as pleasant as always to be with. I'd see him dozing in the La-Z-Boy rocker, and he reminded me of an old dog or cat, sleeping in the peace and comfort of old age. Nothing much disturbed him. He was very attached to my mother, who looked after him now that he couldn't quite look after himself. When she drove to the beauty parlor one day, he rushed to the front window, and watched her back out of the driveway and turn onto Jones Street. He wanted to make sure she made it safely into the street. When they went somewhere, my mother told me, he always had to keep her in sight. In his old age my father was becoming a bit of a child himself again.

One night Jeff, Mother, and I played three-handed bridge. All four of us had had a good time before dinner watching the news and having cocktails, cheese and crackers, green pepper jelly over cream cheese, and cocktail wienies with hot sauce. My parents loved a good cocktail hour, and so did we. My father never played bridge, so after dinner my mother and I tried to teach Jeff. We sat in the living room on the needlepoint dining room chairs at a card table. Jeff found a piece of old chewing gum stuck to the bottom of his chair, which he promptly displayed. He teased my mother about which of her bridge-playing friends stuck gum under her chair. We were all laughing, having a good time, and I felt more relaxed, I realized, than I had in a long time. For a moment at least life was not some monumental problem to solve, there were no hard decisions to make, no hard realities to face, no grief or pain, just a three-handed bridge game with my mother and Jeff and a piece of old gum stuck under a chair.

That night I had the "provided for" dream. In the dream I was struggling. A lot of people were going to show up at our cabin, and I was going to have to feed them all. But when they arrived, they were all carrying food. I didn't have to do anything; it was being taken care of. The people were from all different parts of my life, time ran together, the past and the present were one.

Aunt Grace and Uncle Perry came over before we left. Two years ago they had moved to a retirement home and they were finally making the adjustment. They looked frail in their old age, but they were alive, they were still themselves. I hugged my mother good-bye in the house, and then Daddy, along with Aunt Grace and Uncle Perry, who were driving us to the airport, went out with us to the car. I hugged my father good-bye. March 18, 1990. I felt how small he was. I felt his bony loving hands on my back. I smelled the skin of his face. Good-bye, Daddy, good-bye. I climbed into the car, and as we were pulling down the driveway, I turned to see him once more. He stood watching us go.

We flew on to Florida, to see Jeff's parents who were wintering there. One morning before we were to leave, I woke up early. Jeff was still sleeping, and I looked across to the twin bed where he lay on blue sheets, beautiful in the early light. It came to me that it really was a choice between two good things—having a child and not having a child. Our life without a child seemed good to me. I caught a glimpse that it was what was right for us, for the best. But who can say what is "best"? Maybe it's possible to get to a place where what is best is simply *what is*.

Forty, Trembling

Wendy Rose

She bore no children
but ghosts emerged
from between her legs.
Dare to believe
that roots can be built
like a clay pot
in ascending circles
and that skin just
naturally forms
copper sheets
on the bones.
Promise that a name will appear
blazing from the cliff,
that the harvest is great enough
and her life not empty
when she has so much farther to go.
Step softly.
She is not of this world
and no one rides to the rescue.

The Wash House

PAMELA WALKER

*I*n my line of work you meet all kinds from the low to the high on the social ladder of our Catskills town. At the Wash House I do the drop-offs and oversee self-service, selling detergent to transients, making change and cleaning lint filters, which may not sound like much but it's good, steady work that occupies my hands while freeing my mind.

I have my speculations on the regulars, from the clothes they bring, of course—workmen's dark twills with AmeriGas or Getty patched above the pocket, a doctor's dress shirts monogrammed at the cuffs in with white coats—but I get the whole picture from the cars they drive, the way they walk. I size up each face as its owner walks through the door, hefting bags of dirty laundry. This is why I'm accused of staring. Faces are important but they're not everything. A tall girl hunching her shoulders tells me she wishes she were shorter, or the way pretty girls whisper when they don't believe in their beauty. You have to be ready for the contradictions. That's what I like, devising a life for a character only to have it shattered by simple truth.

For instance, I surmised this one with the curly black hair and horn-rimmed glasses was a college professor as I shook out his chinos and plain shirts after the dry. I'd never seen him, but that was September when everyone's back for school, so it was the obvious guess.

"Haven't I seen you on campus?" I asked when he came back late afternoon for pick-up.

"I doubt it," he tells me, pushing his glasses up his broad nose. "I'm just passing through."

"On business?" I ask sweetly.

"Ah, yes." He had a quiet way as if to apologize. "Explosives."

"Excuse me?"

"Explosives."

"That's what I thought you said. What do you explode?" I was getting interested.

"Buildings, mostly."

"Oh, yeah, I've seen it on TV. The way a whole building sucks in and collapses, there must be quite an art to that."

"Implosion," he nods.

I handed him his laundry and his eyes lit up. "Hey, no ironing." He took the shirts and slacks on hangers covered with plastic. "Most services don't do it so nice. Thanks," he said, as if I gave him special treatment, which I didn't.

I give everyone my best work. A cold water wash—I swear by cold water with a powdered bleach to get at the dirt, it's cheaper with no shrinkage—a perma-press dry and timing are my tricks, knowing when to take out shirts, then pants before wrinkles set in. You have to get them right for a good hand press and they're ready to wear. That's my method. It brings me constant compliments from my customers. We're on first names and they know my schedule, eight to six, Monday, Tuesday, Thursday. Wednesdays, Harry's bowling night, I take the late shift, closing up at ten thirty.

Harry's my husband. Harry Ganakis. I call him Hare because I don't find Harry an appealing name, not that I ever told him. Hare's Greek and he's proud. I was an Allegretti until Hare and I married. My father said no but he couldn't stop us.

"Marry a Greek and live in a trailer?"

"It's a brand new trailer on our own piece of land."

"In the middle a nowhere!"

"Nine miles out of town."

Hare's dad runs the luncheonette, mine owns a pizza parlor. My father, you can't reason with him, but I lived to see him eat his words. Not a peep from him when he sees Hare and me owning the trailer outright, our fields leased to a farmer for hay—that pays the taxes. Hare has the knack. Granted, his father—all generosity, Hare's dad is—gave us ten acres, but we did our share. For my part flowers bloom all over the yard. You ought to see my daffodils poking through fresh snow in yellow clumps of little horns, a sight to break the hardest heart in spring. Hare and his dad laid down railroad ties three foot high for the garden, trucked in rich topsoil so black it looks charred, and layered manure with com-post. There's an art to everything.

Our space is raw, no shade trees yet, just the four baby poplars Hare gave me for Mother's Day the past two years. I was pregnant. Hare planted with an eye to the future, placing them at the beginning of our drive, which will curve back to the house we'll build someday near the tree grove. Most Mother's Days are win-try affairs, but we bundled up and Hare dug holes, the trees on the ground, their roots tangled in big dirt balls. Hare told me his plan.

"Every year, Roseanna, we'll plant two poplars on Mother's Day until they line our drive."

That's how sweet my Harry is and it doesn't embarrass him like it does most guys. "When our baby is grown," he dreamed, stepping the shovel into the earth with a muddy clodhopper, "these trees will stand tall and we'll be old."

"Oh, Hare, we'll still be young." I stomped my feet to keep them warm. "When our kids are grown, we can travel."

"Well, that's true," Hare admitted, but I could see he liked the idea of growing old as he shoveled dirt out of the hole.

The Wash House

As we head into winter, the trees stand bare and spindly. We live on a hill exposed to the wind from the north and I fear for the trees. Though Hare chose Berlin poplars, a hardy variety, there's always a gamble. We meant to name them for the babies, but we didn't get the chance to settle on our choices.

I don't know what went wrong and neither do the doctors.

"You must understand," the bald doctor said, "this baby was not meant to be born." He was a hefty man with the smooth, pudgy face of a farm boy who watched his father drown the lambs born maimed. I didn't need him to tell me the obvious. "You're young, try again."

This was after my second. One, you accept. Hare's mom and his sister lost one apiece. With one I grew closer to true womanhood. My baby lived and died inside me. But two at my age? I'm twenty-three and strong though small and fine-boned like my mom. I couldn't face the world. I didn't want its pity and couldn't bear the thought of babies in their mothers' arms at The Wash House.

The other girls took my shifts and called with messages from my regulars. Mrs. Craver had her baby. The dentist Dr. Grogan was leaving town. Their names sounded strange as if I never cared who they were or where they went between drop-off and pick-up. This never happened to me before. As a little kid bringing silverware wrapped in napkins to Daddy's customers, I eavesdropped on conversations. Even then I had my speculations. I always wanted to know.

It was June. I let the weeds take my garden. The groundhogs ate our lettuce. Hare picked bushels of tomatoes and peppers but I couldn't stand them, ripe and shiny in the baskets. I made Hare give them away. I didn't pick flowers and I never split the bulbs.

Sometimes I sat out front in a lawn chair and watched cars pass, a blur of speed and purpose. If they honked, I waved but I didn't look at faces. Our trailer sits at the edge of fields that border the old highway to Cooperstown. Across the road green hills rolled one into another like gently pregnant bellies. Sometimes I had myself a cry when I was small before the mountains, beneath a sky too big. I never saw Hare cry, though he told me how he sobbed by himself for hours the night we lost the first when he had to leave me at the hospital. Still, Hare awoke each morning at the crack of dawn like a farmer. He works the eight-to-four at Deltown and he has a forty-minute drive. Every night he worked his other job—splitting timber for the sideline firewood business he and his uncle run—till darkness drove him home to me, resentful of his will to keep on going.

"Rosie," Hare reached across the table as we were drinking morning coffee and he touched my hand, shy as if we barely knew each other anymore. "It would've been worse if they'd been born. It's going to work, Rosie. We'll have children."

I squinted at the summer sun resting in a pale sky as though it were a face softened by a gauzy curtain and we were in some childish contest I was determined to win. When I looked back at the table, bright flecks danced red and green across Hare's hand and the room grew darker. My head throbbed and Hare's fingers were rough against my skin.

"Hare, my children died and I couldn't bury them."

I didn't know I meant to hurt Hare until my words hung cold between us, and Hare pulled his hand away.

"They were my babies too." I heard a tremble in his voice that made me glad even as I wished to swallow back my words.

Hare sighed and slapped his knee before standing and trudging into the bedroom. His bare feet pounded the floor, his butt tight in his jockey shorts like he was sucking in his cheeks. He slammed drawers and banged the closet door, emerging in his Deltown blues. The trailer shook with each step of his work boots. He took his lunch box from the fridge and I followed to the door. I hooked little fingers with him, but I couldn't look into his eyes.

"I won't be home for dinner. It's bowling night." Hare pecked my forehead and walked to his truck.

As he drove off, I waved, clutching my flimsy nightgown to my naked body. The air tickled my neck and the sun warmed my arms. Our little trees quivered in the slightest breeze, leaves like whispering hearts, the first two pert and taller teens leading the babies.

I came in and called my boss.

"Rosie, how ya feelin?"

"Okay, Gary."

"It's not the same without ya, Rose. When ya comin' back?"

"How about tonight?"

"You'll close up?"

"Sure, it's Hare's bowling night."

"Oh, that'd be fine. I was gonna stay, but with you here I'm clearing out."

"Okay, Gary."

"See you at five."

"I'll be early."

I arrived at The Wash House at four on the dot. The day girls had hung a sign on the door, "Welcome back, Rosie!" and Gary gave me a hardy hug, lifting my feet off the floor. My back eased beneath the strength of his arms. Gary has the body of a wrestler, squat but powerful with thighs that strain his jeans and forearms rippled with muscle.

Patty ran to the Dairy Queen, bringing back an ice cream cake which we shared with self-service. I was glad to be home in a way I had not felt with Hare. No one mentioned the baby. At five Patty and Angela left for the day, and Gary showed me the drop-offs due the next morning, six orders of two to three bags each. I'd had it worse. I claimed machines before the evening traffic started. After my first washes came out, I noticed dryer one in the corner was full and unclaimed.

"Gary, whose clothes are in number one?"

Gary came out of the office. "I hadn't noticed them. Someone must've left them. They'll be back."

I started my dries with machine number two. Gary left at seven and I was on my own with a full house. I was busy and no one asked to use dryer one, so I didn't think a thing about it until nine-thirty when last washes go in. The morning pick-ups were bagged and I was sweeping.

I wondered what kind of person would leave a load all day. It looked like linens, sheets and towels expensive to replace. Some kind of fool, the type to scream high heaven when they find their load missing though they're asking for trouble to leave in the first place. Or it could have been a woman hassled with kids and too much to do in town for the day, who thought she could dovetail the laundry with shopping, only to forget her last stop at The Wash House when the baby was screaming and the older kids arguing. She had a headache, all she could think of was getting home, where the baby would sleep and the big ones run wild in the woods. Still, you'd think she would've called to claim her load, unless of course she didn't have a phone. I finished the clean-up, wiping out each washer and emptying filters. About ten-fifteen I locked the door after the last customers, a couple of students with books and looseleafs on top of sheets in their baskets.

I rolled a cart to dryer one, planning to leave the load in the office with a note for the morning girls. I'd be out before ten-thirty and I'd stop for a quart of Hare's favorite chocolate swirl as a peace offering.

The clothes were wet. You idiot! I cursed, leaving me to finish up your chores. I dug into my pocket for some quarters. A heavy load of towels could take three-quarters of an hour. I couldn't wait. I'd have to leave the dryer running, something Gary told us never do. It wasn't safe. I thrust the quarters in the slot, turned the knob and was heading to the office to write a note to Angela when the dryer started tumbling. *Clunk-clunk,* it went, *clunk-clunk.* I thought, she has shoes in the load. Gary will not hear of drying sneakers. They dent the drums. I opened the door, the tumbling stopped with one last *clunk* and I started tearing out tangled sheets and towels in fistfuls, heaping them into the cart. She had me in a fury now.

My hand fell on something rounded like a ham, wrapped inside a clammy sheet, and I drew in my breath the way you do when you come upon an animal, newly dead in the woods. You stop against your will, avert your eyes, then keep on moving. Yet I held tight, I couldn't walk away. I grabbed a plastic basket, then gently picked the bundle out of the dryer, its weight solid in my hands. I untied the knot and the sheet fell away on a tiny hand, blue-veined and clenched except the thumb extended toward a hidden mouth. The perfect nail was paper-thin. I read when I was pregnant that the fingernails grow last. This baby went full term.

I looked out the huge windows at the front. Exposed beneath fluorescent lights, I feared the mother's return. Full of guilt and loss, she would claim her baby to bury. But Chestnut Street was calm. Cars passed slow and steady, the drivers knowing who they were and where they headed at the end of a long June day. The tires whirred a lullaby. The house across Chestnut was dark.

I switched off the lights from the office and picked up the basket. The lone blue light we left on all night at the back of the shop guided me to the front. I held the basket on my hip and locked the door with my free hand like any night I close up, my own laundry done, the basket no heavier.

My heart beat hard as the night I lost my first. I set the basket in front beside me. My first had gone a full twelve weeks, too small to hold but not to see in my blood on the bed, soft and crescent like baby moles the cat leaves dead on our front step. I wanted to touch it, to place it in the palm of my hand and know that it was mine, but this was at the hospital. The aide swooped down and took away the bloody pad before I could protest.

After bowling the guys go for beer. Hare's not a big drinker but tonight he'd go the extra round. I took the interstate and stayed in the middle lane, the needle hovering on red fifty-five. I signaled for my exit and took my left onto the county road, blackness deep to either side. The moon was small and useless but the car traveled through its own lighted tunnel. I pumped the brake before the curves, bringing the speed down gently and my car hugged the road. The wind was mild. I turned in our drive and coasted into the ruts my tires made in spring when I got stuck in mud.

Hare was not home. I turned the key and the engine puttered off. The spot-light Hare hung from a telephone pole lights our yard behind the trailer with one large yellow circle. I stepped out of the car and for a moment watched the poplars sleeping, dreamy forms that swayed in balmy shadows.

I knew exactly what I needed, though I hadn't thought this out. I ran into the trailer for a blanket in the trunk beside our sofa. It was my baby blanket Mom gave me the night we told her I was pregnant. Warm in my arms, it smelled of cedar. I hurried to the tool shed, the basket pressed against my chest, the sheets damp through my shirt. I lighted the Coleman and I was ready, matches in my pocket, lantern in hand, the basket hefted on my hip, shovel upright like a sword.

I walked through the field toward our tree grove, the grasses stubby beneath my sneakers. I could not make great time though my feet quickened each time I was bathed in the brights of oncoming cars. A slow, steady pace would take me to the place among our trees more than halfway, yet not too close to the marshy earth above the springs that feed our well.

Within the trees the air was close and musty. I hadn't stepped into our woods since an early spring Sunday when I was pregnant. Hare was chopping wood and I was keeping up my exercise. I'd never walked our woods at night and yet I feared nothing. The black enveloped me, my feet moved sure. I knew the roots that rose in loops. The lantern light was white and hot as if it beamed from a picnic table at camping grounds. Hare and I load up his truck with gear and take our KOA guide. We've camped all over New England and as far south as the Outer Banks. We hiked the White Mountains and next we went to see the Everglades.

We're going to do things different than our folks. Hare and I have had our share of the food business. We'll take our kids on trips, not just Howe Caverns and the Baseball Hall of Fame. We're going to show our kids their heritage. We'll take them on our backs to Greece and Italy.

I reached the spot where an oak stood tall and set the lantern on the ground. Lowering the basket, I smoothed my blanket, tucking its edges. Though I wished to look and see it whole, its sex, its skin, I could no more raise the cover than I could touch my grandma's hands clasping her rosary as she lay dead and powdered.

I began to dig. My foot drove the shovel into the earth. The ground was soft and the pull felt good between my shoulder blades as I hefted and dumped each scoop. I dug deep, a good three feet or more. My breath came in gasps and sweat tickled down my face. Another couple shovelfuls and I'd have the depth to keep it safe from animals. I would return to this spot, covering it with dirt and leaves as soil settled. I knelt beside the basket, wanting to tell this baby something, but even in our grove alone with the arms of grandpa trees reaching to hold me, words stuck in my throat, throbbing silently.

I touched the mound beneath my blanket, then lowered the basket into its sorry little grave, no tight pine box. I shoveled dirt back in the hole, rocks grating against metal. One huge scoop soiled my blanket, then I began to heap the dirt in fury, suddenly afraid of time and Hare. Had I heard a voice, distorted by the wind and distance, from our field? Were those Hare's feet scuffling through the brambles?

I snuffed out the lantern and crouched behind the oak. Hare's flashlight beamed in the dark. "Rose!" The panic in his voice made me want to yell his name but I was frozen to the tree. Branches broke and leaves crunched beneath his boots. He had circled the field and was coming up behind me. I could not run. I could not hide. I had to let him find me.

Hare's light fell on my face and I turned away.

"Rosie!" He ran to me and touched my shoulder. "What happened?"

"Nothing, Hare."

I was still hunkered on the ground. Hare's body towered above me, his jaw set tight. Dark eyes darting, they settled on the new-turned earth at my feet.

"Rosie, what is that?"

"A grave, Hare."

"You buried an animal?"

"No, Hare."

"What, then?"

Stuck between the truth and a lie I could not fabricate, I said, "It's mine, Hare."

"What, Roseanna? What's yours?"

"This." I patted the dirt, tidying the edges as best I could.

Outside Pisa

CHITRA BANERJEE DIVAKARUNI

Above the Boca del Arno the sky
bleeds its last red. The sea gives up
its colors to the dark. On the barren shore
we stand trying to hold hands,
to smile like lovers. The fishermen
have left their nets and poles, black and jagged
against the night's coming. Nothing
left for us to say. Smell of salt
and death, older than this broken harbor, older
than the white tower
this morning by the cathedral

After all the pictures, how small it seemed,
how fragile in its leaning. Dark slits of stairs,
the sooty upturned spiral, the holding on,
walls damp and slippery to the palm,
surface-scratched with names and hopes:
Lorenzo e Rosa. Pietro. Clementine. Sally
loves Bill. And when we came out
into the hot light, all around us
the breathless rainbow sheen of pigeon wings,
couples kissing, mouth to moist
rose-mouth. This same death-smell.
The floor tilted away
from my feet. No railings, just
the adrenaline rush of white edge
into nothing. You were taking pictures. I
kept my face turned away in case
you saw my eyes, my longing to jump.

When the doctor said
I couldn't have children, I sensed
the stiffening in your bones. We never

spoke of it. Deep
bell-sounds from the baptistry
where they say Galileo discovered
the centripetal motion of this world,
the headlong, wheeling planets held
arc upon arc, calm and enormous,
without accident.
Now I let go your stranger's hand,
the unfamiliar callus on your thumb.
We are suspended as dust
in this dark river air, floating
away from each other, from the other shore
where we cannot be,
its gleam of fairy lights
that we would die for.

The Deferred Dream

TORY DENT

*W*riting about my living with AIDS is always painful for me. But it is—always—what I write about; I can't think of anything else to say. In the desire to write is the desire to communicate, I believe. I'm sharing with someone and in that process trying to understand myself what it is I'm thinking or feeling. I'm compelled to share sincerely, intimately, these efforts made in order to create closeness. By writing I hope to feel closer to the world. Its what I want. Its more and more what I want as I lose slowly, incrementally, unpredictably, and of course, unfortunately, my physical grip on the world. It is AIDS that weakens my grip, and therefore the world I reach out to becomes more oblique as I struggle to sit up and look at it. I hope that by trying to describe this struggle I will connect, and that the power of connection will succeed in making me feel more a part of the world, enfolded within it rather than rejected by it.

My organic body, born into this world and made up of this world as its by-product, is the rejecting factor. My female body, whose destiny (although not its only destiny, as reaping the privileges of a more feminist Western culture taught me) would be to contribute, likewise, another organic being, to make along with poems and essays and friendships and salaries, goulash and huckleberry pie, in addition to the other goals or objectives toward which the idiosyncrasy of my individuality has motivated me, something, someone, inside me. I could give birth. I would give birth. And for as long as I can remember torturing my Siamese cat by dressing her up in doll's clothes, I've wanted a baby. I have always wanted to have a child. And just as importantly, I have always wanted to be a mother.

The most profound challenge in living with this disease is the effort to accept that I may well die from it while simultaneously remaining hopeful that I may survive. The most mundane challenge is balancing the many affronts to my superego which the physical and mental limitations of AIDS impose. But for all that I feel I have failed to do (which includes defeating the virus by responding to drug treatment), I have attained much of what I've always wanted in life as well. I have wonderful friends, a partner I deeply love, work that satisfies me, as well as the many levels of enlightenment I have experienced. This optimistic mind-set, focusing on the gain and not the loss of the past ten years, is the act of ascension within the echelon of pain. The descension, of course, is the litany of loss into which I tumble from exhausted time to time. Not a dream has been spared some change or another in these travels, as if jammed into one burlap sack heaved over my shoulder, pulled upward and then dragged downward. Not a dream has been spared completely, except one: the dream of having a child.

I'm not sure why this is so. Perhaps this dream has been spared because I have spared this dream: I have never contemplated having a child unless HIV be far behind me. Hence "the child" becomes the center of all my dreams representing the penultimate dream of survival, operating like a centrifugal force toward which all of my other dreams and their various subsets whirl and pulsate. For having a child, biological or adopted, would mean that I could rely on my body again. It would mean that the most egregious aspects of living with HIV are no longer a threat—the tenterhook lifestyle in which rare infections lure in the background waiting to seize their "opportunity" for attack.

To myself, I do not describe my dream of having a child as such, but rather in the stark shorthand of "the child"—as if there were a specific child. The child waits for me somewhere in the netherland of spiritual entity, orphaned in that she or he is without me. It's as if I have a relationship with this child already, and the child is missing. It is in a state of suspension, its destiny decided by the fate that finally chooses to look benevolently on me again, and brings us together. Therefore, it seems as if I am always aware of the child's vicinity. Indeed, all other children connect me to the child, unwitting envoys of sorts. This must be why, when I find the crosstown bus suddenly packed with kids at around three in the afternoon—swapping seats, screaming to each other, whispering, gossiping, mocking, or (one or two) contemplating—I'm thrilled to be inundated with their chaos, no matter my mood. It's like swimming and then suddenly stopping for a moment, in order to allow one's body to be carelessly battered about by the waves. Children always bring me closer to life.

Perhaps I have spared this dream, or rather reserved this dream, the way many women do, contextualizing it within the confines of their biological clock, thinking that they still have this many years to procreate. For this time period the child always hovers in the realm of possibility. Perhaps because I tested HIV-positive in 1988, six weeks after my thirtieth birthday, I allowed myself to follow such culturally conventional thinking. Although I knew that my body, for the short term, was not fit for gestation, I believed it, and I would be, eventually—if I were to live at all. This year I turned forty, and I am no closer to cured than I was ten years ago. It never dawned on me (incredible as that might seem now) that I would find myself in this position. Either I would become ash or I would survive fully, completely, resuming all the dreams and potentials I assumed myself capable of experiencing before I tested. Certainly in ten years some miracle would occur—if I were to live that long.

When I was first diagnosed, I remember seeking out a female doctor, ostensibly for a second opinion but in actuality to express this concern about children, since I didn't feel I could discuss the topic in depth with a male doctor. Male doctors would get angry, trying to scare me out of my "denial" of which they interpreted my focus on the subject of children to be a manifestation. They wanted to wake me up to the reality of the life-threat of HIV: "You'll be lucky if you live! Let's just deal with that for now," they would say gruffly, or cynically, and what I felt to be a tad mysogynistically. I'm awake, I wanted to say. Wide awake. I just want some reassurance. So during the physical examination with the female doctor, I mustered up the courage to ask her about kids. I didn't know how she'd react. Luckily, she was nice. And she did reassure me. She waved her hand in a gesture of dismissal and said that of course I could have children if I continued to remain asymptomatic. "Oh, in five years they'll have a vaccine and that'll be that. Sure, you'll be able to have kids." And she went on to tell me a couple of stories of other women, one a patient, one a friend, who for this or that reason didn't think they'd be able to conceive and "now she's got a beautiful baby boy and complains about how tired she is all the time!" We laughed together at this.

Perhaps I have spared the dream of a child because living with a life-threatening illness like HIV for ten years appears (in terms of the emotional and physical weariness I feel) to be tantamount to caring for a child who is just as seriously sick. When I dream of a child I cannot separate the happy fantasies from the worst-case scenarios that quickly co-opt the bliss of illusion. Wouldn't I therefore become a terribly overprotective parent, instilling in the child a fretful, obsessive fear of life? And then whenever I allow myself to entertain the idea of having a child, adoring and enjoying my child, suddenly I envision my child becoming critically ill like me. And I think: Could I do it again? Could I tolerate more pain? If I ever get beyond this, wouldn't I want to choose the easiest life (as if such choices can be made)? Yet, what of the joy, the pleasure, the rewards of a child? It would seem that weighing these checks and balances is part and parcel of the decision-making process in becoming a parent, but—with a background of this kind? I have experienced the somatic reality of what life is like when it goes terribly wrong. It eats me alive to imagine my child enduring such suffering. Then I become doubtful and mistrusting of my ability to make such a judgment. I admit that the thought of encountering all over again hospitals, doctors, medical tests, labs, bloodwork, insurance companies, homecare nurses, pharmacists (and we're not talking cotton balls and nail polish remover here), IV poles and syringes, makes me shudder to the very depths of myself. But worse than all that would be the sadness, the sense of lost potential, the way in which I would need to be again what I've already been to myself—a parent who gives all to this one specialized problem. My sick body has been a kind of child, in that this disease makes me as helpless and vulnerable as a child. Indeed, I have the immune system of a newborn. To be healthy and have a child, only to have that child become ill would be as if a dream were granted but heinously realized, like the fulfillment of a wish in Poe's short story "The Monkey's Paw," where impossible requests are bestowed but in their presentation become the inverted horror of what was originally hoped for: the son wished back from the dead, who does return, but only as a dead man bloodied and partially devoured by worms.

But perhaps this dream has been spared for one reason only. I have spared this dream because once I was forced by my better sense to literally spare the child. In 1991 I underwent an abortion because of my HIV status.

•

It took me a little while to realize I was pregnant. Before I tested HIV-positive, pregnancy was always the first, alarmed thought when my period was late. And when I was in college this fear was once founded, and I had an abortion. I was very upset for a long time about it, because of my ultimate desire for children, and because I loved and had been in a long-term relationship with the man whose child it was. But we were too young, everybody said. The child would screw up our graduate school aspirations, and as the words of wisdom from Planned Parenthood would remind me, every child should be a wanted child, meaning a planned child. Was I really ready to have a child? All that responsibility? I was twenty. No, I guess not. But I vowed to never let that happen to myself again. I became someone who would both take the pill and use a diaphragm.

Somehow in the adjustment to living with HIV and all that this entailed, including a sex life, safe sex, rather than pregnancy prevention became the focus. My objective in using condoms and spermicide was to protect my partner, no longer myself. Stricken by a disease that affected so many gay men, as well as living in NYC where the disease was politicized and protested in the context of gay rights, the underlying prejudice against homosexuality exhibited in the passivity of the Regan/Bush administration, I came to forget I was a woman in a way. I felt both caught up in the tidal urgency of AIDS activism and yet utterly isolated in my position as a heterosexual female, wanting to delineate my own path of reaction and response that was not only just true to myself but respected the integrity, the solidarity of the persecuted class. I was not a gay man. As a woman I had experienced the expectations of a patriarchal society. I knew I was subjugated, robbed of rights and privileges, but my fight was a different fight from that of homosexuals.

The closest I could come to understanding would be to witness the hardened faces and accusatory looks, the implicit repulsion when I revealed that I was HIV-positive. More often than not, I encountered this tenor of recrimination in the medical community, from nurses and technicians and even doctors. Then people would ask me how I was exposed (I wondered how often they would ask a gay man that). I would answer that I had a boyfriend who was a hemophiliac who died of AIDS in 1984. (To the best of my knowledge this was true, since my other boyfriends, whom I had to "notify" eventually tested negative.) I would watch their hardened faces immediately soften and reformulate into expressions of deep sympathy and compassion. Subsequently their manner shifted completely; they treated me gently, caringly, with pity rather than resentment. The change in their reaction would fill me with wild indignation, a fiery, violent anger. "I don't see why it matters," I would add. After a while, I would decline to answer when they asked how I was exposed. I knew I was opting for the rougher attitude by not complying with their need to know if I was one of the "true victims," but it didn't much matter since life had become so much rougher anyway.

So in my sense of extreme isolation, I naturally gravitated toward the gay community for terms of support and solidarity. This is how I came to forget I was a woman. This is why when the condom broke while my boyfriend and

I were making love, my attention remained focused on him and on our mutual fear of his possible exposure. We rationalized all night how unlikely it would be, reciting statistical data on the low risk of infection from women to men. It never occurred to me that the accident might also have impregnated me. When my period was more than two weeks late and I experienced vomiting, low-grade fevers, and sudden fatigue I was certain it was HIV related. This is why I sought out my physician, an infectious disease specialist, at the time to investigate these symptoms.

It was mid-October, and it was an overcast, blustery afternoon. It was cold and had rained on and off all day. It was the end of the day; my doctor's secretary had squeezed me into his schedule, and I had waited the requisite two hours for such an accommodation. The waiting room, at this hour, was almost empty. I regarded the other patients with sidelong glances. I was the only woman. One man, very thin and well-dressed in a three-piece business suit read the *New York Times*, folding the sections precisely into half-page columns, a technique perfected on commuter trains. Two men sat to my right, a couple, one very anxious and attentive to his partner, who stared straight ahead, holding a cane between his legs, his eyes glazed over with what looked like cataracts. "Advanced CMV," I remember thinking. Another patient slept, in jeans and sneakers, hooded sweatshirt and leather jacket, his face and scalp and neck spotted with dark purple, amorphous KS lesions. I wrapped my cardigan tighter around what, unbeknownst to me then, was my pregnant belly.

It never occurred to my doctor that I might be pregnant either. Instead he rebuked me for not seeing him more regularly, for not capitulating to the aggressive protocol of full doses of AZT which was the AMA agenda for treating HIV in 1991. He thought the symptoms indicated my first opportunistic infection, and when we sat down in his office for the consultation portion of the visit after the physical examination, he leaned way back in his desk chair, his face now partially obscured from the lamplight on his desk, the only illumination in the room. The daylight had almost disappeared entirely from the single window. His arms were folded across his chest, not in a position of relaxation and familiarity, but in defense. We were about to enter combat. He paused and breathed deeply, as if to exemplify in his exhalation the prolonged sense of frustration he had been forced to manage as a forerunner in the treatment of AIDS patients. His sense of defeat and anger at the disease was palpable—I could touch it in the air—and equally evident and implacable was his intolerance for patients who did not "fall in line" with his recommendations, as if they formed a platoon, an attack unit in which orders must be followed. His frustration was so profound, so long-standing. I felt the compounding despair behind it. I felt compassion for this wearied warrior, although he had no compassion for me. He had used it up awhile back, perhaps after his fiftieth patient died of AIDS. Or was it his hundredth? Or his thousandth?

He stated his limits bluntly "So. You're back. . . ." Sighing again with exhausted emphasis, he added the icy supplement, "And you want me to pick up the pieces."

I said nothing, but stared into his eyes, which in turn communicated back to me "well, you can forget it." I realized he was terminating our relationship. The wearied warrior explained to me why, softening a bit at my frozen expression. I listened to his explanation, my eyes wide with disbelief: I was sick and he was dismissing me. The window was entirely dark now, a void where he was expelling me. I listened to his explanation in part not wanting to leave, hoping to change his mind, and out of fascination for what it has been like for him. Suddenly he confessed all, perhaps because he was terminating our relationship, telling me things I doubted he shared with ongoing patients; he couldn't expose such lack of confidence, such unswerving discouragement and emotional entanglement with them.

"You see," he began "I've lost so many patients over the past eleven years." I listened while I noticed, briefly, a photograph on his desk of two young girls, roughly ages eight and eleven, laughing, heads tilted toward and touching each other: his daughters. It was a happy picture that made you smile to look at it.

Ten days later, I took a home pregnancy test and it was positive. I was so amazed that I bought five more tests after reading the positive outcome on the first.

My visit to my gynecologist's office to confirm the pregnancy was opposite in every way from my experience at the infectious disease specialist's. The waiting room and reception area, round in shape and pink in color, evoked a womblike sense of security. I took my seat amid a crowd of pregnant women, either Hasidic, with husband and children in tow, or very Upper East Side, with Chanel bags and sunglasses, reading a magazine or chatting away with another pregnant girlfriend. I was the only flat-stomached woman in the room, although I too was pregnant. It was both refreshing and foreign to be enveloped in the world of ob-gyn, a world in which the female body predominates, after the stark and scary male-dominated waiting room of my infectious disease specialist. I was struck to the core by the gender change in the atmosphere, as if experiencing some kind of gender change taking place inside myself as I waited. I felt a renewed awareness of my breasts, of my belly, of the complex workings of my reproductive system, and I was startled by it. It felt good, despite my predicament. I felt attractive and proud of my body for the first time since I had tested HIV-positive. But the discrepancy between me and the other women in the room short-circuited this confidence as I remembered the reality of what would lay ahead: I had already decided I would have an abortion.

The atmosphere of this office is one of friendliness and warmth. A patient, no matter how frequent or intermittent her visits, is treated with a sense of intimacy and community, and quickly transitions from being called "Miss" to "Tory" to "Honey" or "Sweetheart" by the nurses, of which there are many, all young and smart and extremely efficient. Yet there is never a sense of superficiality to this swift encircling as one is ushered from waiting room to exam room. In my case, everyone seemed to know I was pregnant (although my gynecologist kept my HIV status confidential), and as I was called from the waiting room this knowledge was conveyed in a way that made me feel comforted by their familiarity. The retesting took a few minutes, and I sat in a lab area with at least three or four nurses in attendance, in the midst of accomplishing other tasks. They flattered me ("great jacket!") and asked polite but sensitive questions like, "So Tory, Honey, will this be good news . . . you know . . . if you are pregnant?" I said nothing, but stared with fear at the petri dish that seemed to glow extraterrestrial under the fluorescent counter light.

The nurse in charge of monitoring the results read my face and glanced a bit nervously at the other nurses, alerting them to the possibility that this might not be good news. She double-checked the petri dish again and said in a neutral tone, "It's positive." The nurses all turned to me in unison, eyebrows raised, eyes searching, half-smiles on their faces, looking to me for the conclusive reaction. I couldn't look at their sweet faces, and imagined very briefly how this could have been a happy moment, a flash of congratulations and embraces and phone calls made to relay the good news. They waited patiently, while I stammered with my explanation.

"I'm HIV positive" I murmured, addressing my words primarily to the floor. There was a beat of silence, during which I watched the nurses look at each other with pained expressions; then they responded with a rush of sympathy and compassion.

"Oh, Tory, I'm so sorry," they said in one form or another, creating a kind of music with the partial synchronicity of their voices. Their kindness gave me leave to feel the full thrust of my emotions, and I burst into tears.

In a huddle with me sobbing at the center, the nurses escorted me to my gynecologist's private office, where I waited for him. Periodically nurses would knock, then stick their heads in to ask how I was doing, tell me that the doctor would be a few more minutes, that I should hang on, or hang in there, and did I want something—water, coffee, soda, something to eat? At one point the nurse checking in on me caught me in the uncensored throes of crying, my head buried in a clump of tissues. "Tory, Hon, can I come in?"

I nodded, lifted my pinched face up to look at her, my eyes swollen, the attempt to focus stinging a bit. She shook her head as she made herself at home in my gynecologist's desk chair.

"Oh, what tough luck you're having." Her attitude was open and embracing, but breezy and not falsely maternal. "Jesus," she began again, "the way people perceive this disease really pisses me off. You know? Like Magic Johnson coming out? Now the whole world cares. And I don't have to tell you how many people I've lost, and I'm sure you have too, to this illness because the government couldn't give a shit." Her modulated anger and feistiness, plus the carefree use of profanity in this setting, sobered me up, and I listened with relative calm and interest to her argument.

She took a deep breath, having exhausted her rant for the moment, and looked at me, not inquisitively or suspiciously, but with genuine curiously. "So how old are you?" I was thirty-three, I replied. I didn't look thirty-three, she said. She thought I was in my mid-twenties. I smiled sadly in rehearsed gratitude. People always tell my I look younger than my age.

"Eye cream," I stated flatly, supplying the secret, and she laughed.

"No kidding, eye cream. I'm going to start using it!" Then on a more serious note, "So when did find out you were HIV-positive?"

"Nineteen eighty-eight," I answered. She did the arithmetic quickly in her head,

"Christ, you were thirty years old." She shook her head again. "That's tough. That really stinks." All her modifications on the adjective *lousy* were starting to cheer me a little. It was comforting to hear someone else voice the self-pity I was feeling. She didn't ask me how I had been exposed to HIV, and also didn't inquire how I got pregnant—as people would later, always with an attitude of incrimination, implying that I had been lax in my responsibility to have safe sex. When I would answer that the condom broke people would look disgusted, click their tongues, and say nothing more.

At this point, my gynecologist entered the room carrying several files, greeting me with his usual broad smile. He has a debonair South African accent that lends a certain savoir-faire to the patient-doctor interaction, compensating somewhat for the indelicacies of his job. I'd been his patient since my early twenties, and have always been impressed by the sensitivity with which he treats his female patients, as if instinctually aware of the invasive aspect of a checkup.

I remember when I told him of my HIV status. He leaned against the counter in the examination room for a moment, seeming a bit taken aback, eyes instantly filled with depth and sorrow. "If there's anything I can do for you," he said, "you must let me know. We're here for you, Tory." Now was the time he could do something for me, as he had offered four years earlier. He could take my hand, so to speak, and lead me through this diabolical situation as quickly and caringly and professionally as possible. And that's what he did.

The nurse gave up his chair to him and left the room, shaking my hand and wishing me good luck with a warm smile. Not until she had closed the door did he broach the subject. "Tory, dear, have you decided what you want to do?" There was no judgment and no implication of what he thought I should do. If I had said I wanted to try to have the baby, I know he would have helped me. And when I responded that I thought I should have an abortion, he asked me three more times if I was certain. Was this really what I wanted?

"I think so," I answered, tears starting to well up again. "I mean, it doesn't really seem to be an option. . . ." He looked back at me, never losing eye contact while I grappled with this important choice. "It would be a risk, wouldn't it?" I asked him. "The baby would be at risk for HIV, wouldn't it? Too high . . . the risk . . . right?"

I was starting to cry but trying hard to keep my composure so that we could work productively together. He took a deep breath while still looking at me, glanced briefly down at his desk as if to collect his thoughts, and then looked back at me. "There are things that can be done to reduce the risk, you know. For instance, high doses of AZT at the beginning can reduce the chances of transmission somewhat."

"How much?" I asked, my voice high and small.

"We don't really know," he replied gently.

I knew all this already, and I knew what had to be done. I blew my nose, cleared my throat, swabbed my face with the damp clump of tissues I had been clutching all this time, and took a deep breath, my spine arching in the process. And then, forcing my head back, I spoke in an even, deadpan tone: "I can't risk that."

He nodded in acknowledgment, not necessarily in agreement. He looked troubled, as if he wanted to provide a consoling answer but couldn't. It didn't exist. And then, in one fell swoop of a single breath, I said "I could never forgive myself if I gave HIV to my baby."

I searched his face for understanding and support and he nodded again. Then the tears overwhelmed me, as if I had suddenly gotten sick to my stomach. But we had done it; we had decided.

From then on I followed his lead. The abortion had to be done in the hospital under general anesthesia because I had a history of epileptic seizures. I waited in his office while he left to organize some things and then returned. He caressed my sobbing shoulder on his way out and solicited my attention softly when he returned.

"Tory, dear, please follow me. I'm going to introduce you to a friend of mine. Her name is Rosalind, and she'll take care of everything. Tory, you're going to be fine. We're going to take excellent care of you."

I mumbled some inaudible thanks before Rosalind's arm wrapped around me and shuffled me into her office. She handed me a square box of tissues leaving it in my care, assuming (and rightly so) that I would use up its contents within the duration of our visit. Rosalind, who was in her late fifties, was more matter-of-fact than my gynecologist, but equally compassionate. Her style of consoling was that of an earth-mother-matriarch, with many years of experience under her belt. She punctuted the visit with reassurances and words of wisdom: I was young, life was tough, we have to get used to it, I would get through this, it would all be over soon enough, would be but a bad memory in time, but I would find myself happy again, we never know what will happen in life, I shouldn't blame myself, where's the man in this, is he going to own up to his responsibilities, he'd better—all the while filling out forms, checking insurance cards, helping me schedule payments, pre-op dates, the abortion date, and reminding me more than once that when I left here I should get something to eat, take a hot bath, treat myself to some ice creams, and call a girlfriend. I loved her.

I obediently followed her advice, both in the short-term and in the long, and her words of wisdom on all accounts continued, through the weeks, months, and years, to prove themselves accurate. The bath, ice cream, and phone call to girlfriend did help me to feel better that night. I did "find myself happy" again, perhaps happier than I had ever been, more than once, more than twenty-five times. I did learn to accept, slowly but surely, how tough life could be, never underestimating how much tougher life can still be. And Rosalind was right about something else as well. I was young then, particularly in the sense of what I perceived as intolerable. Since then I've come to understand that everything, ultimately, can be tolerated (not that all should be), even though that process of toleration may feel like a sweatlodge initiation, a vision quest embarked upon involuntarily. And the abortion itself became over time a just a memory, it's true—less painful than it once was, though never entirely painless. I don't blame myself.

And when I look at a calendar—whether it be the calendar that hangs in the lab as the technician draws blood from my foot (since I have no more useful veins in my arms); or whether it be the little week-by-week pocket calendar that's continually inscribed beyond decipherability with medical must-dos as well as the skeletal schedule of a normal life; or whether it be simply the sky, and the sun in its rise and its fall, which ordained the original calendar for us all—I always remind myself, even if only subliminally, that we never know, for sure, what life will bring us. We know it can bring pain. Therefore, pleasure, too, may be in our path—in the cards, in fact, just around the bend.

The Childless Woman Poems

BECKY BIRTHA

I
Childless Woman in a Playground

The children would let me be.
It is the mothers,
fathers who
stare at me.
Their bald curiosity
confronts across the box of sand
demands my justification.

There is no role for one like me
in this place.
I become a woman
who has lost her only child.
A daughter,
she would have been three this year.
I would have brought her here
to play with the others
in the sand.

The children's voices leap and fall
call to the fathers, the mothers.
It is my own child's voice
calling
crying
finally
pulling me away.

II
Habits

This is the woman who turns
    saucepan handles inward on the stove,
    has done so for years
This is the woman who has memorized
    lullabies all her life
This is the woman who collects
    second-hand picture books,
    shelves them close to the floor
This is the woman who saves
    the prizes from cereal boxes,
    keeps a crate full of toys wherever she lives
This is the woman who places poisons and
    breakable objects high out of reach,
    leaves on a light in the hall
This is the woman who has
    no children in her life
This is the woman who waits
    until her lover goes to sleep
    before she cries

III
The Childless Woman Meets an
Old Friend on the Street

in the moment
when the baby turns
away from the stranger
to hide its face
in its mother's shoulder
I want
to be the mother
and not the stranger

IV
The Rest of Your Life

Ask yourself
why you want this.
Who is it for?

The simple fact that you
carried her until she could walk

and even after,
that you consoled her
nursed her ills and
nurtured her well-being
delighted in her little hands and feet
her first few words
or that she hugs you freely
at three
is no guarantee
that at any time
in the rest of your life
you will be loved.

V
Thirty-two

Sixteen and sixteen are thirty-two
old enough to be a grandmother now.
Among my people
in any other generation
I would not have had these choices.
The first Rebecca
raised on a slave plantation
bore nine children and
delivered ninety more
knitted socks
sewed dresses by hand from
feed sack prints
cooked over an open fireplace
chopped wood
butchered pigs
slaughtered chickens and
never learned to read.

The Mother

Joyce Carol Oates

A long time ago when she was a girl she lay in secret with a photograph cut from a pulp-paper magazine smoothed carefully on the pillow beside her head; now she lies awake past midnight, past one o'clock in the morning, listening for her son to come home, waiting for the head-lights to startle her skimming the ceiling and the noise of the tires in the gravel drive and the footsteps at the rear of the house that sound so shy and cautious. Then he will go to his room, he will close the door quietly behind him, she must imagine his warm flushed skin, the bruised look of the mouth, the quivering eye-lashes, eyes lidded with secrets, the smell of the girl on him that he won't wash off until morning, so many hours away. If she stares at him, it must be in secret, he won't allow it otherwise, the soft down on his upper lip, the pale silky hair that is neither hers nor his father's, Why are you looking at me? Jeesuz!—but with a light nervous laugh, he isn't her baby any longer but a baby sleeps coiled up inside him, that deep clammy-still sleep of an infant whose breath you must check by leaning close, your ear turned to its mouth. The girls he sees don't wear lipstick so there won't be lipstick on his face, she can't allow herself to be angry.

Years ago she first turned a doorknob to discover it locked against her and she drew away frightened, ashamed, now she dreams of a hallway of doors locked against her, she calls out her son's name but no one answers, the voices are sud-denly hushed, someone giggles softly, they were sitting atop a picnic table, her son and a girl she'd never seen before and whose name she did not know, she saw her son's arm slung about the girl's shoulders, she saw their heads nudging together, his blond hair gleaming bright as it did in a snapshot taken when he was nine years old. Do you think I don't know what you do with your girls, she whispered, do you think I can't guess . . . ?

So many mirrors in the house, upstairs and down. But none shows her true face.

At meals the son and the father get along companionably, the son and the father and the mother, there is the exchange of news, there is chatter, laughter, both men are good eaters which pleases the mother though even now, at his age, the son must sometimes be chided for eating too fast, and for dropping his head toward his plate.

Once she asked him why he was going out again so soon after he'd just come home, hadn't he been gone all day, at home for no more than forty minutes, why

134

was he going out again, where was he going, she kept her voice light, calm, amused, in truth she was amused, it was so transparent, his lying. She saw how his eyes were hooded with secrets, how a pulse beat in his throat. She saw only that he wished to be gone since his life was elsewhere. She was pointing out that he'd been out late the night before, that it was raining, that he'd only just come home, it was all so childish, the game he played. A flush began in his face, that look of swallowed fury, shame, but she kept her voice light and unaccusing, she said, You're going to a girl's house, aren't you, please don't lie, isn't that where you're going, I'd like to know her name and I'd like to know if her parents are home and if they're not, I'd like to know if they know you're there, and though she was speaking calmly tears spilled from her eyes, her son backed away in shame, in embarrassment, in rage, as if he didn't trust himself closer to her.

Afterward every room in the house was a room he'd just slammed out of, the air was queer and sharp, as during an electrical storm, she saw her son's face growing smaller and smaller until the features were indistinct, she had to imagine the eyes, the set of the mouth, and cried out that he was so beautiful: so beautiful.

She would smooth the photograph out carefully on her pillow and lie down beside it, carefully, not daring to breathe.

Rain blown against the windows, spilling noisily out of the gutters. The most secret time.

At night the father sleeps heavily while she waits for the flash of the headlights, the sound of the tires in the drive, minutes sliding into minutes, hours into hours, the father's breath is usually hoarse, rasping, dry, and only when he swallows it, when she becomes aware of an arrhythmic patch of silence, does she hear him, or, rather, she suddenly hears the silence, his terrible absence, like a heart that has ceased to beat. But in the next instant there will come a startled little snort, swallowed too, strangulated, and then with an air of surprise the breathing begins again, hoarse, rasping, dry, rhythmic, this too the absence of sound, to which she never listens. Why do you lie to me, she is saying to her son, her fingers closing about his arm as they have a right to close, her nails digging gently into his skin, do you think I don't know what your life is now? the things you do? you and your girls? you alone? in your room? with the door locked against your mother?

His fingers drum on a tabletop, his eyes shift in their sockets, so beautiful, the flush in his cheeks, the soft tawny down of the upper lip, even his raised aggrieved voice as he tells her to let him alone, for Christ's sake please let him alone. And the long sinewy legs, the muscular thighs, arms, the very set of the head, neither hers nor his father's. Who can claim him? Who can possess him? Who dares? She shuts her eyes against the boy and girl, those frantic young lovers, only partly undressed as they couple, eager, impatient, shameless, she hears the boy's life torn from him in a cry of deliverance, a cry of triumph, while she lies sleepless beside a sleeping man, waiting for release, waiting for his footsteps, the soft sound of a door being locked against her.

Cutting My Heart Out

Notes Toward a Novel

SANDRA SCOFIELD

*T*here is a trigger in the woman's body, an impulse set off by hormones as the baby comes to term. "It's time," it tells the womb, and labor begins. Only it doesn't work in me; there is nothing that says, "Let go."

I carried my first baby ten months. I was on welfare; the staff at the clinic assumed I was stupid. Nobody believed I was so overdue. Nobody was concerned that for weeks I had been in pain, I had been leaking. A friend who was a social worker took me to the emergency room. She made a joke: You've got belly power, she said. All you have to do is scream.

I screamed. Once I started—it was easier than I anticipated—I could not stop. I screamed as they brought me a wheelchair, I screamed on the elevator, I screamed until a nurse knelt in front of me and said, We'll take care of you.

When your body doesn't do what it's supposed to do, they give you a drug to start the contractions. They say it's like a skier on a slope. Once you get going, you pick up speed on your own. Only I didn't. I don't.

For twenty hours they drip the drug into my IV. I am crazy with pain. Other women come and go. One, a black woman, says it's time, and they argue that it is not. Laughing, pushing, she wins, and has the baby in the labor room. Another woman shuffles in shackles; she has been brought from the county jail, accompanied by a matron and a male guard. They don't want to take off the chain. The resident yells (there is a lot of yelling in this room): How the hell do you think a baby will come out if the legs don't spread?

I wanted the baby. Not at first, maybe; not when I learned I was pregnant and didn't know if I could make it work with my lover. Not when I thought my life was drowning in a rain of trouble. But a baby fills you up and changes you from the inside. A baby makes you want it. You feel things, you get acquainted; there is somebody made from you. I did want him, but when they rolled me into the operating theater (instantly I understood why it is called that), and I looked up at the plate glass windows and saw interns and students filing in to watch, when I understood that I had messed this baby up somehow, with my bad luck, I was

136

happy for the long needle in my spine, and happier still for the morphine lie that slid down my vein, past caring.

Later, I visited Baby. Before the birthing, he was perfect—handsome, robust, too robust for me to bear—and it was only the moments when he was locked in that changed that. The moments when he was caught, head out, by his shoulders, and there was no breath in him. The moments when he could not pass from me to the world.

When I was pregnant again, I knew better, and I was paying for my care. We made a date, the doctor and I, for January 2. No matter what.

On New Year's Eve my water breaks. My heart is thudding as I ride to the hospital in a cab (everyone has been drinking). They say I can come back later when labor starts, if I want. I start to cry. Read my chart, I say. Please. So they put me in a room to sleep, and in the morning they give me hard candy to suck. The candy contains the drug; contractions begin. This pain is different. This hospital is different. And I deserve this baby.

I will do everything right, I think. I will love her.

I wonder about details—feeding, burping, rashes, and fevers (the baby book business has not yet boomed)—but it never crosses my mind that love itself is a commodity as questionable as aspirin, wine, sun, speed. There is too little, there is too much. Whatever you give, someone will say it was not the right amount. Someone will say you did not give it freely. You wanted it back.

In February I flew to New York City to rescue my daughter, Jessica. She had fallen, not to crime or dissoluteness, but to hepatitis, and so I sat with her each day, horrified by her pale gauntness, tremors, and most of all her rictal parody of a smile, brought on by Compazine and dehydration. At night I packed her things, clearing out the chaos and filth of her careless existence, boxing and taping and sputtering with exhausted tears. Yet I was happy. In the months she would be home, recovering, I would know where and how she was. We would not be separated. She would be safe.

When she was fifteen, I picked her up at school one day. She was crying hard. A girl from her geography class had written her name in a toilet stall, she said. I made her wait in the car. I could not find anything. I told her not to worry. She was not sleeping through the night, nor eating. Her stomach hurt. She thought kids talked behind her back and all her teachers were unfair. She spent days in silence. I began sleeping in her narrow bed with her, so I would wake up when she did, so I could hold her if she wanted. One night she rose without disturbing me and ran a bath. I woke when I heard the water running out of the tub. I looked up, and in the moonlight I saw her standing in the doorway to the room. She was naked and wet. She sat down on the floor, dripping water, and I could not lift her, and she would not stand, and she did not speak, and after all the years when I had been so afraid for myself, waiting for my mother to show up from inside me, I saw it was in Jessica instead. If this can happen, I thought, anything can.

I don't read the newspaper. I watch the news on public television where larger issues merit time on the air. Elections, executions, earthquakes, wars. I don't watch violent movies. But I know what's out there. At night I have woken and felt a presence in the room. It's okay, I want to say. Stay here. I can take it. In the morning, I feel so foolish, to have assumed there is only one of whatever it is, and that I can tell it what to do.

I lived as a child in my grandmother's house in Wichita Falls, Texas. She had a neighbor whose house was like a great Southern mansion to us children. We dared one another to stick our feet across the property line. His house was white with columns, and it had a lawn like a putting green. He had once owned all the land around. He owned grocery stores in colored towns. He shot a little kid— eight or nine—for playing on his yard one day at dusk, and he got away with it because the boy was trespassing. I understood that this was how it was. Between my grandmother's house and the bus stop, I knew children whose fathers beat them with razor strops, and a girl who wasn't allowed to leave her house except to go to school or church. My own mother was crazy enough for shock treatments, pills, my family's constant eye, and, finally, early death. I grew up thinking it was Texas that gave my family so much bad luck. I could not wait to leave. Somehow, the burden my mother was had not eased when she died. My grandmother hoarded her few possessions and never spoke of her, and, I thought, watched me for signs of madness. I woke many nights from dreams I wanted to abandon. But I was an optimist then. I thought it was geography. I thought I could leave bad luck behind.

In May Jessica flies to Philadelphia to visit a new art school. I want her to like it. It is smaller, classical; going there is an act of faith in her talent (no computers, no illustration, no cartooning). I want her to believe in her future. Now the summer will yawn open in pure leisure. I have just completed a novel, and Jessica is well. Now, I imagine, we will talk. We will be close. I have the idea this will be the last of her summers here. She is twenty. When she was fifteen and spent most of the summer in the hospital, she thought she and I were the same. She didn't think she had to tell me anything, she says. She didn't know we were two people.

She calls from Manhattan. She has taken a room in Staten Island and a job as a foot messenger for a magazine she admires. She didn't intend to do this—she took only a single change of clothes—but, she says, she realized as she walked around Philadelphia that it was time. She couldn't come home.

In the days that follow, I lie on her bed in a kind of a wounded stupor. I tell myself what I have told her a hundred times: that she will grow strong by acting as if she knew the way. And, little by little, my focus shifts from her to my mother. Over a course of days, I am so engulfed with memories and emotions, I can hardly stumble from one room to the other. It is as if my life has suddenly been compressed, moving from my own fifteenth year to this, my fiftieth, from one loss to the other, with nothing in between. I go back and forth in my mind.

•

Except for a few stories, I have always resisted the autobiographical impulse. I have thought my life not interesting enough, not intellectual enough, not rich enough in meaning, for fiction. Writing is an invention and an escape. It is about empathy and imagination. It isn't, is it, about me, after all?

I putter through my days. I write late, sometimes all night. I know in those hours that what I have lost, or never had, feeds my work. There is a chance to make things right, to find a new place where I have not been and did not know I wished to go.

In the course of a few weeks, my next book arrives as if by mail, whole and demanding, in my mind. There we are, the summer after my mother died: my grandmother, my sister, my cousins, and I, all of us in my aunt and uncle's home in Monahans. It is the summer I made a list of stories I would someday tell: stories about houses, about photographs, about quarrels, about secrets. Stories about sex (something adults did, to betray one another and their children). I began writing, but with other stories, stories I thought of as fairy tales, stories that had not ever happened, stories about loss and fear, abandonment, and, in the end, safe haven.

I will shape that summer so that it is no longer what really happened. The "true story" does not have a clear narrative arc. The tensions are too muted. I borrow from something that happened when I was nine, something that happened when I was twenty. I fuss and muse and move into the fugue state in which I will write something I do not remember ever having known. This time, I think, I will let my mother go.

My daughter does not get a phone. She does not give me an address. She arranges for voice mail, so I can leave messages. She checks several times a day. She calls when she has something to say. She has some good days and some bad nights, she says, but I am not to worry. Really, she says, there is nothing you can do. Something cold slices through me. I remember how, after they plunged the needle into my spine, I had no more feeling below the waist. What can anyone give me for this, I wonder? What is the analgesic for cutting my heart out?

There is only one way I can accept this. "Do you mind," I ask her, "if I write about you in my new book? It's really about my mother, but with notes about you, too." I must let her draw the line, but I don't know what I will do if the boundary cuts through my vision.

She isn't especially interested. Impatiently, she says, "As long as you don't try to write what you think I'm thinking. As long as you stick to your own story."

And this I do, a little each day, pushing back the boundary that turns out to be inside me, not her, the wall between my safe haven and the story I have not wanted to tell. This I do, because, more than light or exercise or serotonin or even the love of my husband, writing saves my life. And in writing, Jessica, like my mother, is the stuff of fiction. I can make her what I will.

The Weremother

KIT REED

*O*ften in that period in her life, when she least expected it, she would feel the change creeping over her. It would start in the middle of an intense conversation with her younger son or with her daughter, behind whose newly finished face she saw her past and intimations of her future flickering silently, waiting to break cover. Black hairs would begin creeping down the backs of her hands and claws would spring from her fingertips. She could feel her lip lifting over her incisors as she snarled, "Can't you remember anything?" or "Stop picking your face."

She had to concentrate on standing erect then, determined to defeat her own worst instincts just once more, but she knew it was only a matter of time before she fell into the feral crouch. In spite of her best efforts she would end up loping on all fours, slinking through alleys and stretching her long belly as she slid over fences; she would find herself hammering on her older son's window, or deviling him on the phone: Yes we are adults together, we are even friends, but do you look decent for the office? Even when he faced her without guile, as he would any ordinary person, she could feel the howl bubbling in her throat: Did you remember to use your face medicine?

Beware, she is never far from us; she will stalk us to the death, wreaking her will and spoiling our best moments, threatening our future, devouring our past. Beware the weremother when the moon is high and you and the one you love are sinking to earth. Look sharp or she will spring upon you; she will tear you apart to save you if she has to, bloodying tooth and claw in the inadvertency of love.

"Lash me to the closet pole," she cried, knowing what was coming, but she was thinking, "What might happen to the older son if he married the wrong girl, whom he is in love with? Who would iron his shirts? Would she know how to take care of him? It's his decision now; he's a grown man and we are adults together, but I am his mother, and older. I have a longer past than he does and can divine the future."

This is for your own good.

She and the man she married were at a party years before they even had children. Someone introduced the identity game. Tell who you are in three sentences. After you finished, the woman who started the game diagnosed you. She said you valued what you put first. Somebody began, "My name is Martha, I'm a mother." She remembers looking at that alien woman, thinking, "A mother? Is that all you want to be? What does that make of the man sitting next to you?" She thinks, "I know who I am. I know my marriage. I know my ambitions. I am those three things and by the way I am a mother. I would never list it first in this or any other game."

On the other hand, she can't shake the identity.

Here is an old story she hates. It is called "The Mother's Heart." The cherished only son fell into debt and murdered his adoring mother for her money. He had been ordered to tear out her heart and take it to his debtors as proof. On the way he fell. Rolling out of the basket, the heart cried: "Are you hurt, my son?"

Damn fool.

Nobody wanted that. Not him, not her.

As a child she had always hated little girls who told everybody they wanted to grow up to be mothers.

She goes to visit her own mother, who may get sick at any moment and need care for the rest of her life. She comes into the tiny apartment in a combined guilt and love that render her speechless. On these visits she slips helplessly into childhood, her mind seething with unspoken complexities while her lips shape the expected speeches.

What was it like for you?

"How are you feeling?"

Did you and he enjoy it and how did you keep that a secret?

"That's too bad. Your African violets look wonderful."

Why won't you ever give me a straight answer?

"Do you really want Kitty up there with the plants? I wish you'd get someone in to help you clean."

I wish I didn't have to worry. I went from child who depended to woman struggling for freedom to this without ever once passing through a safe zone in which neither of us really needed the other.

"That dress is beautiful, Mother, but you don't look warm enough."

I know you think I dress to embarrass you.

The aging woman whose gracious manner comes out of a forgotten time says, "As long as it looks nice, I can put up with being chilly."

Just before the mother looks away her daughter sees a flash of the captive girl. The old lady's flesh has burned away, leaving the skin quite close to her skull. Stepping off the curb, she is uncertain. Caged behind her mother's face is her own future.

As they go out the door the old mother tries to brush a strand of hair off her grown daughter's forehead; the old lady would like to replace her daughter's wardrobe with clothes more like her own.

Stop that. Please don't do that.

She thinks, "Mother, I'm sorry your old age is lonely," but something else snags at the back of her mind. Why was my childhood lonely? She will lavish her own children with company: siblings, people to sleep over. She will answer all their questions in full.

She will never insist on anything that isn't important.

All her friends have mothers. In one way or another all those mothers have driven their grown daughters crazy.

"She pretended to know me," says Diana, who had flown all the way to Yorkshire to be with her. "Then on the fourth day we were in the sitting room when she showed me a picture. I asked who it was and she said this was her daughter Diana, who was married and living in America. She had erased me."

Another says: "When I was little she praised everything I did, even if it wasn't any good. She praises everything so much that you know she means, 'Is that all?'"

"She says, 'You can't do that,' whatever it is, when what she means is that she couldn't do it. When I told her in spite of the family and the job I'd made Law Review she said, 'You're doing too much,' when what she meant was: 'It's your funeral.'"

"The world has gone past her, and at some level she is jealous."

Every one of the women says, "She thinks my house is never clean enough."

"She thinks families always love each other and dinners are delicious and everything is always fine, and if it isn't, then it's my failure."

We are never going to be like that.

As their children grow older they try to remain open, friendly, honest, tolerant, but behind their eyes the question rises and will not be put down. Will we be like that after all?

Beware for she is lurking, as the full moon approaches she will beg her captors to lock the cell tightly and chain her to the bars, but when the moon completes itself she will break through steel to get to you and when she does she will spring on your best moments and savage them, the bloody saliva spraying for your own good for she never does anything she does except out of love.

And she does love you.

Says her own mother, whom she has just asked what she's going to do when she gets out of the hospital: "We'll see."

It is the same answer her mother gave when she was a child and asking, "Are we going to the movies? Can I have some candy? Is my life going to come out all right?" It infuriates her because it means nothing.

(She will always give her own children straight answers. She will tell them more than they want to know about things they may not have asked.)

She is trembling with rage. The aging woman looks at her with that same heedless smile, magnificently negligent. How will she manage alone with a mending hip?

We'll see. That smile!

She cannot know whether this is folly or bravery. In her secret self she can feel the yoke descending.

I will never be like that.

•

Can she keep her hand from twitching when she sees her daughter's hair out of control? Can she be still when the oldest flies to Europe and his brother wants to leave school/move away/hitchhike to Florida and sleep on beaches? Will she be able to pretend these decisions are theirs to make or will she begin to replicate those maternal patterns of duplicity? Kissing the cheek to detect fever, giving the gift designed to improve the recipient, making remarks that pretend to be idle but stampede her young in the direction she has chosen. She never wants to do that.

She wants to be herself, is all.

Is that such a big thing to want?

Her problem is that she wishes to believe she has more than one function.

Lash me to the . . .

Are you sure you know what you're doing?

Are you all right?

I was just asking.

Beware the weremother, for even when you have hung the room with wolfsbane and sealed the door and bolted it with a crucifix, even as you light the candles she is abroad and there is no power to prevent her. Cross yourself and stay alert for she will spring upon you and her bite has the power to transform even the strongest. Barricade yourself and never take anything for granted even when you think you're safe, for even in that last moment, when you think you have killed her with the silver bullet or stopped her once for all with the stake at the crossroads, her power lives; when everything else is finished there will be the guilt.

Stork Talk

ROCHELLE RATNER

*J*oanie clasps her hands on the table. Tighter. Tighter.

Every finger's trembling.

She tells them slowly, for it seems the hundredth time, "You just don't understand what it was like to grow up in that house."

"You're right," Jim says, calm, controlled, therapeutically correct. "We don't understand. We can't understand unless you describe it for us."

She feels their eyes on her.

Wishes she could bury her head in her hands.

"When I was a kid, three or four, you know, like all little kids I asked my mother where I came from. And she told me the stork brought me."

She tries to laugh, and it comes out sounding like someone gargling.

"What the heck, that's what most people tell kids that age, right? But then I got older. My breasts started to develop. We had health class in school, which included some anatomy. I was in junior high and the kids I played with on the next block were already starting sex education classes. By that time any parents in their right minds are warning their kids about safe sex and birth control. And she was still claiming the stork brought me!"

"How did you find out otherwise?" Jim. It's always Jim who asks those blunt, no nonsense questions.

"My grandparents told me. We were close, you know, my grandfather was the closest thing to a father I had. He'd take me to the museum, or on bird-watching trips in Central Park. And when I was a kid my mother would take me shopping and stuff, but you could see how much she resented having to give up her time like that. Besides, it was always more fun to go with my grandmother."

"When did they tell you?"

"I don't know, maybe ninth grade. I had my period already, I remember that.

"They came into my room while I was doing homework, and started telling me how difficult it's been for my mother to raise me without a husband. And I thought oh no, here it comes, the old guilt trip my grandfather lays on me every so often when he's getting set to ground me or dock my allowance or something. Only I didn't remember having done anything wrong lately, or at least nothing they'd be likely to have found out about.

"My grandmother told me how my mother was always lonely, being an only child, never having many friends at school, overweight, not good at sports, a bad case of acne. She said maybe it was her fault, how she and my grandfather never really sat down and talked things out with her, how they seldom did things together as a family. Then she cleared her throat and commented on how fast I was growing up. She said maybe I was old enough to know. . . ."

She runs the back of her hand across her forehead

Unbuttons the top button of her blouse, half expecting Steve to whisper her breasts are showing. But of course he doesn't.

Christ, is it hot in here, or what?

"Know what?"

"I remember asking that very same question. I thought it might have something to do with my mother hiding her stained underpants in a drawer when she first started menstruating. I found out about that one almost by accident, listening to my grandmother talking on the phone. You know how kids sometimes eavesdrop."

"So, okay. I was a pretty smart kid, but I had no idea what she was getting at."

She takes a deep breath.

"My grandfather said my birth surprised them.
"I told him I'd already figured that out, I mean no father around and all, at least that I could remember. I realized she'd probably never been married. That was okay by me."
Steve comments that several girls in his high school class got pregnant.
"This was Catholic school, remember. But that's not the point. He said my birth came as a surprise. *A shock.* Even to my mother."

She bites her lip to hold tears back

massages her forehead with a palm she can hide behind.

The others in this room must not even be breathing, that's how silent it is.

Eerie.

She shoves the chair back stands up paces the room raises her voice, her arms maybe one beat short of flailing.

"They thought she had a ruptured appendix! Can you believe it? Here I was kicking away at her insides, six pounds at birth, and none of them even suspected it! Jesus! He tells me she had just come back from the beauty parlor, she'd had her hair done that morning!"

Steve places a hand on her shoulder
  Jim gets a cup of water from the cooler
    They draw her slowly back to the table.

She sits down
  Takes a sip
    Lets it slide back.
    Rinsing more than drinking.

"Then my grandfather was talking about that damn stork again. He told me they started it as a game, while she was still in the hospital. They'd lift me up and put on this big smile and say 'Look what the stork brought.' Then sometime after that they realized she really believed that bit about the stork. She refused to admit she'd been pregnant."

Even Steve's finding it hard to contain his laughter. Or what she reads as laughter.

"Yeah. I must have laughed, too. You know how kids do at that age, they don't care whose feelings they're hurting. Anyway, the next thing I knew I was on the floor and he was straddling me, hitting me with the buckle of his belt, again and again. I couldn't sit down for a fucking week! And all the time I was thinking how she's the one who deserved that beating, how it was all her fault."

She looks from one to the other.
Jim's her own age, a certified marriage counselor. Probably with two or three kids by now.
Steve, eyes downcast, always the gentleman, and yes, as she's said here a dozen times over the past month, she loves him very very much and no she doesn't blame him and yes she knows it isn't his fault and oh god she loves him.

Twenty-one months they've been married and she still hasn't slept with him.

Mother and Two Daughters

JANICE EIDUS

I'm going to write a story about two young women, Ronelle and Honey, fairly close to one another in age, who become pregnant fairly close to one another in time. The reason that I write such a story is that I'm the mother of these two women who are sisters, each of them a product of my own womb many years ago.

The names Ronelle and Honey once sounded equally sweet, soft, lilting to my ears. My late husband often said those two names in the morning while shaving; I'd overhear him in the bathroom almost chanting: Honey and Ronelle, Honey and Ronelle. . . .

I didn't even attempt to write until after Dick's death. One day he was around, whistling, returning home at six o'clock with ice cream or a cake for dessert and ready to drink his martini. And then he no longer was: something inside him simply malfunctioned. After his death, though, I felt so like a zombie, watching soap operas every afternoon, checking three, four times an hour for crumbs on the cabinets. Ronelle encouraged me to enroll in evening classes in the local high school's adult education program. She may have sensed that I might have fallen apart unless I went outside myself in order to tap those stifled things inside myself (not that I hadn't been happy as Dick's wife, but there was a time when I, like most young women, had hoped for other things . . .). I took a creative writing class, and there I blossomed. Our instructor, Mr. Jarvis, was a youngish middle-aged man who constantly smoked a pipe and wore herringbone jackets with patches on the elbows; a man of integrity, critical awareness, warmth. Crinkle lines around his eyes contrasted markedly with the two vertical lines, almost *scars*, that ran down the sides of his face. We had coffee together once after class; his car had broken down and I drove him home. He enjoyed my style, my ability to (as he put it) "perceive metaphor where someone else might not." I had written only a few poems before his class, and those during my one year in college. This very ability to put my thoughts down on paper prevents me from being driven insane.

(I sit home, that's all I can do these days, scared to go outside except when absolutely necessary. Pixie squalls constantly from the room we've made into her nursery while I sit in the kitchen writing.)

•

Scene: A kitchen in suburbia. Yellow curtains on two large windows. The sink is sparkling. Colorful wallpaper. At a large kitchen table sits an attractive middle-aged woman reading a newspaper, sipping a cup of tea. She is trim and neat and gives the appearance of sensibility, organization. Ronelle, eighteen years old, wearing wide flowered pants and a loose-fitting man's shirt, enters the room. The woman at the table (her mother) smiles her greeting and returns to the newspaper. The young woman speaks throughout in a monotone.

> *Ronelle:* Just stop reading that paper.
> *Mother:* Whatever do you mean?
> *Ronelle:* I mean that you should stop reading that Daily Rag when your dear daughter is trying to tell you she's pregnant.
> *Mother: (Dropping newspaper to the floor, remaining seated, breathing heavily, smile frozen in place)* No!

My memory goes haywire here: I try to think about it all exactly as it happened, but it blurs. Perhaps Mr. Jarvis would advise me to relieve some of the tension. "Go outside yourself," he might say. "At the most bitter, painful moment, force yourself to make your reader laugh." Should I have the mother slip on a banana peel as she attempts to stand?

Or would Mr. Jarvis have advised the truth at such a moment? I can *force* myself to remember accurately. I'm quite serious about my writing, for my only identity now is that of recorder for posterity. My identity as mother, widow, grandmother, woman: all meaningless.

> *Ronelle:* I mean that you should stop reading that Daily Rag when your dear daughter is trying to tell you she's pregnant.
> *Mother:* I hope for your sake that this is some kind of joke. *(Ronelle remains silent.)* I mean it, this better be some sort of stupid joke. *(Ronelle remains silent. Tears form in Mother's eyes; her voice rises.)* I hope for your sake you at least *know* who did this to you, and how, and why!
> *Ronelle:* You know how. Who cares who?
> *Mother: (Moaning loudly)* Oh!
> *Ronelle:* Don't get silly. *(Eats a chocolate chip cookie, loudly, seemingly savoring each bite.)*

I stood up from the table and called Honey on the phone. She was already married to Bill then, and they lived nearby. Bill repairs air conditioners, and has always seemed to be quite happy in his field. (Now we all live together in this house and he is less happy. At the moment he and Honey are both upstairs in their bedroom with the door closed while Pixie cries in her nursery.) Honey has always loved Ronelle dearly, and she raced over. Soon we were all assembled. Mother and Two Daughters Seated Around a Table. Which artist would have chosen to paint us?

Honey's face was streaked with tears when she arrived. "Ronelle!" she cried. "You're just eighteen!" But she forced herself to take charge. "Okay, listen. Bill knows someone, someone who'll do the job. One of the men he works with got a girl in trouble once; it won't be cheap, but he's no butcher and at least you'll be safe. Bill and I will help with the money if we have to. Bill can contact him tonight. . . ."

Ronelle interrupted. "Jesus Christ, they're *legal* now!"

Honey laughed her tinkly laugh (a sound sorely missed nowadays). "Well, you know how it is . . . you get married, bogged down, you don't have much time to keep up with current events. . . ."

"If I wanted to have an abortion," Ronelle said, "I wouldn't ask *you* for advice. Margot Prester, Lucy Lief, Betty Goldberg, and Didi Retikliano have all had at least one."

(Shall I, at this moment, have the three models stand up at once from the table and simultaneously slip on banana peels?)

Completely at my wit's end, I wrote the advice columnist in the paper:

Dear Charlotte Dexter:

I am a middle-aged, fairly cosmopolitan suburbanite who seeks your advice. I am aware that society's standards are flexible—in other words, I don't think of myself as a stodgy prude. I am worldly enough and don't lack a creative, spontaneous side. My husband passed away eight years ago and I have brought up my two daughters, Paula and Rhonda, (not their real names) by myself. Paula is Rhonda's junior by only two years. Charlotte Dexter, they've always been so different. Paula stays with a wild group of kids who stand in front of the ice cream parlor in our shopping center. She swears that she does not participate in drinking and drug-taking, yet her vocabulary includes words like "busted" and "fag." Rhonda, on the other hand, was a senior queen, a good student, read weekly to a blind woman, and a year after high school married John Porter, who has since gone into the refrigerator repair business and makes good money. Their home is lovely and they are happy and have many friends.

My problem is this, Charlotte: Paula is pregnant and refuses to say who the father is. I don't really approve of abortion myself, but in a case like this, I feel it is the only solution. She disagrees. I might add that she no longer helps with any housework and almost completely neglects her appearance.

The letter was sent special delivery. Ronelle, in the meantime, had taken to coming home only to eat and sleep, and not always that. Obviously, our mother and daughter relationship was finished. One morning, during this jumbled period of time, I woke up early and stumbled out to the kitchen. Light flooded the room and I thought briefly, fleetingly, that the light might symbolize a new beginning. When I opened the refrigerator to take out the orange juice, I discovered a folded piece of stationery next to the carton of eggs. The stationery's design was a blue-eyed brontosaurus in a daisy hat in the upper left corner next to the printed words: "You've sure been gone for a long time!" Underneath the brontosaurus was a pencilled poem:

Mother Mother
curses
heaped on you your eyes
heaped on you your words
You have murdered
each of us.
Your stars are out and they are bloody
mother mother
I have learned to sing
and life
will emerge
from me,
my ripped heaven
will open up.

I scrambled two eggs in margarine in our Teflon pan. Charlotte Dexter hadn't responded to my special delivery letter, and I didn't know where to turn. The orange juice tasted pulpy; the eggs were too moist.

Then, just two days later, also during my breakfast, the phone rang. Honey's voice was ecstatic. "Me too, me too! Oh, Mother, me too!"

What could I say? "Should we arrange a baby shower?"

"Oh, yes!"

Later that morning, Bill's mother called up also, to gush her soon-to-be-grandmotherly-joy into my ears, which *should* have been the receptive ears of an empathetic granny-to-be. And then, just two weeks after that, the following letter from Honey appeared in my mailbox, unpostmarked, in a torn envelope:

Dear Mother,

I went into the city to see a Wednesday matinee performance of "Wait Until Dark," which is about a beautiful blind woman with a tormented soul. After the show, feeling alone and unattractive, despite having on my navy blue pant suit from Macy's which I know is flattering to my trim shape, the trim shape which will leave me once I start ballooning and ballooning and will have to shop at those icky Maternally Yours shops, I decided to ride the subway! I had seen Puerto Rican women pass by the theater as I bought my ticket (Puerto Ricans, Mother. From the island of Puerto Rico, the city of San Juan, from the hot, hot land of exotic fruits and plants) and they are beautiful. Their skin is darker than mine, their lips are fuller, their black eyes are smoky. They descend into the subway. They ride the I.R.T. local and get off on West 137th Street and Broadway. They shop in supermarkets selling *habituelas, Vitarroz, Mi Secrito Sofrito!*

Nearby their homes is the City College of New York. Plump girls from Queens who wish to be lawyers attend classes there; and young black men in dashikis and leather boots, majoring in history and economics; and sad women, bored with home, husband, and children, wishing finally to earn a degree in education. You wonder how I come to know of such people,

Mother. I will only tell you this much: all those students ride the subways, the same cars that the Puerto Rican girls and boys, men and women, ride!

Mother, have you by any chance, ever thought about the excitement that a woman feels when a strange man, a man without a name, becomes wildly excited by the very presence of that woman? The tall dark man with the fierce mustache who sees beyond the conservative outline of her breasts under tailored jacket, the curve of hips beneath the trim slacks. He pushes the woman, down, down, not cruelly, yet of course very forcefully. Those men also ride the subways! They get off at 50th Street, Grand Central Station, Pennsylvania Station, West 4th Street. Their bodies seethe by the train doors.

"Wait Until Dark" had ended; it was five o'clock and I was on West 48th Street. I carefully began to walk downtown. The women who type, the women who proofread and edit magazines, the women who sell lipsticks behind counters, all wait at the corners for the green lights which will free them to walk to the subway so that they may ride home, prepare dinner, make love to their husbands (those husbands who aren't impotent most of the time, anyway) and sleep and dream. (Do *you* dream, Mother?)

I arrived at Times Square. Need I describe Times Square to you? (Once you and Father took us to see "Bambi" at a special one dollar showing.) Dope addicts, drunks, deranged persons. Anyway, I walked down the steps of the Seventh Avenue I.R.T. subway and I dropped my token into the slot and pushed my way (as hundreds of other bodies had done previously, within that very hour alone!) and emerged onto the platform itself. Mother, I stood there for an hour, but I could not board that train and go where they go! Faces changed, the noise became unbearable. Then I turned and ran outside and began to walk faster back to the garage where my car waited. It was six-thirty now and darker and two men said things to me when I passed. I distinctly heard the word "fox."

Bill asked me later what delayed me (he worries so, like you) and I blamed the traffic. "Remember," he said, "we'll soon be three, so you'd better relax now, while you can." He laughed.

Your daughter,
Honey

Everyone in my family was suddenly writing! I sat down, feeling extremely tired, and decided to use again what Mr. Jarvis had helped me to realize was my saving grace: my ability to laugh at myself. "Tsk tsk," I sighed in a cackling old lady's voice, "those darn kids will be the death of their poor old ma yet." Then I tore the letter to bits.

Recently I wrote a letter to Jim Jarvis explaining my present situation and thanking him for having aided me in such a creative, therapeutic skill in the past, but I ripped that letter to bits, also.

There were many times I wanted to give up and simply scream and rant and rip at my hair during that period of time when both my daughters were growing round and buxom and eating strange concoctions of mayonnaise and yogurt. But the baby shower demanded my energy. "A *normal* baby shower," Honey insisted. We had yet another tearful moment at our kitchen table (a rare moment, indeed, that found Ronelle home during daylight hours and actually speaking to her mother and sister) when Honey turned to Ronelle, sobbing, "Why? Why shouldn't I go on with my life as though it's good and normal despite the fact that you've decided to go ahead and have some sort of *abnormal* pregnancy from one of your *abnormal* friends? One of those greasy little boys who watches you because you don't wear a bra!"

Ronelle might have laughed sardonically, while Honey continued sobbing. Ronelle's eyes might have squinted and glittered; her teeth could have been bared for a brief instant. I could have said, "Ronelle, you bad girl, you damaged seedling, how dare you use your father's name any longer?" Ronelle might have stood, assumed a savage stance, shrieked, "I'll avenge myself! Just try to stop me from having my baby or from bringing it up; see if I care about any of you!"

The invitations we sent out were tiny cards: shimmering bits of white boasting drawings of a pink bunny holding an umbrella with the words, "COME to a SHOWER for a CHILD of TOMORROW!" The shower was held in my own home. I ordered cold cuts, set up a miniature bar, cleaned and scrubbed for days in advance. Ronelle sullenly slithered in and out during the preparations. On the day of the shower she sat coldly, never smiling, watching Honey's guests arrive, barely saying hello. Honey's girlfriends (most of them married and potential future mothers themselves) arrived bearing gifts. Honey looked smart in an off-white shirtwaist dress. I drank more than my usual small share of wine.

Sometime during that long afternoon I happened to be standing alone next to Ronelle in the kitchen. She stared at me and asked, "Do you understand a single thing about this planet, do you understand that there are people here who think you're mad?" I walked away feeling wobbly and slightly out of control.

Honey was standing by a cabinet eating a sugar cookie. "Honey," I said, "why are you so interested in Puerto Ricans: I have to know! I'm your mother!" She backed away from me, dropping the cookie on the linoleum floor.

Then I rejoined the giddy group of women in our living room until I began to feel lightheaded and giddy myself. Suddenly I was overcome by joy: I would be a grandmother! Cute little girls wearing pajamas with feet and snaps on their soft, round bottoms. Evening bath; hot cereal in the morning. I would love both those little tykes equally, no matter what! I poured myself another glass of wine, but before I had tasted it, there was the scream. Who screamed first? Was it one of Honey's girlfriends or was it Honey herself? The brunette in pink, or the chubby girl putting on her coat first? No matter. Ronelle was standing by the television set, swaying from side to side; then she fell to the floor in a faint and someone screamed. That was what mattered. An odor filled the room and the rug turned red around her body. Honey sat on the sofa, clinging to a hand-painted cutting board, rubbing her fingers along the painted peaches and pears. Someone took Ronelle in a car to the hospital; I followed in another car; Honey stayed home.

Ronelle miscarried and then slipped out of the hospital behind all our backs the very next day. The nurses take no responsibility. "You should all have your licenses suspended!" I told them; I meant it then, and I mean it still, although I am not by nature a vengeful woman.

Three months after the birth of Honey's baby, the first letter arrived in a blood red envelope. My name and address were printed in black ink; there was no return address.

Mother:

I began when I was feeling extra fine one night. I had just slept with Ronald for the first time. (You know him: the boy with the guitar case at the mall.) Sex had really been fine. So, when I left Ronald, I put on my purple shawl and was just tripping along the street on my way to Betty's apartment. Betty lives downtown and you don't know her because her mother has been labeled "manic depressive" and put somewhere and you don't know people like that. I was humming and walking when I heard a sound. Crackle. Then another crackle. I thought about Rice Krispies and about how good Ronald had been and how nice my purple shawl felt and how warm the evening was and how nice it would feel not to go home that night and see you. I walked only a few more feet before the knife was thrust against my back and an arm thrown around my neck.

"Don't scream," the voice said. "Make a sound and you're dead. Don't scream." He pushed me, hard, but it didn't hurt, into a doorway. "I want all your money, and you better give it to me or you die!"

"Of course," I said. "Don't even think about death." And then, the Ronelle seed which you hate so much–why? something in your past?–said to him, "You can kiss me, too."

"Money."

I handed him the seven dollars I had.

"Okay," he said and began to run away. His last words before he began to disappear from my life were, "Don't scream, mother, or I'll come back and remove all your insides!"

"Let's go for coffee," I said. "You can use my money to pay and it isn't expensive and then we can go to Betty's and she'll reimburse you."

He agreed. Later he said the vibes were right. He made passionate love to me in the men's room of the Simpson Street subway station.

"I love you," he told me when we parted on 149th Street.

And Mother, my baby was conceived magically that night. That same baby which you and Honey tormented me into losing!

After my "miscarriage" I left that white hospital and took to the streets in search of my lover. He was sitting in that same coffee shop, eating a donut.

And now I travel with my mugging man, Mother. Oh, he hates you. He hates you and Honey and Bill and the squeaking little monster they now own. He wishes you all painful deaths. But please don't think that he and I are a revolutionary duo out to avenge the working class of the Third World brothers and sisters. Actually, we're just a couple sharing a deep communication who happen to despise the rest of the world. We hide out and we haunt you and this makes us very happy. Sometimes during lovemaking he says,

"Your mother will bleed, your sister will cry, your brother-in-law will break, the house will rise in flames . . ." and it's fantastic.

Never leave your door open, Mother.

Yet . . . it was you who held me, rocked me, fed me ice cream when I had a sore throat. So what?

Still, you did read me *Sleeping Beauty* when I had the mumps, so I'll offer you these words of advice: Beware and be wary, don't accept unexpected packages, don't allow the plumbers in, the milkman might be a friend of mine.

Pass the word on to Honey and Bill.

> Always,
> Ronelle

So now I wait and watch. Pixie is crying again from the nursery; she's really such a darling. Honey gave birth easily and afterwards she and Bill moved in with me to save money. I must go inside to tend to my granddaughter, wondering if Ronelle will enter through a carelessly open window somewhere in another room.

Perhaps one day Jim Jarvis will receive this manuscript in the mail, neatly typed. How will he feel about himself being such a central character? But I had better go check on Pixie, even though her crying has momentarily stopped.

Taking the Train to Harmon

DANIELA GIOSEFFI

for Thea at three years old

Plowing through snow, sleet taps
at the windows, trying to get into my warmth,
cold trying to melt on me.

The holiday finished,
I left you sleeping in a strange bed,
Daughter of Christmas Trees.
I'm going to buy you words to float in icy branches
to change boredom to mystery.

If there is a moral to the scheme
that brought you from me,
you are temptation undone.
You breathe now without me.
I leave you for awhile to your grandmother
as a gift from me.

A cat slept on my chest through the night.
Its hairs caught in my throat
coughing mysteries.
There is a cold blue
blanketing the windows.

Lights are eyes looking back at us,
stamping our retinas with dazzling imagery.
We are verbs in the dark;
not nouns of insanity.
I'll have told you nothing
unless I reach your secret ears
with poems from me.

Knowing Loss

If I could push you in park swings forever
through the airs of spring,
but I can barely hope,
face to face with these cold blank windows,
that you will not hate
whatever world of you
is to come from the verbal whore of me.

Norton #59900

JUDEE NORTON

"*A*TTENTION ON THE YARD, ATTENTION IN THE UNITS! NORTON, FIVE-NINE-NINE-ZERO-ZERO, OBTAIN A PASS AND REPORT TO THE CAPTAIN'S OFFICE *IMMEDI-ATELY!*" the public address speakers boom. The sound bounces around the yard, boomerangs between the buildings and my ears again and again. I am standing outside the schoolroom, smoking and sweating in the 112-degree summer after-noon, squinting at the sun and wondering whether this kind of weather would be more enjoyable if I were lying on a Mexican beach wearing only a string bikini and a smile, holding a frosty margarita in one hand and a fine, slender stick of India in the other. I have just decided that it most definitely would be when the summons comes.

At once I am approached from every direction by fellow inmates asking, "Did you hear them call you to the captain's office, Jude?" and "What's goin' on? Why does the captain want you?" I feign indifference as I take a long final drag of my cigarette, then flip the butt into one of the pink-painted coffee cans nearby.

"Who the fuck knows," I respond, with just the right degree of flippancy. My voice is sure and steady and that pleases me. I can feel my face rearranging itself into a mask of haughty insolence, a half-sneer claims my mouth, one eyebrow hitches itself a quarter-inch upward on my forehead to indicate arrogant disre-gard. It is my intention to appear poised, untroubled, faintly amused, and slightly bored. I am quite sure I achieve such a look.

My guts belie my measured outward calm. They twist and grumble and roil, threatening to send my lunch to the sidewalk. My heart is beating much too fast. My mouth is dry, my tongue feels like a landed trout thrashing about in that arid place. My hands are trembling, my knees belong to a stranger. I am grateful for the first time that it is so goddamn hot in Phoenix. Everyone glistens with a fine film of perspiration; perhaps no one will notice that I smell of fear.

I affect a hip-slung swagger for the amusement of the gathered crowd, and head for south unit control to ask for a pass. It strikes me that I am asking for per-mission to go to a place I haven't the faintest glimmer of desire to go to, and I gig-gle. The officer issuing my pass looks up at me and says, "Hope you still think it's funny when you get back, Norton." I shrug.

The walk across the yard is a long one, made longer by my determination to stroll casually under the scrutiny of a hundred watching eyes. I can feel them on me, can almost hear the thoughts behind them:

"Poor Jude!"

". . .'bout time that goody-goody bitch got hers."

"Damn, hope it ain't bad news. . . ."

"Gir'fren', please, look who be in trouble now!"

"Sheee-it . . ."

I knock purposefully at the polished wooden door with the brass plate that announces this as the Mount Olympus of Department of Corrections. "CAPTAIN," it says, in big carved block letters. *Fuck you,* I mouth silently.

After just enough time has elapsed to make me feel insignificant and small, the door is opened by a fat oily sergeant. She is damp and rumpled in spite of the cool air-conditioned comfort of the room. She turns wordlessly from me and installs her sloppy bulk at a desk littered with forms—applications, requests, petitions—paper prayers from the miserable and needy. She selects one and peers importantly at it over the tops of her smeary glasses, then picks up a red pen and makes a large, unmistakable, red "X" in a box labeled "Denied."

Having not been invited to sit, I am still standing near the door, feeling awkward and displaced when the phone rings. She picks up the receiver, says, "Yeah?" and after a moment looks at me, nods, and replaces it. She jerks her head in the direction of the door through which I have just come and says, "Go back outside for a minute, if you don't mind." Fleetingly, I wonder what she would say if I responded, "Oh but I *do* mind, I mind very much, in fact; it's hotter than the devil's dick out there, you see, and I *so* much prefer it inside." What I actually say, though, is, "Oh, sure, no problem," and am mortified to find myself blushing.

Once outside, it occurs to me that if this was sly psychological weaponry, designed to unseat and disadvantage me, it is quite effective. I feel humiliated and disgraced in a way I cannot identify. I light a cigarette and arrange my limbs carefully into a posture of indolent apathy. I hook my thumbs in my belt loops and squint with what I hope is an air of unconcern through the smoke that curls up into my face.

At last the door opens again, and I am ushered into the cool depths of the anteroom, and this time I get a nod from the sergeant to proceed into the next room, the sacred chamber where the captain sits, enthroned behind a gleaming expanse of mahogany desk. He is leaning back in a maroon leather swivel chair, rolling a gold Cross pen between his palms. He is a black giant, all teeth and long-fingered hands and military creases. His hair is cut very short on the sides and back, and the top flares out and up several inches. It is decidedly and perfectly flat on top, as though his barber used a T-square. He motions me to a small chair, carefully chosen and placed so that I am directly in front of him and several inches lower. I feel like a beggar, prostrate at the foot of the king. I am determined that he should not know this. I meet his gaze with a cool look of studied dignity.

"You're Norton?" he asks.

No, you moron, I'm Smith, Jones, Appleby, Wellington, Mother Teresa, Doc Holliday, Jackie Onassis, anyone in the world besides Norton, at least I'd like to be right now, dontcha know? "Yes, sir," I say. "I'm Norton."

The chair creaks as he leans forward and picks up a piece of paper, pretends to study it. Without looking at me, he says, "Norton, I called you in to talk to you about your son's at-ti-tude," pronouncing all three syllables distinctly as though to a slow child.

"My son's attitude?" I repeat, feeling exquisitely stupid.

He gives a derisive little snort, as though to indicate that of course we both know what he's talking about and it's damned silly of me to pretend ignorance. Bewildered, I ask, "What attitude, sir?"

The captain closes his eyes and leans back again, rolling the gold pen in his hands. It clicks annoyingly against his rings.

"Your son, Adam," he begins with an air of great forbearance, "seems to cause a problem every time he comes to visit you. My officers tell me that he is rude and disrespectful, a troublemaker." He opens his eyes and looks at me expectantly.

I am dismayed to notice that my mouth is agape, that I have been caught so unaware as to be, for one of the very few times in my entire life, speechless. "A troublemaker, sir?" I say, realizing with no small degree of consternation that thus far I have only managed to echo what has been said to me.

"Ap-par-ent-ly," he replies, again dividing the word carefully into all its syllables, "he demanded a full explanation of the visitor's dress code a couple of weeks ago. And last Sunday, according to the report, he questioned the policy that forbids inmates or their visitors to sit on the grass."

I have a quick vision of an official report, complete with the Seal of the Great State of Arizona, titled "TROUBLEMAKERS," and can see my son's name emblazoned at the top of a long list. His sins are red-lettered: DEMANDING EXPLANATIONS and QUESTIONING POLICY. Suddenly and against all reason and prudence, I have a powerful urge to laugh, to say, "You're kidding, right, dude?" But I fight it and win, and say instead, "Sir?" as though it were a question in its own right, and the captain obliges me by treating it as such.

"Your son, Adam," he says with exaggerated patience, "insists upon knowing the reason for every rule and regulation DOC imposes, which we are in no way obligated to provide to him. He disrupts my officers in the performance of their duties."

I am beginning to hate the way he says my son's name, and I feel the first stirrings of anger. The visitation officers' "duties" consist of sitting in a cool, dark room with a bank of closed-circuit TV screens, looking out onto the baked parking lot where a line of parched visitors wait for the regal nod of approval which will allow them entry into the institution. Their "duties" include watching us chat with our loved ones, making sure that there is no "prolonged kissing," no hankypanky under the tables, no exchanging of other than words. The most arduous task they will perform all day in the fulfillment of their "duties" is bending over to inspect my vagina after I squat and cough and "spread those cheeks *wide*" for a strip search at visit's end. I fail to comprehend how my son's questions interfere with these odious "duties," and I say so.

The captain's response is brusque, and it is obvious that he, too, is becoming annoyed. "It is not your place, Norton, to determine whether or not the officers' duties are being interfered with. It *is* your place to insure that your visitors comply with procedure."

"What 'procedure,' sir, says that my boy can't ask questions?" I challenge, against my better judgment, which has long since flown. A little voice inside my head says, *oh boy, now you've done it, you smartass,* and the voice is surely smarter than I am, for the captain stands up so fast he nearly topples his chair. His breath is coming fast and his eyes blaze.

As quickly as he is losing his calm, I am gaining mine, and from some place deep inside I thought was forever closed to me, I feel a surge of fearlessness. I stand also, and face him squarely and unblinkingly, an intrepid lioness defending her cub. It is a sensation that will not last.

"Sit," he commands.

I sit.

A moment later, he sits, crossing one elegantly trousered leg over the other and picking up the gold pen again. "Tell me," he says congenially, "what happened in the blue jeans incident two weeks ago."

"What happened, sir," I begin reasonably, "is that my son came to visit me wearing a pair of gray Dockers, you know, men's casual pants, and he was told that he could not see me because he was not in compliance with the dress code that specifies 'no blue jeans.' He was understandably upset, and asked that a higher authority be consulted."

"And were they?"

"Yes, sir, someone called the Officer in Charge, who didn't want to take the responsibility for a decision; she in turn called the lieutenant, who ultimately allowed him in."

"So he *was* admitted," the captain says, in a tone that implies that, after all, the whole point is moot, and whyever in the world am I so agitated about it?

Warming to my subject, and not liking one bit the look of smug self-satisfaction on his face, I throw caution to the winds, full speed ahead and damn the torpedoes, devil take the hindmost. All pretense of civility leaves me, my instinct for self-preservation is gone.

"Oh, he was admitted all right," I say, making no attempt to disguise my disgust. I note with detachment that my hands and arms have bravely joined the recitation and are describing sharply eloquent shapes in the air, punctuating my mounting fury. The pitch and timbre of my voice have changed and the words rush from me, unstoppable. "He was admitted, sir, *twenty whole minutes* before the end of visitation, after taking a filthy stinking city bus all the way from Tempe and being allowed to stand in the blazing sun for three and a half hours without a square inch of shade or so much as an offer of a drink of water. He was admitted after he begged, pleaded, cajoled, and tried to reason with every know-nothing brownshirt in this whole sorry place. He was admitted after repeatedly pointing out to every available cretin with a badge that his gray, pleated, slash-pocketed, cuffed, pleated and creased, 100 percent cotton *slacks* were, in fact, neither 'blue' nor 'jeans' and therefore did not violate the 'no blue jeans' rule. He was admitted after being chastised like a naughty schoolboy by that loser of a sergeant, after being called immature, impatient, juvenile, and demanding, after being threatened with dismissal from the premises, after being subjected to an outrageously erroneous judgment call on his goddamn *pants*, sir. Disrespectful? Oh, I hope so. With all due respect to you, sir, I hope to Christ he was disrespectful."

By this time, I am shaking with rage. I am remembering my fair-skinned boy's sunburned face. I am remembering the awful look in his sky-colored eyes, that bright liquidity that tells of a boy perched on the brink of manhood, trying not to cry. I am remembering my own inability to explain, to soothe, to mend as mothers do, as they must, for if not they, who?

It is an omission of some seriousness that I did not notice earlier the twin spots of color that had crept into the captain's cheekbones. On his ebony skin they are the color of dried blood, and his eyes snap and sparkle at me. There is a vein pulsing at his left temple. I have an abrupt vision of myself cutting out my tongue with his letter opener and simply leaving it flopping about on his desk in expiation. Too late.

"Norton," he says slowly, "it is clear to me where your son got his attitude." I notice that he does not divide his words into all their separate parts for me now. He taps his chin thoughtfully with the pen. "It is my feeling that for the continued secure operation of this institution, it will be necessary to discontinue your son's visits until further notice. Perhaps he only needs time away from you to learn to deal with the fact of your incarceration in a mature and sensible manner. An attitude adjustment period." He smiles.

My heart lurches and I feel the color staining my own cheeks even as it leaves his. "Sir," I say, hating the quavering, desperate sound of my voice, "surely you're not saying he can't come to see me anymore." I can hear the humble, supplicating tone I use, and I despise myself for it. "Please," I say, strangling the word.

Having regained his equilibrium, the captain sits up straighter in the chair and allows a wider smile. "That is pre-cise-ly what I am saying, Norton." In control once more, he has gone back to hacking his words apart. I hate him for that.

I am consumed by impotent rage, I wrestle with a crushing and mighty urge to rise and beat that superior face of his into a bleeding pulp. The desire is so intense as to be palpable. I can hear the dull wet crunch of gristle and cartilage, can feel his warm slippery brains between my fingers, can smell the dark coppery odor of his blood, can see it splashing up, up, onto the walls, the carpet, the desk, my face, my hair, crimson and joyous.

I am dazed and shaken by this vision. I sit for a moment, gripping the chair bottom with white-knuckled horror. Then I push the chair back, gently, like a woman preparing to excuse herself from the dinner table, and say softly, "May I leave, sir?"

"Certainly," replies the captain, ever the gracious host. He smiles at me. I do not return the smile.

With the grace and ironclad composure that have saved me from humiliation since early childhood, I hold my head high as I walk through the outer office, past the inquisitive stare of the duty sergeant. I close the big door quietly and slip unnoticed around the corner of the building.

I lean against the sun-baked wall and struggle with a host of emotions I cannot put name to. I feel the wall burning my shoulders through my blue work shirt. My knees become suddenly and utterly incapable of supporting me. They fold up and I slide bonelessly down the wall, heedless of the way its pebbles surface scrapes my back. My teeth are clenched, but my lips part and turn downward. From them comes an awful keening sound I do not recognize. My eyes sting with the threat of unwelcome tears, I beg them silently not to betray me. But they do, traitorous things, and a great wash pours unchecked down my cheeks, off my chin, into my lap, a flood pent up all those years when to cry was a sign of weakness and to be weak was to be a victim. I lay my forehead on my knees and drop my hands loosely to the blistering cement beside me, like useless weapons that would not fire when so much was at stake. I am dimly aware that I am crying in the broken-hearted way of a small child, a sort of hitching and breathless uh-uh-uh-uh-uh, complete with snot running down onto my mother. I feel naked and wounded, exposed by grief and hopelessness.

Finally I can no longer hear the sounds of my own weeping. I turn my head to one side and feel the sun begin to evaporate the tears, leaving my face tight and dry. I spit on the fingertips of my hands and scrub away the trails they left, wipe my nose on my sleeve, and pull a small black comb from my back pocket. I take my sunglasses from the top of my head and run the comb briskly through the matted and dampened strands and stand up. Straight. Tall. Shoulders back. Chin up. I put the dark glasses on my face and the mantle of hard-ass prisoner on my soul.

I saunter nonchalantly around the corner, past the door marked "CAPTAIN," onto the yard. An acquaintance approaches me and asks in an excited whisper, "So, what happened in there? What's up?"

She is immediately joined by a second and a third and a fourth, all eager, questioning. I am comfortable now. This is my milieu, this is where I know exactly what is expected of me, precisely how to behave, what to do and say. I shove both hands jauntily into the hip pockets of my Levi's and allow a disdainful grin to my own face.

"Fuck him," I say with contempt. "He can't touch this."

We all laugh.

The Child Taken from the Mother

MINNIE BRUCE PRATT

I could do nothing.   Nothing.   Do you
understand? Women ask: *Why didn't you—?*
like they do of women who've been raped.
And I ask myself: Why didn't I?   Why
didn't I run away with them?   Or face
him in court? Or—

                              Ten years ago I
answered myself: No way for children to live.
Or: The chance of absolute loss.   Or:

I did the best I could.   It was not
enough.   It was about terror and power.
I did everything I could.   Not enough.

This is not the voice of the guilty mother.

Clumsy with anger even now, it is a voice
from the woman shoved outside, one night, as words
clack into place like bricks, poker chips.

A man mutters: *It's a card game. Too*
candid.   They know what's in your hand.
I look down.   My hands dangle open and empty
in the harsh yellow light.   Strange men,
familiar, laugh and curse in the kitchen, whiskey,
bending over cards.   Or is it something held down
on the table?   Someone says: *Bull Dog Bend.*
Someone says: *The place of the father in the home.*
A woman's voice: *Those women who've never held*
a little baby in their arms.   In the old window,
a shadow.   Two hands, brick and mortar, seal
the house, my children somewhere inside.   The youngest

163

has lost his baby fat, navel flattened, last
of my stomach's nourishing.

                    You say: *Do something.*
You say: *Why is this happening?*

                    My body.   My womb.
My body of a woman, a mother, a lesbian.

                         And here,
perhaps, you say: *That last word doesn't belong.*
Woman, mother: those can stay.   Lesbian: no.
Put that outside the place of the poem.   Too
slangy, prosy, obvious, just doesn't belong.
*Why don't you—?   Why didn't you—?   Can't you
say it some other way?*

                    The beautiful place
we stood arguing, after the movie, under blue-white
fluorescence.   Two middle-aged women in jeans,
two grown boys, the lanky one, the tactful one,
bundled in a pause before cold outside, to argue
the significances: bloody birth, the man cursing
a woman in the kitchen, dirt, prayer, the place
of the father, the master, the beatings, black and
white, home lost, continents, two women
lovers glimpsed, the child taken from the mother
who returns.

              No one says: This is about us.   But
in the narrow corridor, stark cement block walls,
we become huge, holding up the harsh images,
the four of us loud, familiar.

                    Other movie-
goers squeeze past, light their cigarettes,
glance, do not say even to themselves: Children
and women, lovers, mothers, lesbians.   Yes.

In the Garden

GRACE PALEY

*A*n elderly lady, wasted and stiff, sat in a garden beside a beautiful young woman whose two children, aged eight and nine, had been kidnapped eight months earlier.

The women were neighbors. They met every afternoon to speak about the children. Their sentences began: When Rosa and Loiza have come home. . . . Their sentences often continued: I can't wait to show them the ice-cream freezer Claudina bought us. . . . They will probably be afraid to go to school alone. At first Pepi will have to take them in the car. . . . They will be thin. No, perhaps they will be too fat, having been forced to eat nothing but rice and beans and pampered with candy and toys to keep them quiet.

The elderly lady thought: When they come home, when they come home . . .

The beautiful young woman, their mother, said, This pillow cover for Loiza, I don't know if I'll finish it in time. I make so many mistakes, I have to rip. I want it to be perfect.

There were yellow *canario* flowers among green leaves on the pillow slip. There was a hummingbird in each corner.

The two husbands, accompanied by a stranger, came into the garden and waited under the bougainvillea while the father shouted, Coffee! Black! Black! Black! He always shouted these days. His wife retired to the kitchen to make a fourth pot of strong coffee. The father turned to the stranger, speaking as if the visitor were deaf. Now this is a garden, my friend. *This* is beautiful. The life here is good. You can see that. The criminal element is under control at last. The police patrol the area frequently. I can see you're a decent person and I'm glad to have you on this street. We do not rent to Communists or to what you call hippies. Right now in one of my houses the head of the Chicago Medical Center is sleeping. That house across the street there, with the enormous veranda. He sleeps late. It's his vacation from family troubles and business worries. You understand that. We, my colleagues and I, have been responsible for building nearly all the houses you see, the one you've rented. They are well constructed. We want people to come with children and grandchildren. We will not rent to just anyone.

The elderly woman cannot bear his shouting voice. She asks her husband to help her toward home. They slowly move across the lawn.

The stranger sits among the amazing flowers and birds for a few minutes. He is a well-dressed man, middle-aged, who happens to be a Communist. He is also a father of two children who are only a little older than the kidnapped daughters of this household. He is a tenderhearted but relentless person.

In the course of the next few days, as he shops and walks, he speaks to his neighbors, who are friendly. A woman in the corner house often stands at the wrought-iron gate, the *reja,* she calls it, of her veranda. When he asks, did you know them? she bursts into tears. She says, They never cry anymore, I know. The little one, Loi, played with my granddaughter. When they were tiny, they sat with their dolls right there in the hammock in the back, rocking rocking, little mammies. I thought they would grow up and be friends in life.

He spoke to another neighbor whom he met in a shop. Returning together along the street of palms, the neighbor asked, Did he insult you in any way? No, said the stranger. Well, he often does, you know, some people think he's been driven mad. I would be driven mad. I would sell and leave. But he has too much invested here. He hates every one of us.

Why? asked the stranger.

Why not? he replied. Wouldn't you? We are the witnesses to the entire event. Our children are skating up and down the street.

Yes, I see, said the stranger.

A third neighbor was washing his car. (This was another day.) He courteously turned down his car radio, which was singing evangelical songs of salvation. He said, Ah yes, it *is* terrible. Everyone knows, by the way, everyone knows it was his friends who did it. Perhaps he knows too. At least one was deeply involved. We have all been harassed by the police, but I for one am glad to be so pestered. It makes me believe they're doing their work, at least. But one, Carlo—the main one, I think, I'm not afraid to say his name—killed himself under investigation. Just last month. A Cuban. Always laughing.

Was it political? asked the stranger.

No, no, my friend, no politics. Money. Greed. Of course, I'm sure the kidnappers thought: The money will come. What is $100,000 to that person. The children blindfolded a day or so will be returned. No one the wiser. No problem. No one the wiser. They dreamed. A new car—two new cars. An expensive woman in the city. Restaurants. High life. But aha! something went wrong. I'm not afraid to tell you this. *Everyone* knows it. Clearly. The money did not go out quickly enough. Why? Let me tell you why. Because our friend is vain and foolish and believed himself too powerful and lucky to suffer tragic loss. Too quickly (because he is an important man), the police, all, the locals, the federals, moved in. Fear struck the kidnappers, you can see that. You may ask, Where are the children? Perhaps in another country, perhaps kindly treated by a frightened wife. Perhaps they will forget, go to school, they will think—oh, that childhood was a dream. Perhaps they are thrown into the sea. Garbage. Not good, not good.

He turned the radio up. Goodbye, sir, he said.

The very next house belonged to the elderly woman. She sat on the front veranda, a shawl over her knees. Her husband sat beside her. She rolled little metal balls in her hands, an exercise designed to slow the degeneration of her finger muscles.

The stranger stepped up to the *reja* to say goodbye. His vacation was over. He would leave the island in the morning.

Look at this, just look at this, her husband said, waving a newspaper at him. The stranger looked at the article that had been encircled. The reporter had written: "In an interview this afternoon in his summer home in the mountains, Sr. L——, father of the little girls kidnapped almost one year ago, said, Of course they will be returned. If I had less publicity they would have been returned long ago. We expect them home. Their room is ready for them. We believe, my wife and I believe, we are certain they will be returned."

The elderly woman's husband said, What is in his mind? He thinks because he was once a poor boy in a poor country and he became very rich with a beautiful wife, he thinks he can bend steel with his teeth.

The woman spoke slowly. You see, sir, what the world is like. Her face was imperturbable. The wasting disease that deprived her limbs of movement had taken from her the delicate muscular gift of facial expression.

She had been told that this paralysis would soon become much worse. In order to understand that future and practice the little life it would have, she followed the stranger as he departed—without moving her head—with her eyes alone. She watched, from left to right, his gait, his clothes, his hair, his swinging arms. Sadly she had to admit that the eyes' movement even if minutely savored was not such an adventurous journey.

But she had become interested in her own courage.

All the Colors of Sunset

LUCI TAPAHONSO

*E*ven after all this time, when I look
back at all that happened, I don't know if I would do anything differently. That
summer morning seemed like any other. The sun came up over the mountain
around seven or so, and when I went to throw the coffee grounds out, I put the
pouch of corn pollen in my apron pocket so that I could pray before I came inside.

During the summers, we sleep most nights in the *chaha'oh*, the shadehouse,
unless it rains. I remembered early that morning I had heard loud voices yelling
and they seemed to come from the north. Whoever it was quieted quickly, and I
fell asleep. Right outside the *chaha'oh*, I knew the dogs were alert—their ears erect
and eyes glistening. Out here near Rockpoint, where we live, it's so quiet and isolated that we can hear things from a far distance. It's mostly desert and the huge
rocks nearby, *tsé ahit ah neeé*, whale rock and the other rocks, seem to bounce
noises into the valley. People live far apart and there are no streetlights nearby.
The nights are quiet, except for animal and bird noises, and the sky is always so
black. In the Navajo way, they say the night sky is made of black jet, and that the
folding darkness comes from the north. Sometimes in the evenings, I think of this
when the sun is setting, and all the bright colors fall somewhere into the west.
Then I let the beauty of the sunset go, and my sadness along with it.

That morning I fixed a second pot of coffee, and peeled potatoes to fry. Just as
I finished slicing the potatoes, I thought I heard my grandbaby cry. I went out and
looked out toward my daughter's home. She lives across the arroyo a little over a
mile away. I shaded my eyes and squinted—the sun was in her direction. Finally,
I went inside and finished fixing breakfast. We were going to go into Chinle that
afternoon, so I didn't go over to their house.

Later that morning, I was polishing some pieces of jewelry when I heard my
daughter crying outside. My heart quickened. I rushed to the door and she practically fell inside the house. She was carrying the baby in her cradleboard and
could hardly talk—she was sobbing and screaming so. I grabbed the baby, knowing she was hurt. When I looked at my granddaughter, I knew the terrible thing
had happened. Her little face was so pale and wet from crying. I could not think
or speak—somehow I found my way to the south wall of the hooghan and sat
down, still holding my sweet baby. My first and only grandchild was gone.

I held her close and nuzzled her soft neck. I sang over and over the little songs that I always sang to her. I unwrapped her and touched slowly, slowly every part of her little smooth body. I wanted to remember every sweet detail and said aloud each name like I had always done, *"Díí nijáád wolyé, sho'wéé."* this is called your leg, my baby. I asked her, *"Nits'iiyah sha'?"* and nuzzled the back of her neck like before. *"Jo ka i."* This time she did not giggle and laugh. I held her and rocked, and sang, and talked to her.

The pollen pouch was still in my pocket, and I put a bit into her mouth as I would have done when her first tooth came in. I put a pinch of pollen on her head as I would have done when she first left for kindergarten. I put a inch of pollen in her little hands as I would have done when she was given her first lamb, as I would have done when she was given her own colt. This way she would have been gentle and firm with her pets. I brushed her with an eagle feather as I would have done when she graduated from junior high. All this and so much more that could have been swept over me as I sat there leaning over my little grandbaby.

She was almost five months old, and had just started to recognize me. She cried for me to hold her and I tried to keep her with me as much as I could. Sometimes I took her for long walks and showed her everything, and told her little stories about the birds and animals we saw. She would fall asleep on our way home, and still I hummed and sang softly. I couldn't stop singing. For some reason, when she was born, I was given so much time for her. I guess that's how it is with grandparents. I wasn't ever too busy to care for her. When my daughter took her home, my house seemed so empty and quiet.

They said that I kept the baby for four hours that morning. My daughter left and then returned with her husband. They were afraid to bother me in my grief. I don't remember much of it. I didn't know how I acted, or maybe that was the least of what I was conscious of. My daughter said later that I didn't say one word to her. I don't remember.

Finally, I got up and gave the baby to them so they could go to the hospital at Chinle. I followed in my own truck, and there the doctor confirmed her death, and we began talking about what we had to do next. Word spread quickly. When I went to buy some food at Basha's, several people comforted me and helped me with the shopping. My sisters and two aunts were at my home when I returned. They had straightened up the house, and were cooking already. Some of my daughters-in-law were cooking and getting things ready in the *chaha'oh* outside. By that evening, the house and the *chaha'oh* were filled with people—our own relatives, clan relatives, friends from school, church, and the baby's father's kin. People came and held me, comforting me and murmuring their sympathies. They cried with me, and brought me plates of food. I felt like I was in a daze—I hardly spoke. I tried to help cook and serve, but was gently guided back to the armchair that had somehow become "my chair" since that morning.

There were meetings each day, and various people stood up to counsel and advise everyone who was there, including my daughter and her husband. When everything was done, and we had washed our faces and started over again, I couldn't seem to focus on things. Before all this happened, I was very busy each day—cooking, sewing, taking out the horses sometimes, feeding the animals, and often just visiting with people. One of my children or my sisters always came by and we would talk and laugh while I continued my tasks. Last winter was a good year for piñons so I was still cleaning and roasting the many flour sackfuls we had picked. At Many Farms junction, some people from Shiprock had a truckload of the sweetest corn I had ever tasted, so I bought plenty and planned to make *ntsidigodí* and other kinds of cornbread. We would have these tasty delicacies to eat in the winter. We liked to remember summer by the food we had stored and preserved.

When we were little, my mother taught all of us girls to weave, but I hadn't touched a loom in years. When I became a grandmother, I began to think of teaching some of the old things to my baby. Maybe it was my age, but I remembered a lot of the things we were told. Maybe it was that I was alone more than I had ever been—my children were grown. My husband passed on five years ago, and since I was by myself and I had enough on which to live, I stopped working at a paying job.

After all this happened, I resumed my usual tasks and tried to stay busy so that my grandbaby's death wouldn't overwhelm me. I didn't cry or grieve out loud because they say that one can call the dead back by doing that. Yet so much had changed, and it was as if I was far away from everything. Some days I fixed a lunch and took the sheep out for the day and returned as the sun was going down. And when I came back inside, I realized that I hadn't spoken to the animals all day. It seemed strange, and yet I just didn't feel like talking. The dogs would follow me around, wanting attention—for me to throw a stick for them, or talk to them— then after a while they would just lie down and watch me. Once I cleaned and roasted a pan of piñons perfectly without thinking about it. It's a wonder that I didn't burn myself. A few weeks later, we had to brand some colts, and give the horses shots, so everyone got together and we spent the day at the corral in the dust and heat. Usually it was a happy and noisy time, but that day was quieter than usual. At least we had taken care of everything.

Sometimes I dreamt of my grandbaby, and it was as if nothing had happened. In my dreams, I carried her around, singing and talking to her. She smiled and giggled at me. When I awoke, it was as if she had been lying beside me, kicking and reaching around. A small space beside me would be warm, and her scent faint. These dreams seemed so real. I looked forward to sleeping because maybe in sleeping I might see her. On the days following such a dream, I would replay it over and over in my mind, still smiling and humming to her the next morning. By afternoon, the activity and noise had usually worn the dream off.

I heard after the funeral that people were whispering and asking questions about what had happened. It didn't bother me. Nothing anyone said or did would bring my sweet baby back—that was clear. I never asked my daughter how it happened. After the baby's death, she and her husband became very quiet and they were together so much, they seemed like shadows of each other. Her husband worked at different jobs, and she just went with him and waited in the pickup until he was through. He worked with horses, helped build hooghans, corrals, and did other construction work. When she came over and spent the afternoon with me, we hardly talked. We both knew we were more comfortable that way. As usual, she hugged me each time before she left. I knew she was in great pain.

Once, when I was at Basha's shopping for groceries, a woman I didn't know said to me, "You have a pretty grandbaby." I smiled and didn't reply. I noticed that she didn't say *"yée"* at the end of *"nitsóíh"* which would have meant "the grandbaby who is no longer alive." That happened at other places, and I didn't respond, except to smile. I thought it was good that people remembered her.

About four months after her death, we were eating at my house when my sisters gathered around me and told me they were very worried about me. They thought I was still too grief-stricken over the baby, and that it was not healthy. "You have to go on," they said, "let her go." They said they wanted the "old me" back, so I agreed to go for help.

We went to a medicine woman near Ganado, and she asked me if I could see the baby sometimes. No, I said, except in dreams.

"Has anyone said they've seen her?" she asked. I said that I didn't think so. Then she said, "Right now, I see the baby beside you." I was so startled that I began looking around for her.

"The baby hasn't left," she said, "she wants to stay with you." I couldn't see my grandbaby. Then I realized that other people could see what the medicine woman had just seen. No wonder, I thought, that sometimes when I woke, I could feel her warm body beside me. She said the baby was wrapped in white.

She couldn't help me herself, but she told me to see another medicine person near Lukaichakai. She said that the ceremony I needed was very old and that she didn't know it herself. The man she recommended was elderly and very knowledgeable and so it was likely that he would know the ceremony, or would at least know of someone who did.

Early in the morning, we went to his house west of Many Farms—word had already been sent that we were coming. The ceremony lasted for four days and three nights, and parts of songs and prayers had such ancient sacred words I wasn't sure if I understood them. When the old man prayed and sang, sometimes tears streamed down my face as I repeated everything after him—word for word, line for line, late into the night—and we would begin again at daybreak the next morning. I was exhausted and so relieved. I finally realized what my grief had done. I could finally let my grandbaby go.

We were lucky that we had found this old man because the ceremony had not been done in almost eighty years. He had seen it as a little boy and had memorized all the parts of it—the songs, the advice, the prayers, and the literal letting go of the dead spirit. Over time, it has become a rare ceremony, because what I had done in holding and keeping the baby for those hours was not in keeping with the Navajo way. I understood that doing so had upset the balance of life and death. When we left, we were all crying. I thanked the old man for his memory, his life, and his ability to help us when no one else could. I understand now that all of life has ceremonies connected with it, and for us, without our memory, our old people, and our children, we would be like lost people in this world we live in, as well as in the other worlds in which our loved ones are waiting.

Nothing

LINDA HOGAN

Nothing sings in our bodies
like breath in a flute.
It dwells in the drum.
I hear it now
that slow beat
like when a voice said to the dark,
let there be light,
let there be ocean
and blue fish
born of nothing
and they were there.
I turn back to bed.
The man there is breathing.
I touch him
with hands already owned by another world.
Look, they are desert,
they are rust. They have washed the dead.
They have washed the just born.
They are open.
They offer nothing.
Take it.
Take nothing from me.
There is still a little life
left inside this body,
a little wildness here
and mercy
and it is the emptiness
we love, touch, enter in one another
and try to fill.

Mother of Nothing

Naomi Shihab Nye

Sister, the stars have no children.
The stars pecking at each night's darkness
above your trailer would shine back at themselves
in its metal, but they are too far away.
The stones lining your path to the goats
know themselves only as speechless, flat,
gray-in-the-sun.
What begins and ends in the self
without continuance in any other.

You who stand at preschool fences
watching the endless tumble and slide,
who answer the mothers' Which one is yours?
with blotted murmur and turning away,
listen. Any lack carried
too close to the heart
grows teeth, nibbles off
corners. I heard one say
she had no talent,
another, no time, and there were many
without beauty all those years,
and all of them shrinking.
What sinks to the bottom of the pond
comes up with new colors, or not at all.

We sank, and there was purple,
voluptuous merging of purple and blue,
a new silence living
in the houses of our bodies.
Those who wanted and never received,
who were born without hands,
who had and then lost; the Turkish mother
after the earthquake

with five silent children lined before her,
the women of Beirut
bearing water to their bombed-out rooms,
the fathers in offices
with framed photographs of children on their desks,
and their own private knowledge
of all the hard words.

And we held trees differently
then, and dried plates differently,
because waiting dulls the senses
and when you are no longer waiting,
something wakes up. My cousin said
It's not children, it's a matter of making
life. And I saw the streets opening into the future,
cars passing, mothers with car seats,
children waving out the rear window,
keeping count of all who waved back,
and would we lift our hearts and answer them,
and when we did, what would we say?
And the old preposterous stories of nothing
and everything finally equalling one another
returned in the night. And like relatives,
knew where the secret key was hidden
and let themselves in.

Part Three

BEARING LIFE

Land of the Living

Kathleen Norris

Menstruation is primitive,
no getting around that fact, as
I wipe my blood from the floor
at 3 A.M. in the monastery guest room,
alone in this community
of sleeping men.

Once again, I have given up
the having of children,
and celebrate instead
a monthly flowering
of the not-to-be,
and let it go without regret.

Earlier tonight, a young monk, laughing,
splashed my face
with holy water. Then, just as unexpectedly,
he flew down a banister, and
for one millisecond
was an angel—robed,
without feet—
all irrepressible joy
and good news.

The black madonna watched us,
expectant as earth just plowed.

My sister holds her baby
in a photograph. They smile at me
from the mirror I've placed them on.
Lili sits like the Christ Child
on her mother's lap. She sits very straight
in a blood-red dress

and stares into something
that makes her look amused, and wise.

It's here, in the land of the living,
the psalm says we shall see God's goodness.
I'm glad to be here,
a useless woman,
sleepless and kept waiting,
as breath keeps coming,
as the blood flows.

Liferower

Rebecca McClanahan

*T*here I am on the Liferower screen, the computerized woman in the tiny boat, and the little woman rowing below me is my pacer. We look exactly alike, except she does not get tired. Her strokes are even and unchanging. I aim for thirty-three pulls per minute, but if I rest even a second between strokes, I fall behind. I want to train my heart, to make it stronger.

"Keep up with the pacer," blinks the sign on the screen. "Use your legs. Keep your back straight."

You row with your whole body, not just your arms. There is a leaning into, then a pulling away. The filling and the emptying. Systole, diastole. The iambic *lub* and *dub*—and sometimes a murmur, a leak in the heart. My father's valve has been replaced with plastic that clicks when he overexerts himself. Bad hearts run in our family. An infant sister died of a congenital ailment; another sister nearly died from a myocardial infection contracted while she was giving birth to her second child. I have no children, which is why I am free to come here to the Y and row my heart out three times a week. Aside from a husband who can take care of himself—as most second husbands are able to do—I have no one to worry about. This thought disturbs me, wakes me at night. If I have no one to care for, who will care for me? When I was small I shared a bedroom with an old woman, my mother's childless aunt, who had nowhere else to go. I have fourteen nephews and nieces. Will any of them claim me? Each month from my paycheck I put away more than I can afford, insurance against what time will bring. According to surveys, women fear old age more than men do—the poverty, the loneliness. And the hearts of women beat faster and harder, both waking and sleeping, than the hearts of men.

"Keep up the good work. You are one boat ahead."

From the shoreline a crowd of miniature fans waves me on to victory. Each time I pull the rowing rope, the little woman on the screen moves her cartoon arms. The oar dips and lifts and a ripple of water sloshes across the screen, accompanied by a whoosh that is intended to sound like rushing water, but sounds more like the breath of a woman in labor: in through the nose, out through the mouth. Whoosh, whoosh. In the delivery room I smoothed my sister's clenched fist and watched the electrocardiograph as twin waves danced across the screen—the rise and fall of mother and daughter. The heart is a double pump composed of four

179

separate rooms. If I divide my age into four equal chambers, I am eleven again. It is the year I begin to bleed, the year my mother pushes my sister into the world.

I pump my legs and pull the rope. In a large open area beside the rowing machines, a yoga class begins. The instructor greets the sun, breathing in *prana,* the invisible life force: in through the nose, out through the mouth. The other women follow, open their mouths on the first half of the healing mantra *Om.*

I like the sound of *forty-four*—the "o" bell tone, sonorous and deep. The echo. I don't like the way it looks—two fours standing shoulder to shoulder, square and bony, each built from single sticks of one that could easily collapse. Like an awkward stork perched precariously in mid-air, tipping on one thin leg. The yoga master has now become a tree—arms branching into finger leaves high above her head, one leg balanced against a thigh, the other the root sinking her deep into imaginary soil. "You can't learn balance," she is saying. "You can only allow it." The heart is controlled by two opposing bundles of nerves, the sympathetic and the parasympathetic. One slows the beat, the other quickens it. Thus balance is achieved through a back and forth dance, two mutually antagonistic forces pushing simultaneously against and for one another.

On the screen, red buoys bob between my pacer and me, marking off the miles in tenths: one point six, one point seven. The water rolls beneath us and in the distance a miniature skyline looms. It is the kind of city a child might construct from LEGO pieces, chunks of towers and boxy buildings in the shape of bar graphs a math teacher draws on the blackboard. What goes up must come down. My Y locker combination—32-22-32—is easy to remember because those were my measurements half a lifetime ago, when I was being fitted for my first wedding dress. My mother saved the dress. It still hangs in her guest room closet. The marriage lasted three years, three years longer than it should have because I was determined not to fail. My mother was my measure, my pacer, and when my husband began turning from me, I rowed faster and faster toward him. I would work harder, cook more of his favorite foods, iron his khakis with a sharper pleat.

"Lean into the stroke. Keep up with the pacer. You are three boats behind."

On the rower beside mine, a young woman pumps with long, tanned legs and pulls with lean, muscled arms that she probably believes will never soften. Her body is something she counts on—the belly flat, the skin snug and elastic as the spandex leotard glowing in oranges and greens, the neon parrot hues of one whose life does not yet depend on camouflage. The weight instructor, a short, well-built man about my age, bends to speak to her, to comment on her form and technique. He does not see me. When he leaves, she watches her reflection in the floor-to-ceiling mirror as if her body belongs to someone else. Her forehead is prematurely lined with worry; she is not enjoying this. Nearby, the yoga master assumes the lion pose, crouched and ready. She bares her teeth, lifts her mane into the air.

"Use your legs. Keep your back straight. You are five boats behind."

The heart is a hollow muscle about the size of a clenched fist, surrounded by a slippery, loose-fitting sac and protected by three layers of membranes. At five weeks a fetus is barely eight millimeters long, but already its heart is beating on its own. When my sister had her first sonogram, I watched on the screen the undulating blur that would become my niece. The heart cells were already in place, all the cells my niece would need for the rest of her life. Her heartbeat sounded like a train roaring through a tunnel. A child comes into this world hammering its heart out, 160 beats per minute, a teletype machine tapping an urgent message. Deep in the aortic chamber of some adults survives a hole, the *foramen ovale*, remnant of the place where blood passed through the fetal heart.

The child I chose against would have been born into the cramped space of my life between marriages. I still ask myself how it could have happened. *Things happen.* You wake one morning and you know. Your tender breasts tell you and the flush across your cheeks and the feeling of something larger and smaller than yourself moving inside you. Time passes, liquid as a dream, and one morning, because you are alone and your life is a rented room, you make the call. And the next day when it's over and the nurse takes the gauze from between your teeth, the doctor, who is kind and slightly plump, his forehead lined from having seen too much, holds up a glass bottle filled with something bright and red. "This is pregnancy," he says, believing it is for your own good. "Don't let this happen again." And then it is over, it is done. But your legs are still trembling and your tongue is bleeding from where you bit down and missed.

Five boats ahead of me, the pacer slides over the finish line, leaving red buoys bobbing in her wake. I place my fingertips on my carotid artery and begin the count that will bring me back to myself. Easing up on the rope, I pump slower, slower, my boat cruising past the crowd of bystanders waving from the shoreline. The yoga master begins her descent into this world, shifting from eagle to fish to cat to flower, shape by shape removing herself, moving toward a place that knows no shape. When she reaches it, she bows to the altar of Sadguru, the larger self that dwells within the smallest place. Forehead pressed to the ground, she assumes the child position: shoulders down, knees folded to belly, hands and feet at rest, ears open to the slightest sound. The music of a single heartbeat is actually two-part harmony, a duet sung by opposing valves, the low-pitched *dub* of the atrioventricular and the higher pitched *dub* as the semilunar closes down. The yoga master opens her mouth on *O* and the others follow, float on this communal pond until together their lips close on the hum and, one by one, their single breaths give out.

You Remember Sophia

VALERIE MINER

"*D*espina, you remember Despina," says the ancient woman as she sits on the stone steps frying sardines. "Despina has four children. You remember Despina."

"*Nai,*" nods Sophia in the Greek which comes easily to her head but slowly to her lips. Speaking the old language is like trying to communicate through Novocaine. Numbness. She feels such numbness. Her eyes are drawn down to the sea.

"And Eleni. She lives in that big stone house by the *kastro*. Her husband is a farmer and she has five boys."

"*Nai,*" nods Sophia, searching for her mother in this bird wearing thin, black cotton. Her face is struck as coldly as those clay tourist medallions and her silver hair, knotted at the back, is like a miser's purse, deceptively small.

"Yes, Mama, I remember," she wants to say. "And Sophia has no children. But she has a life. Born of farmers on the Island of Lesbos, she is now a doctor in a big American city hospital. She lives with the woman she loves. But, Mama, you are too busy seeing what I am not."

Sophia knew it would be like this. Despite the twenty years away, she knew in that part of herself that was deeper than memory, the part that would sprout red poppies and pink daphne in dark dreams. She is dark enough to be taken for Chicana by the Americans. And Western enough to be taken for American by the shopkeepers here—until they look closely enough to notice she is one of their own, a Greek woman returned to Lesbos.

"You are happy?" Mama considers this prodigal daughter in the crimson trousers and the boy-short hair. She looks into reflections of her own amber eyes and asks, "You are happy, my little one?" Sophia, the red giant, finds a tear on the edge of her smile. "*Nai.*" She feels the numbness wearing away.

After dinner, Sophia says she will visit the sea. Avoiding her mother's hurt, confused glance, she walks quickly from the house. Mama cannot object. Their reunion is too fragile for demands. Questions cause enough strain.

Boys shout in the street. At first, Sophia is charmed by the chords of children's voices, a noise she never hears above the Los Angeles traffic. She is touched by the natural sound. And then she recalls her own childhood inside—practicing quiet over the washing. Murmuring. Always murmuring, even the prayers. Now all around her, she can see boys. Replicas of her old friends, Christophe, Stevenos, and Darius. Boys' voices. She cannot hear the silent, indoor girls. Perhaps, she laughs to herself, they have all gone to the sea.

Sophia can hear it still, the chorus of thirty years before. "To go to school for a girl is a luxury." "Your parents are peasants, not nobility." "The money belongs in your dowry." "Six grades is enough." "Why must you go to Petra, all the way to Petra for school?" "It will turn your head." "It will . . ." Yes, they were right. Ever since Petra, Molivos was too small for her long legs and big feet. It was in Petra that she met Stellio who promised an automobile and a big house, like in the movies, if she would move with him to Los Angeles. After all, Los Angeles was where they made the movies. That she knew, even before Petra.

Walking down through the market now, all she can hear is the simmering of large black flies and fecund bees in the wisteria. The *tavernas* are quiet. Men are still at home eating meals which their wives have spent all day preparing. As she passes the shop called "Agora," Sophia sees her hills have turned a California gold, haze in the background (and beyond that, Turkey. Turkey is just eight miles away. Eight miles to the enemy. Eight miles of brilliant blue between Europe and Asia), reminding her of Los Angeles. Reminding her that it was never like the movies.

The rape scene was the only time Stellio resembled Clark Gable and he was disappointed she wasn't as grateful as Vivian Leigh. Their marriage lasted one year. But it wasn't a complete loss. It lasted long enough for her to learn about community colleges, to meet a few women friends. Hard to write Mama about the divorce. Hard to read back her shame, her bitter "I told you so." How, then, could she write about going to college, about loving Myrna, about her dreams of becoming a doctor? Instead she wrote that she was well, working hard. She said she missed the bird music of Molivos. Mama asked the priest to read and write the letters. (She could have asked the teacher or one of the shopkeepers, Sophia knew, but she chose the priest.) Through Father's tense, spider scrawl, Mama wrote again and again, "I pray for your safe return."

Two American women at Stratos's *taverna* stare and smile. American. They have to be American with that size and bearing— which she herself now shares. Almost. Their smiles blur into uncertainty as they regard each other, wondering if she is, after all, one of them. Sophia understands. She smiles hello. But she cannot reassure them. She does not know if she is American. Another time she might stop to talk ambiguities. Another time she might explain the banking hours and the best shops for jewelry and the statues of Greek women. But now she must reach the sea.

Gulls sail low, scouting the last catch. The sky is washed a dark gray which, Sophia remembers, precedes the false promise of a sunset. Donkey shit on the cobblestones. How could she explain to Myrna that she missed this smell? Overripe plums are splattered on the roadside. Such richness. "Star Trek" blares in Greek from an open doorway. The sea looks rougher than a moment ago, more determined, as if calling for the sun to set, summoning the moon to rise.

"A doctor now," Mama wrote, the priest wrote, both comprehending nothing except new access to her. "So now you can return home and do good." How could she explain her choice to work with immigrant families in America—mostly Mexican and Asian—rather than with her own people? If you were a person, who were your own people? If you were a gull, you were not a dove. If you were Greek, could you be American? Was this the same water that washed through people in Tunisia and Israel and France?

These beach rocks hold her steadier than city pavement. Lapping waves soothe her deeper than Stratos's *metaxa*. Shadowed hills, now almost invisible, call her to join sleeping shapes in the distance. The hills. The sea. She had always been torn, even as a child.

Despina has four children.

Eleni lives in a stone house.

Mr. Spock speaks Greek.

The priest admonishes.

American women nod in tentative complicity.

She knew it would be like this. Twenty years away and she knew she would be drugged by the flowers. She knew Mama would hold her at arms' length like a stranger, her eyes still full of longing for the daughter to return. Sophia knew she would return to the sea.

Here in the moonrise, she sees a face. Just beyond the cove, Sophia sees a moon face shining in the Aegean. Should she slip these fine lavender rocks into her red pants and wade out to this face?

Sophia does not have four children.

Sophia does not live in a stone house.

Closer yet, she finds a seductive smile, which does not question, which does not blur, a clear face beaming from the sea, a reflection not of the moon, but of Sophia.

Sophia has a face which shines in the sea. It has always been there. Waiting for her. Ever since she was "odd Sophia with books." Now she has found it again.

She stands in darkness an hour, beckoned by this luminous face in the sea. Her own moon floating within reach.

Sophia, you remember Sophia. Finally, the face finds a voice. She watches for another hour and decides she does not need to go as far as the cove. She does not need to explain herself to the Americans at the *taverna* or to the priest. She will rest easily at Mama's tonight. She will return to Myrna in Los Angeles. She salutes her reflection and turns back to Molivos.

The face she carries with her, between the lands, behind the shadows, beneath the waters. Sophia, you remember Sophia.

From Obasan

JOY KOGAWA

*T*he town of Cecil, Alberta, is one hundred and fifty odd miles northeast of Granton, and I have been teaching in the same room now for the last seven years. Every month or so, I try to drop in to see my uncle and my aunt, Obasan, who are both now in their eighties. But at the beginning of the school year, I'm quite busy.

It usually takes me at least two weeks to feel at home with a new class. This year there are two Native girls, sisters, twelve and thirteen years old, both adopted. There's also a beautiful half-Japanese, half-European child named Tami. Then there's Sigmund, the freckle-faced redhead. Right from the beginning, I can see that he is trouble. I'm trying to keep an eye on him by putting him at the front of the class.

Sigmund's hand is up, as it usually is.

"Yes, Sigmund."

"Miss Nah Canny," he says.

"Not Nah Canny," I tell him, printing my name on the blackboard. N A K A N E. "The *a*'s are short as in 'among'—Na Ka Neh—and not as in 'apron' or 'hat.'"

Some of the children say "Nah Cane."

"Naomi Nah Cane is a pain," I heard one of the girls say once.

"Have you ever been in love, Miss Nakane?" Sigmund asks.

"In love? Why do you suppose we use the preposition 'in' when we talk about love?" I ask evasively. "What does it mean to be 'in' something?"

Sigmund never puts his hand up calmly but shakes it frantically like a leaf in the wind.

I am thinking of the time when I was a child and asked Uncle if he and Obasan were "in love." My question was out of place. "In ruv? What that?" Uncle asked. I've never once seen them caressing.

"Are you going to get married?" Sigmund asks.

The impertinence of children. As soon as they learn I'm no disciplinarian, I lose control over classroom discussions.

"Why do you ask?" I answer irritably and without dignity.

"My mother says you don't look old enough to be a teacher."

That's odd. It must be my size—five feet one, 105 pounds. When I first started teaching sixteen years ago there were such surprised looks when parents came to the classroom door. Was it my youthfulness or my Oriental face? I never learned which.

"My friend wants to ask you for a date," Sigmund adds. He's aware of the stir he's creating in the class. A few of the girls gasp and put their hands up to their mouths. An appropriate response, I think wryly. Typically Cecil. Miss Nakane dating a friend of Sigmund's? What a laugh!

I turn my back to the class and stare out the window. Every year the question is asked at least once.

"Are you going to get married, Miss Nakane?"

With everyone in town watching everything that happens, what chance for romance is there here? Once a widower father of one of the boys in my class came to see me after school and took me to dinner at the local hotel. I felt nervous walking into the Cecil Inn with him.

"Where do you come from?" he asked, as we sat down at a small table in a corner. That's the one sure-fire question I always get from strangers. People assume when they meet me that I'm a foreigner.

"How do you mean?"

"How long have you been in this country?"

"I was born here."

"Oh," he said, and grinned. "And your parents?"

"My mother's a Nisei."

"A what?"

"N-I-S-E-I," I spelled, printing the word on the napkin. "Pronounced 'knee-say.' It means 'second generation.'" Sometimes I think I've been teaching school too long. I explained that my grandparents, born in Japan, were Issei, or first generation, while the children of the Nisei were called Sansei, or third generation.

The widower was so full of questions that I half-expected him to ask for an identity card. The only thing I carry in my wallet is my driver's license. I should have something with my picture on it and a statement below that tells who I am. Megumi Naomi Nakane. Born June 18, 1936, Vancouver, British Columbia. Marital status: Old maid. Health: Fine, I suppose. Occupation: School teacher. I'm bored to death with teaching and ready to retire. What else would anyone want to know? Personality: Tense. Is that past or present tense? It's perpetual tense. I have the social graces of a common housefly. That's self-denigrating, isn't it?

The widower never asked me out again. I wonder how I was unsatisfactory. I could hardly think of anything at all to ask him. Did he assume I wasn't interested? Can people not tell the difference between nervousness and lack of interest?

"Well," I say, turning around and facing the general tittering, "there are many questions I don't have answers for."

Sigmund's hand is waving still. "But you're a spinster," he says, darting a grin at the class. More gasps from the girls.

"Spinster?" I grimace and have an urge to throttle him. "What does the word mean?"

"Old maid," Sigmund says impudently.

From *Obasan*

Spinster? Old maid? Bachelor lady? The terms certainly apply. At thirty-six, I'm no bargain in the marriage market. But Aunt Emily in Toronto, still single at fifty-six, is even more old-maidish than I am, and yet she refuses the label. She says if we laundered the term properly she'd put it on, but it's too covered with cultural accretions for comfort.

"I suppose I am an old maid," I say glumly. "So is my aunt in Toronto."

"Your aunt is an old maid too? How come?"

I throw up my hands in futility. Let the questions come. Why indeed are there two of us unmarried in our small family? Must be something in the blood. A crone-prone syndrome. We should hire ourselves out for a research study, Aunt Emily and I. But she would be too busy, rushing around Toronto, rushing off to conferences. She never stays still long enough to hear the sound of her own voice.

"What's her name, Teacher?"

"Emily Kato," I say, spelling it. "That's 'Cut-oh,' not 'Cat-oh,' or 'Kay-toe.' Miss E. Kato." Is there some way I can turn this ridiculous discussion into a phonics lesson?

Someone is sure to ask about her love life. Has Aunt Emily ever, I wonder, been in love? Love no doubt is in her. Love, like the coulee wind, rushing through her mind, whirring along the tips of her imagination. Love like a coyote, howling into a "love 'em and leave 'em" wind.

A Lifetime

ANA CASTILLO

*H*e is tubes all over. He is also bald. I think he had been losing most of his hair already anyway, but now his entire body is hairless.

The last time I saw him we rendezvoused in secret downtown at Christmastime. Even though he was afraid that his wife would question him, he bought me perfume on his credit card.

That was five years ago.

Our life together was a lifetime ago.

Since then, he has been married for nearly twenty years. Nearly twenty years, is what his wife must tell everyone, when she shows off pictures of their children, a boy and a girl, when she talks about their home with the new deck he built last summer, when she recalls their honeymoon every anniversary.

But it isn't twenty years because twenty years ago is when we got married. We had no honeymoon.

He doesn't recognize me at first when I come in. I've intentionally gone to the hospital in the afternoon when I believe she may be at work. She is very dedicated to her job. He says she likes money. But she also liked the idea of a life devoted to a family, a husband, a boy and a girl, a house with a new deck, a brand-new fully equipped recreation vehicle. They take trips to Disney World every summer.

I never thought he'd go for that, at least not when we were married. I thought he didn't like kids. I didn't want to have any then, either, so I just figured neither did he. He was a musician.

He became a contractor. He never had much of a mind for business so he has always worked for someone else.

He doesn't recognize me right away, too groggy from medication. He thinks I'm a nurse.

We thought we were all grown when we married. I had been out of high school for two whole years. During our one-year marriage, neither of us held down a job. We had no real skills. I was always a lousy typist. He wanted to get into the union but, in those days, they didn't let Puerto Ricans in unions.

I tried to find out something from the nurse in charge, about the tumor. She said I'd have to talk to his doctor if I wasn't part of the immediate family.

When we got married I was pregnant. We knew we weren't ready for a family. We didn't want to throw ourselves into a factory all our lives as our parents had done.

I've never had a family.

He smiles when he finally recognizes me, but I know he is nervous that his wife will walk in. She has never allowed him to talk about his marriage to me, not to her, not to their friends and family. I was erased from his history. I saw them together in a restaurant once. He looked so upset, I went right by them to my table. He would have introduced us, but what was the point?

He said I was not the marrying type. Each time I get married he says that.

I put the bunch of irises in a plastic container used for collecting urine. Of course, it's clean and I've put water in it. He takes the little notecard, reads it, and slips it under his pillow.

"So how's your career going?" he asks. He is twenty-one years old again. He is cute and charming. He is not middle-aged, tired, and very likely not going to leave this hospital alive.

I nod. I shrug my shoulders. I am pretty. I have the best pair of breasts on anyone we know. I am going to take the world by storm. I am not overweight, wearing bifocals, and looking for a new job.

He puts his hand out and I take it. We both look to the door reflexively. "You look great," he says. I think he means it. He probably means it because I am not the one in the hospital bed dying.

"So do you," I say.

We spend an hour like that, holding hands, me sitting on the edge of his bed, he dozing off, wondering what day it is and if the staff will relent and let his kids come up to see him later.

Hairball

MARGARET ATWOOD

On the thirteenth of November, day of unluck, month of the dead, Kat went into the Toronto General Hospital for an operation. It was for an ovarian cyst, a large one.

Many women had them, the doctor told her. Nobody knew why. There wasn't any way of finding out whether the thing was malignant, whether it contained, already, the spores of death. Not before they went in. He spoke of "going in" the way she'd heard old veterans in TV documentaries speak of assaults on enemy territory. There was the same tensing of the jaw, the same fierce gritting of the teeth, the same grim enjoyment. Except that what he would be going into was her body. Counting down, waiting for the anesthetic, Kat too gritted her teeth fiercely. She was terrified, but also she was curious. Curiosity has got her through a lot.

She'd made the doctor promise to save the thing for her, whatever it was, so she could have a look. She was intensely interested in her own body, in anything it might choose to do or produce; although when flaky Dania, who did layout at the magazine, told her this growth was a message to her from her body and she ought to sleep with an amethyst under her pillow to calm her vibrations, Kat told her to stuff it.

The cyst turned out to be a benign tumor. Kat liked that use of *benign,* as if the thing had a soul and wished her well. It was big as a grapefruit, the doctor said. "Big as a coconut," said Kat. Other people had grapefruits. "Coconut" was better. It conveyed the hardness of it, and the hairiness, too.

The hair in it was red—long strands of it wound round and round inside, like a ball of wet wool gone berserk or like the guck you pulled out of a clogged bathroom-sink drain. there were little bones in it too, or fragments of bone; bird bones, the bones of a sparrow crushed by a car. There was a scattering of nails, toe or finger. There were five perfectly formed teeth.

"Is this abnormal?" Kat asked the doctor, who smiled. Now that he had gone in and come out again, unscathed, he was less clenched.

"Abnormal? No," he said carefully, as if breaking the news to a mother about a freakish accident to her newborn. "Let's just say it's fairly common." Kat was a little disappointed. She would have preferred uniqueness.

She asked for a bottle of formaldehyde, and put the cut-open tumor into it. It was hers, it was benign, it did not deserve to be thrown away. She took it back to

190

her apartment and stuck it on the mantelpiece. She named it Hairball. It isn't that different from having a stuffed bear's head or a preserved ex-pet or anything else with fur and teeth looming over your fireplace; or she pretends it isn't. Anyway it certainly makes an impression.

Ger doesn't like it. Despite his supposed yen for the new and outré, he is a squeamish man. The first time he comes around (sneaks around, creeps around) after the operation, he tells Kat to throw Hairball out. He calls it "disgusting." Kat refuses point-blank, and says she'd rather have Hairball in a bottle on her mantelpiece than the soppy dead flowers he's brought her, which will anyway rot a lot sooner than Hairball will. As a mantelpiece ornament, Hairball is far superior. Ger says Kat has a tendency to push things to extremes, to go over the edge, merely from a juvenile desire to shock, which is hardly a substitute for wit. One of these days, he says, she will go way too far. Too far for him, is what he means.

"That's why you hired me, isn't it?" she says. "Because I go way too far." But he's in one of his analyzing moods. He can see these tendencies of hers reflected in her work on the magazine, he says. All that leather and those grotesque and tortured-looking poses are heading down a track he and others are not at all sure they should continue to follow. Does she see what he means, does she take his point? It's a point that's been made before. She shakes her head slightly, says nothing. She knows how that translates: there have been complaints from the advertisers. *Too bizarre, too kinky.* Tough.

"Want to see my scar?" she says. "Don't make me laugh, though, you'll crack it open." Stuff like that makes him dizzy: anything with a hint of blood, anything gynecological. He almost threw up in the delivery room when his wife had a baby two years ago. He'd told her that with pride. Kat thinks about sticking a cigarette into the side of her mouth, as in a black-and-white movie of the forties. She thinks about blowing the smoke into his face.

Her insolence used to excite him, during their arguments. Then there would be a grab of her upper arms, a smoldering, violent kiss. He kisses her as if he thinks someone else is watching him, judging the image they make together. Kissing the latest thing, hard and shiny, purple-mouthed, crop-headed; kissing a girl, a woman, a girl, in a little crotch-hugger skirt and skin-tight leggings. He likes mirrors.

But he isn't excited now. And she can't decoy him into bed; she isn't ready for that yet, she isn't healed. He has a drink, which he doesn't finish, holds her hand as an afterthought, gives her a couple of avuncular pats on the off-white outsized alpaca shoulder, leaves too quickly.

"Goodbye, Gerald," she says. She pronounces the name with mockery. It's a negation of him, an abolishment of him, like ripping a medal off his chest. It's a warning.

He'd been Gerald when they first met. It was she who transformed him, first to Gerry, then to Ger. (Rhymed with *flair*, rhymed with *dare*.) She made him get rid of those sucky pursed-mouth ties, told him what shoes to wear, got him to buy a loose-cut Italian suit, redid his hair. A lot of his current tastes—in food, in drink, in recreational drugs, in women's entertainment underwear—were once hers. In his new phase, with his new, hard, stripped-down name ending on the sharpened note of *r,* he is her creation.

As she is her own. During her childhood she was a romanticized Katherine, dressed by her misty-eyed, fussy mother in dresses that looked like ruffled pillowcases. By high school she'd shed the frills and emerged as a bouncy, round-faced Kathy, with gleaming freshly washed hair and enviable teeth, eager to please and no more interesting than a health food ad. At university she was Kath, blunt and no-bullshit in her Take-Back-the-Night jeans and checked shirt and her bricklayer-style striped-denim peaked hat. When she ran away to England, she sliced herself down to Kat. It was economical, street-feline, and pointed as a nail. It was also unusual. In England you had to do something to get their attention, especially if you weren't English. Safe in this incarnation, she Ramboed through the eighties.

It was the name, she still thinks, that got her the interview and then the job. The job with an avant-garde magazine, the kind that was printed on matte stock in black and white, with overexposed close-ups of women with hair blowing over their eyes, one nostril prominent: *the razor's edge,* it was called. Haircuts as art, some real art, film reviews, a little stardust, wardrobes of ideas that were clothes and of clothes that were ideas—the metaphysical shoulder pad. She learned her trade well, hands-on. She learned what worked.

She made her way up the ladder, from layout to design, then to the supervision of whole spreads, and then whole issues. It wasn't easy, but it was worth it. She had become a creator; she created total looks. After a while she could walk down the street in Soho or stand in the lobby at openings and witness her handiwork incarnate, strolling around in outfits she'd put together, spouting her warmed-over pronouncements. It was like being God, only God had never got around to off-the-rack lines.

By that time her face had lost its roundness, though the teeth of course remained: there was something to be said for North American dentistry. She'd shaved off most of her hair, worked on the drop-dead stare, perfected a certain turn of the neck that conveyed an aloof inner authority. What you had to make them believe was that you knew something they didn't know yet. What you also had to make them believe was that they too could know this thing, this thing that would give them eminence and power and sexual allure, that would attract envy to them—but for a price. The price of the magazine. What they could never get through their heads was that it was done entirely with cameras. Frozen light, frozen time. Given the angle, she could make anyone look beautiful, or at least interesting. It was all photography, it was all iconography. It was all in the choosing eye. This was the thing that could never be bought, no matter how much of your pitiful monthly wage you blew on snakeskin.

Despite the status, *the razor's edge* was fairly low-paying. Kat herself could not afford many of the things she contextualized so well. The grottiness and expense of London began to get to her; she got tired of gorging on the canapés at literary launches in order to scrimp on groceries, tired of the fuggy smell of cigarettes ground into the red-and-maroon carpeting of pubs, tired of the pipes bursting every time it froze in winter, and of the Clarissas and Melissas and Penelopes at the magazine rabbiting on about how they had been literally, absolutely, totally freezing all night, and how it literally, absolutely, totally, usually never got that cold. It always got that cold. The pipes always burst. Nobody thought of putting in real pipes, ones that would not burst next time. Burst pipes were an English tradition, like so many others.

Like, for instance, English men. Charm the knickers off you with their mellow vowels and frivolous verbiage, and then, once they'd got them off, panic and run. Or else stay and whinge. The English called it *whinging* instead of whining. It was better, really. Like a creaking hinge. It was a traditional compliment to be whinged at by an Englishman. It was his way of saying he trusted you, he was conferring upon you the privilege of getting to know the real him. The inner, whinging him. That was how they thought of women, secretly: whinge receptacles. Kat could play it, but that didn't mean she liked it.

She had an advantage over the English women, though: she was of no class. She had no class. She was in a class of her own. She could roll around among the English men, all different kinds of them, secure in the knowledge that she was not being measured against the class yardsticks and accent-detectors they carried around in their back pockets, was not subject to the petty snobberies and resentments that lent such richness to their inner lives. The flip side of this freedom was that she was beyond the pale. She was a colonial—how fresh, how vital, how anonymous, how finally of no consequence. Like a hole in the wall, she could be told all secrets and then be abandoned with no guilt.

She was too smart, of course. The English men were very competitive; they liked to win. Several times it hurt. Twice she had abortions, because the men in question were not up for the alternative. She learned to say that she didn't want children anyway, that if she longed for a rug-rat she would buy a gerbil. Her life began to seem long. Her adrenaline was running out. Soon she would be thirty, and all she could see ahead was more of the same.

This was how things were when Gerald turned up. "You're terrific," he said, and she was ready to hear it, even from him, even though *terrific* was a word that had probably gone out with fifties crew-cuts. She was ready for his voice by that time too: the flat, metallic nasal tone of the Great Lakes, with its clear hard *r*s and its absence of theatricality. Dull normal. The speech of her people. It came to her suddenly that she was an exile.

Gerald was scouting, Gerald was recruiting. He'd heard about her, looked at her work, sought her out. One of the big companies back in Toronto was launching a new fashion-oriented magazine, he said: upmarket, international in its coverage, of course, but with some Canadian fashion in it too, and with lists of stores where the items portrayed could actually be bought. In that respect they felt they'd have it all over the competition, those American magazines that assumed you could only get Gucci in New York or Los Angeles. Heck, times had changed, you could get it in Edmonton! You could get it in Winnipeg!

Kat had been away too long. There was Canadian fashion now? The English quip would be to say that "Canadian fashion" was an oxymoron. She refrained from making it, lit a cigarette with her cyanide-green Covent Garden–boutique leather-covered lighter (as featured in the May issue of *the razor's edge*), looked Gerald in the eye. "London is a lot to give up," she said levelly. She glanced around the see-me-here Mayfair restaurant where they were finishing lunch, a restaurant she'd chosen because she'd known he was paying. She'd never spend that kind of money on food otherwise. "Where would I eat?"

Gerald assured her that Toronto was now the restaurant capital of Canada. He himself would be happy to be her guide. There was a great Chinatown, there was world-class Italian. Then he paused, took a breath. "I've been meaning to ask you," he said. "About the name. Is that Kat as in Krazy?" He thought this was suggestive. She'd heard it before.

"No," she said. "It's Kat as in KitKat. That's a chocolate bar. Melts in your mouth." She gave him her stare, quirked her mouth, just a twitch.

Gerald became flustered, but he pushed on. They wanted her, they needed her, they loved her, he said in essence. Someone with her fresh, innovative approach and her experience would be worth a lot of money to them, relatively speaking. But there were rewards other than the money. She would be in on the initial concept, she would have a formative influence, she would have a free hand. He named a sum that made her gasp, inaudibly of course. By now she knew better than to betray desire.

So she made the journey back, did her three months of culture shock, tried the world-class Italian and the great Chinese, and seduced Gerald at the first opportunity, right in his junior vice-presidential office. It was the first time Gerald had been seduced in such a location, or perhaps ever. Even though it was after hours, the danger frenzied him. It was the idea of it. The daring. The image of Kat kneeling on the broadloom, in a legendary bra that until now he'd seen only in the lingerie ads of the Sunday *New York Times*, unzipping him in full view of the silver-framed engagement portrait of his wife that complemented the impossible ballpoint pen set on his desk. At that time he was so straight he felt compelled to take off his wedding ring and place it carefully in the ashtray first. The next day he brought her a box of David Wood Food Shop chocolate truffles. They were the best, he told her, anxious that she should recognize their quality. She found the gesture banal, but also sweet. The banality, the sweetness, the hunger to impress: that was Gerald.

Gerald was the kind of man she wouldn't have bothered with in London. He was not funny, he was not knowledgeable, he had little verbal charm. He was eager, he was tractable, he was blank paper. Although he was eight years older than she was, he seemed much younger. She took pleasure from his furtive, boyish delight in his own wickedness. And he was so grateful. "I can hardly believe this is happening," he said, more frequently than was necessary and usually in bed.

His wife, whom Kat encountered (and still encounters) at many tedious company events, helped to explain his gratitude. The wife was a priss. Her name was Cheryl. Her hair looked as if she still used big rollers and embalm-your-hairdo spray; her mind was room-by-room Laura Ashley wallpaper: tiny, unopened pastel buds arranged in straight rows. She probably put on rubber gloves to make love, and checked it off on a list afterwards. One more messy household chore. She looked at Kat as if she'd like to spritz her with air deodorizer. Kat revenged herself by picturing Cheryl's bathrooms: hand towels embroidered with lilies, fuzzy covers on the toilet seats.

The magazine itself got off to a rocky start. Although Kat had lots of lovely money to play with, and although it was a challenge to be working in color, she did not have the free hand Gerald had promised her. She had to contend with the company board of directors, who were all men, who were all accountants or indistinguishable from them, who were cautious and slow as moles.

"It's simple," Kat told them. "You bombard them with images of what they ought to be, and you make them feel grotty for being the way they are. You're working with the gap between reality and perception. That's why you have to hit them with something new, something they've never seen before, something they aren't. Nothing sells like anxiety."

The board, on the other hand, felt that the readership should simply be offered more of what they already had. More fur, more sumptuous leather, more cashmere. More established names. The board had no sense of improvisation, no wish to take risks; no sporting instincts, no desire to put one over on the readers just for the hell of it. "Fashion is like hunting," Kat told them, hoping to appeal to their male hormones, if any. "It's playful, it's intense, it's predatory. It's blood and guts. It's erotic." But to them it was about good taste. They wanted Dress-for-Success. Kat wanted scatter gun ambush.

Everything became a compromise. Kat had wanted to call the magazine *All the Rage,* but the board was put off by the vibrations of anger in the word "rage." They thought it was too feminist, of all things. "It's a *forties* sound," Kat said. "Forties is *back.* Don't you get it?" But they didn't. They wanted to call it *Or.* French for *gold,* and blatant enough in its values, but without any base note, as Kat told them. They sawed off at *Felice,* which had qualities each side wanted. It was vaguely French-sounding, it meant "happy" (so much less threatening than rage), and, although you couldn't expect the others to notice, for Kat it had a feline bouquet which counteracted the laciness. She had it done in hot-pink lipstick-scrawl, which helped some. She could live with it, but it had not been her first love.

This battle has been fought and refought over every innovation in design, every new angle Kat has tried to bring in, every innocuous bit of semi-kink. There was a big row over a spread that did lingerie, half pulled off and with broken glass perfume bottles strewn on the floor. There was an uproar over the two nouveau-stockinged legs, one tied to a chair with a third, different-colored stocking. They had not understood the man's three-hundred-dollar leather gloves positioned ambiguously around a neck.

And so it has gone on, for five years.

After Gerald has left, Kat paces her living room. Pace, pace. Her stitches pull. She's not looking forward to her solitary dinner of microwaved leftovers. She's not sure now why she came back here, to this flat burg beside the polluted inland sea. Was it Ger? Ludicrous thought but no longer out of the question. Is he the reason she stays, despite her growing impatience with him?

He's no longer fully rewarding. They've learned each other too well, they take short-cuts now; their time together has shrunk from whole stolen rolling and sensuous afternoons to a few hours snatched between work and dinnertime. She no longer knows what she wants from him. She tells herself she's worth more, she should branch out; but she doesn't see other men, she can't, somehow. She's tried once or twice but it didn't work. Sometimes she goes out to dinner or a flick with one of the gay designers. She likes the gossip.

Maybe she misses London. She feels caged, in this country, in this city, in this room. She could start with the room, she could open a window. It's too stuffy in here. There's an undertone of formaldehyde, from Hairball's bottle. The flowers she got for the operation are mostly wilted, all except Gerald's from today. Come to think of it, why didn't he send her any at the hospital? Did he forget, or was it a message?

"Hairball," she says, "I wish you could talk. I could have a more intelligent conversation with you than with most of the losers in this turkey farm." Hairball's baby teeth glint in the light; it looks as if it's about to speak.

Kat feels her own forehead. She wonders if she's running a temperature. Something ominous is going on, behind her back. There haven't been enough phone calls from the magazine; they've been able to muddle on without her, which is bad news. Reigning queens should never go on vacation, or have operations either. Uneasy lies the head. She has a sixth sense about these things, she's been involved in enough palace coups to know the signs, she has sensitive antennae for the footfalls of impending treachery.

The next morning she pulls herself together, downs an espresso from her mini-machine, picks out an aggressive touch-me-if-you-dare suede outfit in armor gray, and drags herself to the office, although she isn't due in till next week. Surprise, surprise. Whispering knots break up in the corridors, greet her with false welcome as she limps past. She settles herself at her minimalist desk, checks her mail. Her head is pounding, her stitches hurt. Ger gets wind of her arrival; he want to see her a.s.a.p., and not for lunch.

He awaits her in his newly done wheat-on-white office, with the eighteenth-century desk they chose together, the Victorian inkstand, the framed blowups from the magazine, the hands in maroon leather, wrists manacled with pearls, the Hermès scarf twisted into a blindfold, the model's mouth blossoming lusciously beneath it. Some of her best stuff. He's beautifully done up, in a lick-my-neck silk shirt open at the throat, an eat-your-heart-out Italian silk-and-wool loose-knit sweater. Oh, cool insouciance. Oh, eyebrow language. He's a money man who lusted after art, and now he's got some, now he is some. Body art. Her art. She's done her job well; he's finally sexy.

He's smooth as lacquer. "I didn't want to break this to you until next week," he says. He breaks it to her. It's the board of directors. They think she's too bizarre, they think she goes way too far. Nothing he could do about it, although naturally he tried.

Naturally. Betrayal. The monster has turned on its own mad scientist. "I gave you life!" she wants to scream at him.

She isn't in good shape. She can hardly stand. She stands, despite his offer of a chair. She sees now what she's wanted, what she's been missing. Gerald is what she's been missing—the stable, unfashionable, previous, tight-assed Gerald. Not Ger, not the one she's made in her own image. The other one, before he got ruined. The Gerald with a house and a small child and a picture of his wife in a silver frame on his desk. She wants to be in that silver frame. She wants the child. She's been robbed.

"And who is my lucky replacement?" she says. She needs a cigarette, but does not want to reveal her shaking hands.

"Actually, it's me," he says, trying for modesty.

This is too absurd. Gerald couldn't edit a phone book. "You?" she says faintly. She has the good sense not to laugh.

"I've always wanted to get out of the money end of things here," he says, "into the creative area. I knew you'd understand, since it can't be you at any rate. I knew you'd prefer someone who could, well, sort of build on your foundations." Pompous asshole. She looks at his neck. She longs for him, hates herself for it, and is powerless.

The room wavers. He slides towards her across the wheat-colored broadloom, takes her by the gray suede upper arms. "I'll write you a good reference," he says. "Don't worry about that. Of course, we can still see one another. I'd miss our afternoons."

"Of course," she says. He kisses her, a voluptuous kiss, or it would look like one to a third party, and she lets him. *In a pig's ear.*

She makes it home in a taxi. The driver is rude to her and gets away with it; she doesn't have the energy. In her mailbox is an engraved invitation: Ger and Cheryl are having a drinks party, tomorrow evening. Postmarked five days ago. Cheryl is behind the times.

Kat undresses, runs a shallow bath. There's not much to drink around here, there's nothing to sniff or smoke. What an oversight; she's stuck with herself. There are other jobs. There are other men, or that's the theory. Still, something's been ripped out of her. How could this have happened to her? When knives were slated for backs, she'd always done the stabbing. Any headed her way she's seen coming in time, and thwarted. Maybe she's losing her edge.

She stares into the bathroom mirror, assesses her face in the misted glass. A face of the eighties, a mask face, a bottom-line face; push the weak to the wall and grab what you can. But now it's the nineties. Is she out of style, so soon? She's only thirty-five, and she's already losing track of what people ten years younger are thinking. That could be fatal. As time goes by she'll have to race faster and faster to keep up, and for what? Part of the life she should have had is just a gap, it isn't there, it's nothing. What can be salvaged from it, what can be redone, what can be done at all?

When she climbs out of the tub after her sponge bath, she almost falls. She has a fever, no doubt about it. Inside her something is leaking, or else festering; she can hear it, like a dripping tap. A running sore, a sore from running so hard. She should go to the emergency ward at some hospital, get herself shot up with antibiotics. Instead she lurches into the living room, takes Hairball down from the mantelpiece in its bottle, places it on the coffee table. She sits cross-legged, listens. Filaments wave. She can hear a kind of buzz, like bees at work.

She'd asked the doctor if it could have started as a child, a fertilized egg that escaped somehow and got into the wrong place. No, said the doctor. Some people thought this kind of tumor was present in seedling form from birth, or before it. It might be the woman's undeveloped twin. What they really were was unknown. They had many kinds of tissue, though. Even brain tissue. Though of course all of these tissues lack structure.

Still, sitting here on the rug looking in at it, she pictures it as a child. It has come out of her, after all. It is flesh of her flesh. Her child with Gerald, her thwarted child, not allowed to grow normally. Her warped child, taking its revenge.

"Hairball," she says. "You're so ugly. Only a mother could love you." She feels sorry for it. She feels loss. Tears run down her face. Crying is not something she does, not normally, not lately.

Hairball speaks to her, without words. It is irreducible, it has the texture of reality, it is not an image. What it tells her is everything she's never wanted to hear about herself. This is new knowledge, dark and precious and necessary. It cuts.

She shakes her head. What are you doing, sitting on the floor and talking to a hairball? You are sick, she tells herself. Take a Tylenol and go to bed.

The next day she feels a little better. Dania from layout calls her and makes dove-like, sympathetic coos at her, and wants to drop by during lunch hour to take a look at her aura. Kat tells her to come off it. Dania gets huffy, and says that Kat's losing her job is a price for immoral behavior in a previous life. Kat tells her to stuff it; anyway, she's done enough immoral behavior in this life to account for the whole thing. "Why are you so full of hate?" asks Dania. She doesn't say it like a point she's making, she sounds truly baffled.

"I don't know," says Kat. It's a straight answer.

After she hangs up she paces the floor. She's crackling inside, like hot fat under the broiler. What she's thinking about is Cheryl, bustling about her cozy house, preparing for the party. Cheryl fiddles with her freeze-framed hair, positions an overloaded vase of flowers, fusses about the caterers. Gerald comes in, kisses her lightly on the cheek. A connubial scene. His conscience is nicely washed. The witch is dead, his foot is on the body, the trophy; he's had his dirty fling, he's ready now for the rest of his life.

Kat takes a taxi to the David Wood Food Shop and buys two dozen chocolate truffles. She has them put into an oversized box, then into an oversized bag with the store logo on it. Then she goes home and takes Hairball out of its bottle. She drains it in the kitchen strainer and pats it damp-dry, tenderly, with paper towels. She sprinkles it with powdered cocoa, which forms a brown pasty crust. It still smells like formaldehyde, so she wraps it in Saran Wrap and then in tinfoil, and then in pink tissue paper, which she ties with a mauve bow. She places it in the David Wood box in a bed of shredded tissue, with the truffles nestled around. She closes the box, tapes it, puts it into the bag, stuffs several sheets of pink paper on top. It's her gift, valuable and dangerous. It's her messenger, but the message it will deliver is its own. It will tell the truth, to whoever asks. It's right that Gerald should have it; after all, it's his child too.

She prints on the card, "Gerald, Sorry I couldn't be with you. This is all the rage. Love, K."

When evening has fallen and the party must be in full swing, she calls a delivery taxi. Cheryl will not distrust anything that arrives in such an expensive bag. She will open it in public, in front of everyone. There will be distress, there will be questions. Secrets will be unearthed. There will be pain. After that, everything will go way too far.

She is not well; her heart is pounding, space is wavering once more. But outside the window it's snowing, the soft, damp, windless flakes of her childhood. She puts on her coat and goes out, foolishly. She intends to walk just to the corner, but when she reaches the corner she goes on. The snow melts against her face like small fingers touching. She has done an outrageous thing, but she doesn't feel guilty. She feels light and peaceful and filled with charity, and temporarily without a name.

Chick Without Children

The Latest Celebrity Interview

NIKKI DILLON

I met the Chick Without Children on a recent Friday afternoon at her cozy apartment in a Brooklyn brownstone. She's a youthful woman in her thirties, with long dark hair framing an oval face. When I arrived, she galloped down the stairs to let me into the building. I could see her approaching through the circular, frosted glass window. She opened the door, grinning and barefoot. Her toenails were painted silver, just like mine. In fact, to my utter astonishment, the Chick Without Children looked exactly like me.

While I'd long admired the work of the Chick Without Children, I'd never seen her in person. She's confident and poised. Well-spoken, brilliant, and vivacious, the CWC, as she asked me to call her, is everything I wish *I* were. She's a woman with enormous drive, talent, and a sense of purpose. In addition to writing witty, taboo-busting fiction, the CWC is a self-appointed Gender Pioneer. She considers her childless condition to be a round-the-clock work of living, breathing performance art.

The sun-drenched apartment where the CWC lives, together with the GWC (Guy Without Children), is the combined workspace and residence of two urban artist/writers on the cutting edge. It's chock-full of furniture, books and photographs collected during the couple's extensive travels—a testament to their wide-ranging and eclectic interests. Above one scratched, pitted wooden table hangs an elegant black-and-white poster—a still life by Robert Mapplethorpe. A collection of commedia dell'arte masks, from Venice, adorn the hallway. The blue-glazed ceramics, covered with a pattern of yellow lizards, are from Tuscany.

As president and founder of Childless Chicks of America, a grassroots organization promoting the benefits of childlessness, the CWC is on the cusp of a new era. In the twenty-first century, she believes, more and more feisty, irreverent, creative women like herself will choose to bypass parenthood in favor of greater freedom. Outside the window of her book-lined study, new mothers were pushing baby carriages along the sidewalk. Two toddlers were at play in a small garden across the street.

Ironically enough, throughout our two-hour conversation, the CWC was supportive, warm and—dare I say it?—motherly to me. For example, she insisted that I drink decaffeinated coffee, telling me that I seemed "stressed out." She served banana muffins, made from scratch, hot from the oven. She told me to eat three of them, with real butter and rich imported marmalade, and not to *ever* worry about getting fat. "Dieting is dangerous," she said, adding that if we're fighting stereotypes, we have to keep our strength up. She told me I should put on a couple of extra pounds, and offered to make me a mushroom omelette with some hash browns.

I asked when she had decided that she didn't want to have kids, and she said she's always known. "Ever since I was a kid myself, I had an idea I wanted to do something different with my life. I was born in the sixties, so maybe I picked up on the turbulence of the times. When I was small, feminism hadn't made an impact on the culture yet. It didn't hit until the seventies. My girlfriends in elementary school were hooked on reruns of 'Bewitched' and 'I Dream of Jeannie.' Those shows bored me to death. I didn't want to wear a bare-midriff top that showed my belly-button, or say, 'Yes, Master.' I wanted to be the Lone Ranger, on horseback, with a cowboy hat and a black mask. The only female television character I could identify with was Catwoman."

The CWC told me about her aunt Susie, an early role model. "She was a painter and, guess what? She was childless. I used to visit her in her studio. It smelled of turpentine. She kept her brushes on a work table, arranged by size, from thickest to finest. She had an exercise bike next to her easel, and she'd ride on it and listen to jazz whenever she needed inspiration. She gave wild parties, with artists, playwrights, and flamboyant theater people."

She went on to comment that many of the men her parents knew did interesting things. They were musicians, filmmakers, anthropologists. "The primary goal of the women—as far as I could see—was taking care of *us*. It just got lodged in my head—a link between freedom and childlessness. I didn't want to be like most of the women I knew. I didn't want to be like the men, either. I wanted to be my own person. I had megalomaniacal tendencies. When I was five years old, I stood up on a table and announced to my family that I was part of 'A Mod, Mod World.' I thought it was the dawn of a new age. Revolution was in the air. I imagined myself to be the leader."

Asked about other women with whom she could identify, she mentioned Virginia Woolf, Margaret Atwood, Martha Graham, Louise Nevelson, Edith Wharton, and the Bronte sisters. "They were—or are—all childless, I think. If I'm wrong, don't correct me! If they *did* have kids, I don't want to know. I'm still kind of bummed out about Courtney and Madonna. It disturbs me a little when I read about anyone famous—like Susan Vega and Sigourney Weaver and Frances McDormand—who says her children are her most important achievement, and that she's gladly set her own creative work aside to focus on motherhood. I just don't get it."

I asked the CWC if she's actually opposed to motherhood, or if she just wants to see women multiply their options.

"Look," she said. "I'm not opposed to it. You've got to be true to your own vision. Not having kids reminds me, for some reason, of going to high school.

There was this guy I fell madly in love with. Everyone called him 'Beak,' because he had a large nose. My friends warned me not to go out with him. They claimed he was a social reject, because his pants were too short and his hair was too long. Or, was it the other way around? I ignored their advice, and asked him to go out with me. They were aghast. They saw a reject. I saw a poet. It's totally subjective."

She commented that, at heart, many of us are cowards and conformists. "We need to see that other people are out there, doing what we do, confirming our decisions. That's because human beings are gregarious creatures, and we operate in groups, not in isolation. But childless chicks don't have a spokesperson. That's why I became one.

"Motherhood's almost a political movement to my peers. Parenthood now! It's like a cult. They can't understand why I don't want to join the cult of parenthood. They're intensely into it. You try to be diplomatic. If you say, 'Look, kids just aren't my thing,' they're insulted. They think you're saying you don't like *their* kids, that their kids aren't wonderful enough to convince you to have your own.

"There are just too many other things I want to do. But, when you say say, 'There are too many other things I want to do,' it makes you sound like a bad person some-how—you're self-centered, or a workaholic, or overly ambitious. But, like a lot of people, I had a difficult childhood. And it's taken me a long time to learn that my mission in life isn't to make *other* people happy. I don't have to please anyone."

"Anyone?"

"My husband matters to me. He's my best friend, and I like spending time with him. I enjoy being romantic. One thing new parents aren't always forthcoming about is the way children can affect your romantic life. They *have* to. They require work and attention, they create a certain amount of strain, and quite frankly they put pressure on an adult relationship. If you ask a new parent who you know really well—no matter how content they are, no matter how ecstatic or gung-ho about parenthood—they will tell you that."

We talked about how difficult it is to "come out" as childless and proud of it. "First of all, you're up against a major sacred cow in our society. The myth of motherhood. We're experiencing an antifeminist backlash in this country. But what if there were no such thing as a biological clock? We wouldn't need to *settle down* unless it suited us. Maybe we wouldn't need to buy big houses, or station wagons, or climb corporate ladders to pay the kids' tuition. So what *would* we do? We'd be free agents. Making art and causing trouble."

As the interview was drawing to a close, I asked her what's been most difficult about remaining childless.

"My in-laws. The Guy Without Children comes from this big, boisterous, tra-ditional Italian American family. From their perspective, having kids is the best thing, the only thing, that anyone can do. Italy has a very child-centered, family-oriented culture. Interestingly, though, Italians—along with the rest of Europeans—aren't having kids now. Their birth rate has slowed remarkably. But with Italian Americans, it's a different story. I go over to my in-laws' house, and virtually every person there has got two or three children. Infants and toddlers are everywhere! It's hard, in that environment, not to feel like a misfit or a freak.

"The absolute worst moment was, right after we got married, when my female in-laws—a bunch of aunts, cousins, and my mother-in-law — pulled me into the kitchen and closed the door. They started poking at my abdomen and grabbing at it, whispering and laughing. I had no idea what was going on. I felt really self-conscious and embarrassed. I barely knew them, back then. 'Your belly's getting bigger!' someone said. Everyone was murmuring in Italian. I hadn't learned the language yet. Finally, one of the aunts said, in broken English, 'There's something inside you, isn't there? A baby!' And I said no. Their faces fell. They were visibly disappointed, even shocked. My mother-in-law said, 'I thought that's why you came over here! That's why I invited all these people, all the relatives, all my sisters. We were throwing you a party!' I have no idea how she arrived at this misunderstanding. I went upstairs and cried. I was angry at them for butting into my business and invading my privacy, but also ashamed. I didn't feel like the Chick Without Children, a woman making a choice, shaping her own identity. Nope. I felt like a failure. I'd let them down.

"On my thirtieth birthday, my sister-in-law sent me a card. On the front of the card was a photograph of a little boy and girl looking inside an empty baby carriage. I opened the card and inside she had written, 'What's missing from this picture? Happy Birthday.' Thanks a lot, I thought, and fuck you too. That card enraged me."

Cherry-Shiree

Shylah Boyd

*S*he looked like something out of a 1950s motorcycle movie. Blond cotton-candy hair, a size twelve poured into tight jeans, and beefy breasts with a long ample cleavage under the V-neck jersey, and you just knew she had a tattoo hidden somewhere inside all that. Anyhow, Faye liked her.

She liked Faye too—you could tell. She said "Sure honey, sure I got rosé, and if I don't got it here, I'll go next door—hole on a sec."

This was some bartender. Faye was the only woman customer. Six guys. The pits. A nervous coke-head who phoned his sister (who wasn't there) outside Seattle about every five minutes, and asked Faye if she was "actually *from* the Florida Keys," three times. Then you had the professional drunks who washed for one of three local restaurants in return for half a trailer and fun money. The name of the joint was the U Bet Bar.

"Shit, this rosé's a little warm, hon—ice it down for you?"

"No thanks."

She wanted to talk. She saw the look in Faye's eye strangers always misjudged as compassion. Actually the look was curiosity. Anyhow—she talked.

"Yup—far as I'm concerned you can slide the whole state of California into the sea an I woun't blink an eye—except to get my kid and run, that's what I think of the whole thing—goddamn son of a gun gets custody—a felon! You believe that—they give him custody—a felon? Hell, worst thing I ever done was shoplift—and this is no-shit shoplift—Tangee lipstick from Woolworth's when I was twelve. Fifteen when I had her, see . . ." she says with the cracked color snapshot out from her hip pocket. She had a problem getting the thing out, her pants were so tight, "Cute in't she. She is, God bless her."

"Yah, she's beautiful. What's your name?"

"Cherry-Shiree. What's yours?"

"Faye. I hate my name. You've got a great name."

"Yah? Think? My mom named me after a boutique in Laverne, Mississippi—some life, huh."

"Hell yes."

"So what do you do Faye?"

"Depends. Write I guess."

"Yah you a writer? You look like a writer."

"How's that?"

"Smart. You look smart."

"You been on the Keys long, Cherry-Shiree?"

"Coupla years, you include Key West. Big man, big promises, usual story."

"Uh huh."

"Just gettin' it together, get my kid—"

"I'm sorry."

"So you married, hon?"

"Divorced, usual."

"Yah, join the human race huh. Hell, I get off in an hour, you wanna toss a few at Zips?

"Zips? Sure. Zips."

"I'll give you some stories to write—tell you that much."

"I believe it—Zips," Faye said, and tipped her the price of the wine, then went home to feed the animals.

After she fed the dogs, the two stray cats, hers and Ralph's pet rat snake, her toucan, and Ralph's tarantula, there was thirty minutes before the ride up to Zips, so she skimmed the pool, called Mike the mechanic to ask about her ailing BMW, and read the Sunday *Book Review*. Then she took Ralph's Porsche out and said the hell with the loaner.

Cherry-Shiree was already at Zips, though Faye was a couple of minutes early. A greaser was buying her drinks—another guy standing behind, had his eyes down her jersey. The place was a jumble of dope smugglers, college kids, and Moms and Pops for Saturday night rum and cokes.

"Hey."

"Hey Faye. Meet the guys."

She met the guys. They exuded that kind of oily politeness like they'd been told she was not just a "nuther dumb cunt."

"Yah we already knowed who you were—din't we, Cherry-Shiree. . . ."

"Yup, God's truth, Faye—whatcha drinkin'?"

"Coke."

"Coke?"

"Yah, Coke."

"Honey, coke's somethin' you put up your nose."

"Oh yah . . . nose huh. . . . No, seriously—Coca-cola's fine."

"Faye here's my new friend, guys. Hey, Don, show how you make an elephant disappear."

Don, who was tall, thin except for his gut, and sported a greasy black Prince Valiant, leaned towards Faye.

"Oh yah," she said, "that's how you make an elephant disappear?" Faye was sorry she'd come.

"Wanna see how I make the elephant come back?"

"Not on one Coca-cola. That was truly spectacular, Don."

Cherry-Shiree said as how her and Faye had girl-talk to make and whyn't they excuse them for a minute—they'd be right back.

Upstairs at Zips the Tahitian girl was doing her rope dance with the tourists and there were children around. Downstairs was "local" and where the boats pulled in. Downstairs was also known as the Free Fire Zone.

"Listen, I did a lot of things in my life, but never for money. You do it for money, it changes you."

"Sounds right to me. . . ."

". . . See I figure, anything I do bad'll reflect on my kid and I want her. I want my baby."

Cherry-Shiree pointed to one of the big Magnum boats docked by itself at the end of the longest pier. "That other guy, Rick? That's his—said how'd I like to make ten thou—all I need is a driver's license . . . follow me?"

"Sure."

"Ten thou'd buy my kid back from that bastard. He don't love her—he's got her but he don't really love her. Guy can't love shit, man. Hey, right now I need a friend—I don't need no one-night thing and I don't need a lot of booze . . ." she said, looking over at Faye, as straight in the eye as she could since Faye figured she'd already done something, and her eyes had that wine-stain coloring around the retinas. "Look, I trust you, Faye—you meet someone once a blue moon you trust even though you don't know shit about them. So I know you'll tell me what I should do, and it'll be all right if I do it."

"I don't know what you should do, Cherry-Shiree. All I can do is maybe help you see things the way they are—that's the best friends can do I think. . . ."

"Hey . . . *see*, you're already helping—you know how to make things clear—see if I got the ten thou and I went back to California and just said, 'Hey, you take the ten grand and I'll take the kid'—if I got the ten that is—I mean, what would you do?"

"If I were you?"

"Yah, if you were me, and you could think like you—wanna drink?"

"Now I do—I'll treat," Faye said and ordered herself a Bacardi Anejo on the rocks, Cherry-Shiree a Canadian Mist and Seven-up. The Tahitian dancer had taken a break because of the sunset. It was one of the better ones this time, lots of thunderheads and red and orange covering the water. "Wellll," she said after the first sip, the Anejo burning a little, "Well, what I think you have to consider is the law of probabilities here—the first probability is whether or not they'd actually pay you your ten thousand. I'd say that's doubtful, and it's probably dangerous. Then, even if you got the money, you don't know how your ex-husband would react. Here you go all the way back to California and he's moved, or has an unlisted number, and maybe you find him and he takes your money but doesn't give you your daughter. Then again you could steal your daughter and go live somewhere in hiding—you could try that—but see, you stand out, Cherry-Shiree—people see you fast, the way you look. . . ."

"You think I look like a pro, Faye?"

"I don't know. I saw some pros in Amsterdam once who looked like they taught sixth grade, so I don't know. Let's just say you're provocative. Listen, you want to come back to my house? We can talk better."

"Sure. Who needs those creeps."

So Faye took her back. She hadn't the foggiest why. She didn't know why she'd more or less picked up this bleached blond person or why she'd agreed to Zips or why she was thinking of a plan. Driving down the four-mile strip—then the Old Road—then opening the gate which was half-hidden to the double lot with the trees making a jungle of it and the two-story house with the verandas full round, the pool, the Spanish chairs, and carved oak bed—the whole nut of the advance she and Ralph had gotten on the movie—throwing it in her face—only Cherry-Shiree had the kid and Faye didn't and wouldn't and maybe couldn't without some fancy procedure she was going to go through anyway—maybe that was what Cherry-Shiree'd call the bottom line. And Ralph'd been gone for a week. Maybe a week. Maybe forever.

"My God," Cherry-Shiree kept saying. "My God!" Both of them floating in the pool naked with the moon at quarter wane overhead and that pitch with all the stars. "I guess if I didn't like you so much, I'd sure hate your guts."

"It's not what you think. By the way, my animals like you—they don't like that many people. You're very kind to animals aren't you, Cherry-Shiree?"

"Oh yah—even throw bugs out stead of squashing them—you believe that?" She smiled with her poufed hair flat and wet down her back, and her mascara streaked. She looked younger. "You always live here?"

"No. I've lived here four years. Before that I lived in France."

"Paris, France?"

"No. A small village right above the coast," handing her a towel. It struck Faye, the pink skin—like Monroe was said to have had, that luminescent pink skin.

"You gotta boyfriend, right?"

"I did. I may still have. I'm not sure—"

"But no kids."

"No. No kids."

"You want kids?"

"Who knows. Anyway, it's unlikely I can, at least not without going through this procedure, so. . . ."

"Yah—I don't know why I figured that—but I figured that. Well, it isn't glory, that's for sure."

"No. Nothing is. Even this isn't. But I think you could get your daughter back if you want. I think you could do that."

They were sitting on the veranda. Faye had grilled the fish caught earlier and filleted by her day-worker. It was good mahi-mahi with a lime sauce. She made a green salad and poured her some of last night's Pouilly Fumé. Cherry-Shiree made a face at first, then said she liked it. Faye drank Coke.

"How could I?"

"Write down all the information you have on your ex-husband and daughter."

She handed her the legal pad and pencil, and while Cherry-Shiree wrote, cleared away the dishes. When Faye came back, she'd finished.

"Okay, now what?"

"Now, I make a phone call."

Faye called the lawyer in California who'd said "I owe you one" a couple of times and who'd made a considerable sum off of two movie deals with Faye and Ralph. She told him she didn't understand how you do these things, but to do it. He said he'd just gotten back from a party with the Oscar nominees and it was a crashing bore, and it made him feel a lot better to hear Faye sounding so well.

"My lawyer's going to get on it," she said while Cherry-Shiree played with her hair at the bedroom mirror.

"I always wanted a canopy bed when I was a kid." She turned around, smiled. The blue jeans seemed looser.

"So did I. That's why I have one now . . . listen, Cherry-Shiree, don't do your hair."

"Why?"

"You need to change your image. It'd help. It'll make or break you through the system. And at least until you get your daughter back."

"But then I won't be myself."

"Yah you will. Just be in disguise for a while then. Can you do that? And you should get some community credentials—church or something. And stop working as a bartender—particularly where you are now."

"Just like that? I can't."

"Can you type?"

"Nuh uh. Quit school in the ninth grade."

"Can you clean house? Shop? Domestic stuff?"

"Oh sure."

"Well, you can work here. You can do all the house shopping, and clean five days a week, and take care of the animals—see this . . ." Faye brought out a shirt-waist cotton dress Ralph's mother had forgotten to take back with her. "Put it on, and I'll do your hair—come on, this is a dry run—what have you got to lose?"

"And this'll get her back and then I can be myself again?"

"Yup."

"Maybe I shouldn't be exactly myself again—Hey, you know what—I always got religion—shit, I'm always prayin' and I'm a lot nicer than some of those bitches who just pretend."

"Yes, you are. Will you do it?"

"Yah. Yah, I'll do it."

Six months later, Cherry-Shiree got her daughter back. She was a terrible house-keeper, but good with the animals. The whole deal cost Faye ten thousand dollars—four for her, four for the father, and two for the paperwork; the lawyer was a freebie. Now Faye gets letters from Missoula, Montana, with pentecostal pamphlets, and snapshots of her newborn, Faye Hope Charity Ruskin—and her husband the Reverend Charles Ruskin—and her older daughter, Letitia.

But Ralph and Faye were quits like she thought.

Parent as a Verb

DONNA BROOK

*I*n Pathmark, I run into this acquaintance/neighbor/peripheral person who says to me in hushed tones what is so often said to me in hushed tones and always makes me angry:

"You're so good at mothering. It's too bad you never had kids of your own."

Now I'm not exactly alone here. Within the range of my bellow are fifteen-year-old Thandi, who needs ginger beer and coconut cookies, and thirteen-year-old Matthew, who needs soda and ranch-flavored chips, and eleven-year-old Jesse, who needs whatever I won't buy. Not to mention the shadowy troops of middle school students past and present and the future readers of my children's books. Lady, I've got kids. Or to be more precise, I've got interest in kids like money in the bank and joy of kids like pennies from heaven. What I've never had is pregnancy.

So I reply to the "kids of my own" as I always reply.

"Haven't you heard about Lincoln's Emancipation Proclamation? You're not supposed to own anyone."

So I seem the rude bitch, don't I? But something is required to balance this other view of me as so good I run around requisitioning children. Yes, Thandi's parents returned to Durban and left her with us so she could get a better education, and she's only on loan, and yes, I had the bad form to become a stepmother, but I didn't kill the woman. She died of all too natural causes and, OK, I prefer to teach ten-year-olds over college and high school students, but I have my reasons, and I don't have a heart of gold. I don't even have any more time to explain this because I've got three kids wandering around a supermarket.

While you may have heard that it takes a whole village to raise a child, or however that goes, it actually takes a whole society, and the recognition that childhood is a stage through which everyone passes, and never quite leaves entirely. *They* don't get cranky when they are sleepy or hungry. *We* do. Don't get me started.

When I was eight years old, I saw a TV documentary about a family composed of children adopted from all over the place. One of those a-dozen-at-dinner families. I became an adoption fanatic. I'd sit in the back seat looking at the rain and street lights as my father drove through the dark, and I'd list to myself all the wonders I'd share with my new formerly poor and lonely sibling. I was besotted. Obsessed. When my parents felt no pressing need for more than the two children they already had, I resolved that when I got to be a grown-up. . . . But by the time I grew up, I wasn't any family service's ideal, and I'd learned the costs of college and dentist, discovered the limits of time and self-determination. So I meandered into parenting as previously discussed.

Now I use *parent* as a verb because my friend Nell told me that, somewhere, Anna Freud wrote that the person who does the parenting is the parent. The word *caretaker* enjoys a current vogue in terms of children, but it reminds me of someone who trims hedges on English estates, and *caregiver* isn't right either because children require a lot more than care. Thought helps. Patience comes in handy. I mean, this is about people who, if they don't lose or destroy them, outgrow their shoes in months that seem like minutes. Let's pay some attention to detail.

So if I buy the only plastic tray of coconut wafers on the shelf—jumbo enormous— Thandi cannot possibly eat a worthy percentage of them before she as usual abandons them to a state soggy or stale. Ditto huge plastic go-flat-immediately bottles of Pepsi versus cans and any overpriced box of cereal that contains Dayglo pebbles. I am wavering between budgetary concerns and whining. Maybe the problem is that I haven't accumulated enough children for modern packaging methods, or enough children who'll all eat the same things. Kids are out there waiting to be collected like trash at the curb, God knows. And if not picked up, they will be beaten or sexually assaulted or taken to Disney animations. All worse than my caving in to junk food cravings when, on rare occasions, I do not shop alone.

"Alone" is what's easier. "With" can feel like surrounded-fraught-with-guilt. Are there others like me who so carefully avoided bringing one more soul into this world of forgotten souls, who got a package deal in marriage and liked it that way, who admit that they don't feel that they've missed out on an essential by never giving birth but would hate a life lived always and only in one's own age group?

Motives are never clean or unconfused. I've missed out and gotten freebies. Probably, to drag in that doctor and poet, nobody's driving the car. Or pushing the cart. But we are proceeding toward checkout.

The Question of Children

JANE RULE

*I*t is fashionable in some circles to speak of children as the blight of the heterosexual world, burdening those of more enlightened sexuality with noise pollution, road hazards, and school taxes. One of the "benefits" of a gay retirement home is that one wouldn't have to sit in a rocking chair next to someone with a wallet full of pictures of grandchildren. Having visited several retirement compounds on the southern desert, I've noticed that even heterosexuals in no small numbers want to escape the sound, sight, and cost of children.

Barbara From said to me defensively, "I suppose you think having children is an ego trip." Quite the opposite. Now that children are not needed as unpaid farm workers and cannot be sent out at six or seven to work in factories and mines, now that birth control gives people some choice, children are neither necessary nor inevitable. They are, instead, a luxury that some can ill afford and others simply don't want. Abortion is more often the answer to those women who try the pregnancy route to marriage.

Yet, as a gay lifestyle becomes increasingly an open option for people, those who at first conformed to heterosexual expectations bring children with them into their new lives. And custody cases are being won now by gay parents who insist that their obligation to and love for their children is in no way altered by their claiming of their own sexuality.

Some lesbians are arranging pregnancy by otherwise uninterested men or sperm banks. I have talked with men who would like to adopt children.

I suspect a disproportionate number of us work with children as educators, social workers, nurses, and doctors. And many of us who don't have children participate in the raising of our nieces and nephews and our friends' children. A friend of ours with a six-week-old baby phoned at midnight and said, "You like this kid, don't you?" We agreed that we did. "Well then, come and get him before we kill him."

The difficulty of combating the notion that all of us dislike children is the conflicting but even more deeply held conviction that we seduce children. Most of us who have or work with children feel we have to stay in the closet in order to be allowed to continue to care for them.

211

Yet, as in every other area where we are working for our rights, only visibility will bring about change. The twenty or so children who use our pool every afternoon from three/five will have a harder time growing up fearful and bigoted about lesbians, and their parents are being educated at the same time. When a couple of the little girls announced that when they grew up they were going to live together like Helen and me, there was no parental outcry.

Before we settle for being the smug answer to the population explosion, let us acknowledge that we have parents among us, that many of us have a sensibility which makes us particularly good with children, being less apt to make rigid role requirements, more sensitive to their bewilderments and need for reassurance, able to establish relationships with them that don't have to be rebelled against because we know, at first hand, the value of accepting difference and are not allowed to forget it.

The only love in which possessiveness is generally frowned on is that of adults for children. We learn to take responsibility for their safety, well being, and education whether they are ours or not, even without knowing them. Far from being an experience to avoid, it is the model for the concern we might feel for adults as well.

I don't mind looking at pictures of other people's grandchildren, but I hope where I am I'll see the kids themselves.

All My Kids

ELIZABETH MARRAFFINO-REES

*A*t fifteen my best friend Terry Sheridan and I were voracious readers. With our Holy Cross Academy blazers flapping open to reveal plaid skirts rolled up to miniskirt length, our black tights hiding our regulation panty hose, we'd raid the Donnell branch of the New York Public Library. It was a weekly ritual, like Friday night dances, Saturday afternoon confession, or Sunday morning mass.

Our goal: to read in alphabetical order every book on the fiction shelves of the Young Adult section on the second floor.

Beginning with A, we divided the books. I'd take ten; Terry, the next ten. Between us we may have even made it up to Dostoevsky—the details are hazy after all these years. But sometimes we each, separately, "cheated" and read something out of alphabetical order. *Please Don't Eat the Daisies* by Jean Kerr was one of those harmless books making the rounds of Catholic school girls in the early sixties, alongside forbidden fruits like *Franny and Zooey* and *Catcher in the Rye.* Salinger affected the poet and writer I later became, but Jean Kerr's classic light-hearted interpretation of 1950s suburban domesticity shaped the vision of the life I was supposed to lead.

A big family, a huge house filled with cheerful commotion, a dog, size extra large, and a car too small to hold us all. An assembly line of Wonder Bread, twenty slices arranged in two neat rows on the kitchen counter together with a jumbo jar of peanut butter and family-sized grape jelly. I would be efficient, smiling, perfectly coiffed, and running my own daily pb and j sandwich assembly line for my personal platoon of kids.

Being an only child I craved a big family. Back then I'd never heard that a person should be careful what they wish for.

Some years ago I was complaining to a friend at a party about how hard it was to dress all my girls for their junior prom. Chris needed something white, filmy, and all-American; Brenda, something mysterious, dark, and offbeat, but without the barest whiff of her old bad-girl image, now that she'd gotten her act together; but Phoebe—Phoebe of the red hair and faded pink overalls—Phoebe was on the brink of everything. Her dress should reflect the state of her life, the state of her heart.

A woman, tall, forty-something and perky, interrupted our conversation. "So how many kids *do* you have?"

I stared at her, confused.

"I have a daughter myself," she confided. "Shopping with her turned into pure torture the day she turned thirteen. How do you ever deal with three teenagers at once?" She glowed with admiration.

"I don't," I told her.

Her face fell. "But the prom dresses—I couldn't help but overhear and. . . ."

"Oh, *those* kids. They're not my kids. They're my characters."

She looked at me like I had downed one too many glasses of punch.

"I write books for kids. Young adult novels, mainly serial fiction. The heroes and heroines, well, I guess they are like my kids." I realized this for the first time.

The conversation veered neatly into the usual exchange about writing for teen readers and the pressures of earning a living as a commercial writer to support my painting, pottery, and poetry habits, as well as to pay a skyrocketing Manhattan rent.

But I went to bed that night thinking not about my painting or rent, but about my kids. *All* my kids. That's how I've thought of them ever since: some adopted— or perhaps fostered is a better term—some natural born.

The foster kids, they were created by someone else, the authors of the first books in any given young adult romance series, like *Sisters,* or *Couples* or *Freshman Dorm.* Some of these authors bestowed upon me kids whom I will love for the rest of my life, though among them were, for me, some difficult children, souls I couldn't quite fathom. Nicole, the oldest, sophisticated sister; Chris and Greg, a couple I never could quite understand; K.C., the earnest college freshman. These were among the ones who stormed my heart but stayed virtual strangers. I never caught the drift of their language, their tastes, their take on life in general. They were the overachievers, kids armed with briefcases in high school, hearts set on Harvard, visions of M.B.A.'s from Wharton dancing through their attractive heads.

But others, though not my creation, seemed to have sprung right from my own womb. The outcasts like Brenda, Winnie, or Matt; the boy-crazy flirts, slightly floozy and frothy and often comic relief, like Esme, or Jessica or Molly who got into endless scrapes that made me cringe and laugh and cry; the shy ones, poets or artists or just sensitive souls who still at sixteen loved fairy tales, girls like Sasha, or Elizabeth, or Janie, the ones still looking out at the big world called Life from the shelter of their safe homes, their schools, their forever friends.

Phoebe was one of those. But with Phoebe it was head-over-heels in love at first sight. She was the foster child I longed to adopt as my own. Except for her red hair and green eyes, Phoebe was me reflected back in the mirror. She was the daughter I once was, the daughter I always dreamed of having. Popular, vulnerable, happy, insecure, amazed and full of wonder as her world expanded from the comfortable, habitual niches of home and school, from the heart of the in-crowd to the fringe of everything. Danger twined with hope when she fell in love with the wild, romantic Griffin who spun her life around like a glass soda bottle. Phoebe spiraled joyfully from the safety of her old boyfriend, steady, doctor-to-be Brad, to the take-a-chance-on-life Griffin. Griffin was not a bad guy at all, just one so possessed by dreams that he would skim by yet touch her soul so deeply she would never be the same. Then, of course, he moved on, breaking her heart into a thousand pieces that even a new, nice boyfriend and five or six more books about her couldn't really put back together again. Phoebe after Griffin was never quite as carefree again.

Ten years ago, when I wrote the story of these two impossibly beautiful kids, I was convinced that they should rush off together to make it on their own in New York. They would not bother to finish high school. They would encounter innumerable obstacles, all in the name of being romantically irresponsible—and so what I wished I had dared to be at sixteen or seventeen.

Today I'm old enough for Phoebe to actually be my own child, for my own kid to be in her last year of high school. I am glad some editor made me make Phoebe come to her senses, and stay home when Griffin cruelly—as heroes with huge dreams do—had to take larger-than-life giant steps forward and move on.

It is still hard to think of Phoebe and Griffin as among those kids I fostered, nursed for a while, then lovingly relinquished to other caring hands.

Fortunately, I never suffered "empty nest" syndrome for long. Other kids sprung from my own literary womb. I've created my own worlds in novels like *How to Kiss a Guy,* where shy, good girl Naomi falls for another actor type, Dylan, and defies family and friends and finally even heartthrob Dylan to find out who she is and what she wants for her life and herself.

My own kids have grown too numerous to count. But at the moment it's one particular bunch of ex-rug-rats that rule my life: Sophy, Daly, Inez, Roxanna, Jen, Carlos, Ray, and another guy called Cat. All of them, an entire family, I have grown to know and love. They live in High Falls, a blue-collar, riverfront town in the mountains of Pennsylvania. They are dancers, most of them, and go to a school called Dance Tech. Their series, *Heart Beats* is drawing to a close. I am within weeks of finishing the final book, aptly titled *The Last Dance.*

Still I tell everyone about this series, about the whole world I made. A one-woman soap opera. It makes me feel strong, but leaving my world will make me feel lonely, as if somehow, behind the scenes, beyond the last period on the last page, it will go on. Sophy will turn seventeen, Carlos eighteen; Roxanna will continue to wreck lives or find love; Jen will continue to wish that Carlos had never happened: Daly will heal and love again, and again, and again.

I've lived with these kids since March of 1998, yet writing them is still a process of discovery. Even though they are among my natural born babies—like good strong characters, and real kids—they've revealed themselves to me slowly, reminding me that they have sides and corners and recesses of their beings that I still know nothing about.

Sophy, the ballet dancer heroine, so private, so poised, so cool in some ways, is a bit of a stranger to me, as she is to the mother in the books she inhabits. I am beginning to know her, but even as I write her story, she turns and surprises me, and makes me follow her down alleyways and passages. I never imagined the Sophy of the first book ever daring to travel. Hey, she's sixteen. At sixteen souls, flower fast. At sixteen, life is forever.

Carlos, my seventeen-year-old salsa king, he is no mystery to me. I have adored him forever. He is the hero I always wanted to write about. The boy of my high school dreams. Handsome, sensitive, all guy. Carlos, controlled and great on the dance floor, can't help but move much too fast on the stage of life, not noticing the small things, thinking the world is his oyster. He is mad for girls. Not just because of sex, but because somehow being with them makes him better, completes him.

Carlos will always outrun me. I struggle to keep up with his energy, his drive, his determination. But sometimes he brakes to a sudden stop. Halfway through a door, or up a flight of stairs, he turns, and gazes back at me over his shoulder. For a moment the little boy in him looks out of the hunky guy he's become, as if he is deep down inside, wavering, uncertain of something. Whatever it is, he is still just for a moment, then keeps pursuing love. And now pursuing Sophy, who to my surprise, and to his, brings out new, deeper facets of him, steadies him, becomes the fulcrum around which his passionate, dancing soul spins.

I am nearing the end of the last book in the series. The woman in me knows exactly what Sophy and Carlos are probably up to.

The mother in me hopes I'm wrong.

My feelings are a jumble as I go to sleep tonight. The mom in me is worried: sex in the age of AIDS and bondage. Will Sophy use protection? Prayers rattle my soul: Please let Carlos be the Carlos I breathed life into, a passionate guy, full of life but kind, kind—and willing to hear the word *no* should Sophy even whisper it once. Please let all his previous girlfriends be healthy, sensible, and have insisted on condoms.

How will Carlos treat her, afterward? Is he, after all is said and done, only out to score? Does even this woman, the writer-mother who birthed the character, really know what he's about? Is the only problem, as I wrote at the end of *Face the Music,* that he is compelled to move this quickly, too quickly for my little Sophy? Sweeping Sophy not just off her feet but off the path of her own life? Has Sophy's destiny shifted to the fast lane, distancing itself with the speed of a meteor from the one I plotted?

Sophy is nervous, scared, confused, wishing she had a mother to talk to. Or that she could talk to the mother I gave her. But Sophy's mom, Anne, is a reserved woman, with her feelings tucked inside herself like folds in stratified rock, much like her own daughter. Or like Sophy was until Carlos came along, nuking her into total plutonium melt-down. Could Mom—could *any* mother— ever have felt this fire inside?

Sophy doubts it.

Mostly Sophy is desperately wanting Carlos, in ways she never imagined wanting anyone or anything in her life. If she were a real kid would she pull back?

Not on your life! I know I wouldn't. But like Sophy, I would read every romance ever written, hoping love at sixteen can at least once turn into happily ever after.

It's true that a writer *is* her characters—or vice versa. Sophy, her mom, Carlos, and all the rest are facets of me. But because somehow, in the mystery of writing, life is breathed into characters and they take off on their own, I am also separate, and their mom.

So the mom in me waits up, pretending to work late, but always listening—for the sounds of a car pulling into the driveway, for footsteps, the click of high-heeled platform shoes against the flagstones of the front walk. Listening for the jiggle of the key in the lock, the squeak of the heavy oak door, and hoping, when it opens, not to hear tears.

Imagining Motherhood

Julia Alvarez

*F*inally, late fall 1995, my last child-
less sister became a mother. Forty, single, unlucky in finding a lifelong match, she
decided to have a baby on her own. In anticipation of the phone call from the
Dominican Republic that would let her know a baby had been found, my sister
painted her spare bedroom a soft lavender; she went shopping for baby clothes;
she considered a dozen names and heard feedback on possible awful nicknames
that might come of them; she baby-proofed her house. And she talked and talked
and talked about the upcoming baby.

Every time she'd start in, I'd feel my chest tightening. Pushing its thorny head
through the veneer of cheeriness and encouragement was that old monster all sisters are well acquainted with: jealousy. It was like being back in childhood, in the
full of summer, with my sister anticipating her big birthday party in July while
mine had already gone by way back in March.

My other two sisters had raised their babies in a flurry of diapers and photo
albums full of the cute little critters. That was back in my early thirties. I loved my
niece and nephews to bits. I uncurled their tiny infant hands, smelled their baby
powder skin, wrote them poems on every occasion, but I was glad to hand them
over at the end of the visit and get back to my writing.

You mean they didn't stop howling like that when you wanted to finish a chapter? They had to be driven to what? Suzuki recorder lessons, just when your editor called with a request you had to mail out that night? No, thanks. I'd gladly be
the godmother, sending birthday checks and little gifts, but as for being the good
mother, well, I just didn't have the time.

Then suddenly mid-forty, I realized what most of my women friends must
have realized in high school. We *are* mortal. We don't have an endless supply of
time. By now, I'd already used up half of mine or more, and I had only a couple
of years left if I truly wanted a child. I could always adopt, but I had to make up
my mind soon or I'd be following that poor kid to school on my walker, for
heaven's sake.

But it was more than a biological clock that was ticking away; it was a familial
one as well. In my family of four sisters, two and two is a fine balance, but if three
sisters go a certain route, the fourth sister can't bear the loneliness and caves in to

the majority choice. It's the old story of women living together in a house; their menstrual periods will eventually synchronize.

With us, it went further—we all got married within the space of a few years, at least the first time around. Overnight, we all had the same sensible short haircut because our sixties' manes were just too hard to keep up (and made us look passé). Then, we all seemed to find silk one Christmas, shimmering loose outfits that freed us to move without constraints (no funny bras safety-pinned to things we had to be careful not to tear, no tight waistlines reminding us that we were eating too much of Mami's flan de guayaba). Only two stayed in long-term marriages, leaving the other two to commiserate over the dearth of good middle-aged men.

Then last November, my compañera in childlessness, my baby sister and fellow maverick, became a mami. When she called from the Dominican Republic with the news, I burst into tears. "I'm so . . . happy," I sobbed, "so, so happy."

And I was. Who wouldn't be? To have my beautiful niece suddenly bringing up the rear of the next generation of our family! Had any child ever been so cute! I mean, Benetton babies, beware! I went through my town, showing off photos. On the way home, it struck me that I was acting as if I were the proud mother. But it was my sister's birthday party. Again, I burst into tears.

"Nothing in the world compares to this, nothing," my sister kept saying. I finally asked her to please stop saying so, please.

Because the yearning hit strong. Suddenly, I noticed there were babies everywhere. Every junior colleague had a babe in her arms—and these moms were getting their writing done as well. How did younger women learn to do that? As for my women friends— those old-world fems, as these younger women now refer to us— my "old" friends were suddenly busy with babies, too. Most of them, having reared their children, had joined me in our knockabout middle years, their empty nests looking a whole lot like my one-person one. But now they were becoming grandmothers of beautiful grandbabies they couldn't stop talking about.

By this time, I had remarried, but alas, my husband's two daughters were grown girls I couldn't sit on my knee and cuddle. So, of course, the question came up: Why not have or adopt our very own child?

"What do you think?" I kept asking Bill.

His face would get a stricken look. He had already raised his babies, and though it was worth (almost) every minute of it, he didn't want to start all over again at fifty. He was at the stage I was in my late twenties and thirties when I wanted to give these pooping, wailing babies back to their mothers.

But hearing my tearful plaints month after month, he finally caved in. "If it's something you really think you have to have, I'll do it for you."

With the choice presented in terms of what *only* I wanted, the same indecisiveness struck again. Oh, I knew Bill would rally 100 percent to become a father. Still, hadn't I been inside marriages where my life's direction was dictated by a partner's passion, not my own? How long and dreary that road can become! And at our age—a phrase I find myself saying more and more— there just isn't time to be taking too many tangents away from where we have left to go.

But my decision was not ultimately a submission to Bill's preference. I had to face the fact that it had been my own choice not to become a mother. The thought of putting aside—even for just a few years—what I had always considered my real calling, the writing, putting it aside now in my mid-forties when I was finally hitting my full stride, gave me cold feet. I came to realize with that straight, clear-eyed vision of a writer analyzing her fictional characters that I didn't really want to be a mother solely for the sake of being a mother.

Yet I still felt the pressure to at least say I wanted to be a mother. For all our talk of feminism and pro-choice, willful childlessness continues to have a bad reputation. That Victorian view of childless women as not fully realized lingers. A woman who doesn't care to have a child is considered foolish at best. At worst, as I heard one lecturer proclaim, she is "committing genetic suicide."

Among my friends and acquaintances here in rural Vermont, the rearing, educating, and taking care of children has been a major focus of their lives. "You're lucky," they tell me, but beyond a momentary weariness, what I hear in their voices is a secret pride at the fecundity of their lives.

And if being childless is unusual in rural Vermont, it is mucho más odd in my own Latin culture, where being a woman and a mother are practically synonymous. Being childless—by choice—is tantamount to being wicked and selfish. Marriage is a sacrament for the procreation of children, how many times have my old tías told me that? Even the one family holdout, my maiden aunt who grew orchids and read books and knew Latin, finally married in her thirties and had her one child. "I won't deny," she has told me, "that this has been the most significant event of my life."

Ever since I married Bill, the pressure has mounted. On my annual visit to the Island, the inevitable question pops up, Don't I want a child? More tactful aunts approach the topic through my eating habits. Don't I know I have to put aside that vegetarian foolishness in order to strengthen my body for a child. "But you have to have your niño," my aunt's maid told me. It's mandatory, she might as well have said. Last year, when my sister adopted, I almost canceled my trip.

"That'll make you feel even worse," my husband wisely counseled. He was right.

The only way to come to terms with the yearning was to accept that it was a loss. Just as never having learned a musical instrument or never having become a bullfighter or a ballerina is a loss. As is never having grown up in the Dominican Republic amid my own people; never having learned the languages to read Dante, Tolstoy, Rilke in the original. All these are losses now—instead of possibilities to be left open—because I know that given my age, there isn't time enough for all that I once meant to do with my life. You can't have everything, our mothers used to tell us. So why *is* it that our me generation tends to feel cheated if we can't have everything? Maybe part of accepting childlessness is accepting this rude fact.

But in accepting my chosen loss, I've come to realize that, ironically, I was grieving over the loss to my writing more than anything else. A good part of my sudden, last-minute reconsideration of motherhood has sprung from a writer's approach to life: I do not want to miss out on a valuable experience that might help me to understand people better, that might inform my spirit and intelligence, make me a better human being, and (dare I say it?) a better writer.

As my best woman friend, thrice a mother, and recently a new grandmother reminds me: What is the imagination for if everything requires life experience? She's right. I can imagine motherhood. I don't need to subject a child to my writerly personal growth experience, if that's what I'm after. Spare the poor kid a grandmother-mother who wears dentures. (I can just imagine a whole new category of your-mamma-wears-army-boots jokes!) Now, when I travel to my native Dominican Republic, and my tías inquire after my sister and her new baby, and winking at Bill, ask us if we don't feel inspired, I will have to say, "Yes, I feel inspired."

Inspired, that is, to come home and write about it.

From Black Woman Artist Becoming

BELL HOOKS

July 30, 1979. Late Saturday night.

I sat up reading a biography of Käthe Kollwitz—I am more and more interested in reading about the life stories of women artists. Reading about their lives I learn about their struggles, how they coped with sexist sex-role patterning that makes it difficult for women to motivate ourselves to do art in a serious manner. Somehow it seems cliché given all we know to be true of sexism to wonder why there are not as many women artists visible in the art world as there should be. (I was about to say why there are no "great" women artists—but that term "great," what does it mean?) To me the term "great" means the work of such artists demonstrates profound sensitivity and beauty—and for that reason they have been selected to represent greatest. Ah! but men and only men were doing the selecting.

I feel strongly that one cannot have a family, even a nontraditional one, and be a committed artist without tremendous struggle—a tremendous giving of one's self. I had a discussion with Hannah a couple of weeks ago in which she talked about doing it all, motherhood, work, writing. I believe doing it all, trying to do it all, is a trap women fall into. Why do it all!!!! Then one is running around like a chicken with its head cut off accomplishing things. But what of the quiet moments—the necessary leisure to just experience without structure—Life. If you try to do it all that is gone. Nor do I admire those men, like Rilke, who were able to leave wife, women, children, whenever they felt like it to do art—then return to find them waiting, there to love and give to them. Are we to admire Rilke's commitment to art that was so great he boasts of his inability to attend his daughter's wedding. Well, I say, perhaps he should have been really strong and not had a daughter. A recognition of limits is so much more important than exploiting people. And not just Rilke, not just men, occasionally women do it too. Louise Nevelson also talks of leaving husband, children to pursue Art. I feel as if N. and I have tried in his having a vasectomy to acknowledge our realities as people committed to Art, to writing—to absorbing ourselves in various works. It is not that we would not love children. Certainly, I feel torn. But I am not a romantic. I know that in life we have to choose if we are not to bring unhappiness to others.

Writing is a lonely process. Writing little poems and stories, however "great" in the anonymity of closed-in rooms, no, that cannot compete with intimacy with humans. It can never be as fulfilling as touching another person, holding them close. But it is a life-affirming energy. Oh me! a necessary energy. I have felt it driving me since I was very young. And the conflict over which world to live in was evident even then. To be outside playing with friends or inside writing and reading. To be clustered with family around the television or upstairs dreaming of words. Perhaps it was the unhappiness of that childhood struggle that has caused me to feel it is better to choose, to accept limits, and live through the pain of choice. And that means choosing to create other forms of human contact and intimacy that become just as significant as the having of one's own children. I believe children bring one into community and connection with others in a way that art does not. You take children to school, meet other parents, especially other women, and share similar concerns. It is a unifying experience. An experience of "togetherness" that is really important to women. It is difficult to know such intimacy when doing art.

Artists approach their work in so many different ways. Some are just driven by the idea of fame, thoughts of money, and greatness. With others the process of making art is a spiritual undertaking, not freely chosen by them, but like a cross taken up, because a higher power called them to art as a vocation. I feel that I am this kind of artist, called to my work by higher powers. And it is so profoundly obvious that there are higher powers in the world than just people, why we alone are very small, very insignificant. It is only that we are present on this earth in such vast numbers that makes us seem important. But is that not the very nature of illusions? Even though I accept the call of Art, I know it's harder for women to walk this path and find fulfillment. I want to be fulfilled in life and art. But when I look around me, so many women seem really unhappy with the choices they have made. Sometimes, I do not see any women doing things differently in a way that works, that satisfies, and I need to see this for it to be real.

I know in my heart that it is important for women to see other women doing many things. It gives one a sense of infinite possibilities. Women have not always seen the infinite possibilities, how freeing it is. I feel just now the ability to shake off the depression that for many years has been a burden in my life, weighing me down, and I want to explore every possible path to artistic and personal fulfillment. . . .

August 7, 1979.

Late nights, reluctant days. Have not made it in here to the typewriter. I have been thinking and talking again about the issue of why there are not many committed women artists who achieve their full potential. Having spent much of the summer reading the life stories of male artists it appears that one characteristic of their life experiences that is different from biographies of women (and it is so hard to even find the recorded life stories of black women artists) is that they, these men, irrespective of race or class, approach life with a total lack of restraint. It seems that so many female children, from the very onset of our lives, are being taught the subtle art of restraint, limits, how to exist comfortably in small spaces, how to accept confinement, so much so that it becomes a habit of living. Not at all conducive to creative exploration.

Some women like to suggest that it is because men have had wives to care for their daily practical needs that women have been unable to totally commit themselves to art. While I think this helps most men, I do not think it is the decisive factor. (Let's face it, there are a lot of male artists that aren't into women who make it.) I believe there are crucial factors that make it easier for men to realize artistic potential, to fulfill themselves through work, only I have not discovered them all yet. But I am looking. One awareness that comes from my own life experience is that I seem to have a much harder time validating my creative work than males I know—that is, to self-validate. I tend to seek some approval from outside myself. When that approval is not forthcoming I am not so motivated. And yes, to really sustain creative work one must be inwardly motivated. The inner impulse that compels one to create is totally necessary. I have met so many women who have talent but are not motivated. They create, but in a half-assed way. On the other hand I think many of us look at how men create, achieve, and do not like what we see.

Women pay attention to how men live and work. And women pay particular attention to how men who are dedicated artists live. And we rarely like what we see. We do not like the fact that their individual creative work is often deemed more important to them than all else in life—family, children, wife, lover/s, friends, whatever—maybe even more important than their health. Women look at that, and while we admire the steadfast dedication, we get suspicious. We feel the coldness of those "creative" hearts, their indifference to others, and we are afraid to be like them. In fact, even when we overcome our fears we don't want to be like them because they seem to be experiencing life in fragments. They seem to compartmentalize everything in ways that are dangerous. And yet many of us, women, have not found a way to keep alive responsible, loving relationships with others and work in a dedicated manner.

It seems to me that there exists a higher, more life-affirming work order than the one men have established as the norm. I see it as the holistic work order. Using that as the model, one would struggle to attain the discipline and energy necessary to be wholly alive both in art and in other daily experiences. I think that men who give all and everything to art have been pushed to an extreme just as limiting and possibly unsatisfying as women who sacrifice all for home and family or material desires. I think some of that feeling of lack, of an enormous void, that art with all its greatness and wonder could not fulfill has never been acknowledged by most male artists. This recognition comes through in the writing of Van Gogh. Of all the male artists I have read about recently, I think he is one of the most sincere. He does not try to pretend that painting pictures is analogous to women having children. But I do not think that women's ability to have children is better or more fortunate (as Van Gogh suggests—that smacks too much of patronizing sentiment) but simply that the two experiences are not the same. And the lack he felt was surely caused by the terrible one-dimensional nature of his life, the door opening only to one room—the one window in the room, looking out to the same old scenery. At least Van Gogh had the courage to admit that art was not enough, that he wanted and needed something more.

Surely there must be another way. There must be a way that men can create art without exploiting women (who bring them other dimensions of life served on silver platters when they take a break from their "real" work). Women who serve in the roles of mothers, sisters, wives, daughters, or friends. Such men act as though everything that exists apart from art is mere entertainment. Look at Picasso, or Romare Bearden. And there must be a way for women to create Art without having to be cheap imitations of alienated, emotionally retarded men. I suppose that is what we women fear, being so estranged and alienated from Life. I reread Tillie Olsen's *Silences,* in which she attempts (makes what I think is a rather feeble attempt) to understand why it is that white women or black people don't write. Her analysis disturbed me because she wants to blame it all on no money and lack of leisure time. But I've seen too many talented women and black men who do not do art even though all the right conditions exist in terms of economic and material comforts. And I think what she leaves unexplored is the question of self-esteem and self-confidence—that feeling that one has something to offer that is worthwhile, that will be acknowledged and affirmed. Since so many men (especially white men) are taught from childhood on that that anything they do is potentially important, valuable, they may not consistently ask themselves questions about worth the way women, and many black men do. Like Midas, some men feel that whatever they touch will become gold. And even if it's really dirt, or shit, they see it as important and are able to make other folks see it as important. I know we women artists on the fringe, and especially us black women artists, judge ourselves very harshly sometimes and fear the harsh judgments of others. We want to create only the best. And this longing for excellence torments, sometimes it prevents us from producing anything at all, as nothing we do seems good enough. Oh well, silence and sleep, have to do more typing on the *Ain't I a Woman* manuscript tomorrow.

From Journal of a Solitude

MAY SARTON

January 2

Begin again where this long hiatus of Christmas and the book's publication began just a month ago.

I can understand people simply fleeing the mountainous effort Christmas has become even for those, like me, without children. Everyone must feel revolt as I do about the middle of December when I am buried under the necessity of finding presents, immense effort of wrapping and sending, and the never-ended guilt about unsent cards, about letters. But there are always a few saving graces and finally they make up for all the bother and distress.

One such moment came as I turned into Harrisville from Dublin and saw what looked at first like a prehistoric animal coming toward me. Then, I realized that it was a Christmas tree carried on a man's shoulder, pointed toward me. There he was, bringing home the tree through the silent, woodsy, white world. We had a huge snow, fifteen inches, December 16th. Luckily it had been announced and I managed to get Judy and the two cats up here a day early; so we enjoyed it in perfect peace, open fires burning, and the moony, whirling world outside as if we were in the center of a "snowing" glass paperweight.

Before that, since a lunch was cancelled because of the snow, I was suddenly given a few hours of unexpected time and managed to get down a poem that had been pursuing me for days.

What other saving graces in the welter of *things*? The dear presents made for me by friends, often far away, sometimes friends I have never seen who know me only through my work—a knitted waistcoat, a lovely soft white wool sweater, a strawberry-pink turtleneck. How cherished they make me feel! Eva Le Gallienne made me a superb long heavy wool scarf to wear when I go out to feed the birds. Anne Woodson designed and worked a small petit-point pillow, quoting the last lines of the Kali poem —a bold design of light and dark with two Shirley poppies woven through it. I wept with the sheer joy of it, and the love it represents, when I opened it:

> Help us to be the always hopeful
> Gardeners of the spirit

From *Journal of a Solitude*

> Who know that without darkness
> Nothing comes to birth
> As without light
> Nothing flowers.[1]

This December I have been more aware than ever before of the meaning of a festival of light coming as it does when the days are so short, and we live in darkness for the greater part of the afternoon. Candlelight, tree lights—ours, tiny ones—are reflected in all the windows from four o'clock on.

Then, there are the great presents of long letters from former students and friends from whom I hear only once a year. They bring me a tapestry of lives, a little overwhelming, but interesting in their conjunctions. Two of my best poets at Wellesley, two girls who had something like genius, each married and each stopped writing altogether. Now this year each is moving toward poetry again. That news made me happy. It also made me aware once more of how rarely a woman is able to continue to create after she marries and has children.

Whatever college does not do, it does create a climate where work is demanded and where nearly every student finds him- or herself meeting the demand with powers he did not know he had. Then quite suddenly a young woman, if she marries, has to diverge completely from this way of life, while her husband simply goes on toward the goals set in college. She is expected to cope not with ideas, but with cooking food, washing dishes, doing laundry, and if she insists on keeping at a job, she needs both a lot of energy and the ability to organize her time. If she has an infant to care for, the jump for the intellectual life to that of being a nurse must be immense. "The work" she may long to do has been replaced by various kinds of labor for which she has been totally unprepared. She has longed for children, let us say, she is deeply in love, she has what she thought she wanted, so she suffers guilt and dismay to feel so disoriented. Young husbands these days can and do help with the chores and, far more important, are aware of the problem and will talk anxiously about it—anxiously because a wife's conflict affects their peace of mind. But the fact remains that, in marrying, the wife has suffered an earthquake and the husband has not. His goals have not been radically changed; his mode of being has not been radically changed.

I shall copy out parts of one of these letters, as it gave me much to ponder on and I shall refer to it again in the weeks to come, no doubt. K says,

> It has been a year of unusual branching out, and I feel quite young. You will laugh at that, but many of our friends now are pathetically worried about aging and full of envy for young people and regrets about wasting their own youth—and these are parents of small children, under thirty! I think it is a very destructive system indeed that worships youth the way we Americans do and gives young people no ideals of maturity to reach for, nothing to look forward to. (Adolescence is often so miserable that one needs an incentive to get through it!)

1. "A Grain of Mustard Seed"

Well, I'd better stop, because I feel a harangue coming on; I'm so hope-lessly out of tune with these times and it's a temptation to join the haranguers. . . .

As for the writing of a poems, I'm beginning to see that *the* obstruction is being female, a fact I have never accepted or known how to live with. I wish that I could talk to you about it; I know that you are into insights that I'm only beginning to realize *exist*. (And that's why Sylvia Plath interests me; Robert Lowell describes her as "feminine rather than female," what-ever that means; but she strikes me as breaking through the feminine to something natural that, while I suppose it still has a sex, can't be called feminine even.) At least I can see the inadequacy of that male and very Freudian psychiatrist, trying to help me accept or do something with this burden of femininity that marriage had seemed to finalize. I am grateful to all the crazies out there in Women's Liberation; we *need* them as outra-geous mythical characters to make our hostilities and dilemmas really vis-ible. As shallow as my contact with the Women's Liberation has been, I have really seen something new about myself this year; the old stalemated internal conflict has been thrown off balance and I am surprised to under-stand how much of my savage hostility is against men. I have always been rejecting language because it *is* a male invention. My voice in my own poems, though coming out of myself, became a masculine voice on the page, and I felt the need to destroy that voice, that role, in making room for D in my life. It is not just my equation but a whole family tradition, which decreed a deep and painful timidity for the women; and for me this was always especially intolerable, since the personality I was born with was the very opposite of passive! It is very fortunate for me that, of all my friends, excepting you, D is the only one who seems to understand, or at least to sympathize with this—a fact which violates the principles of psy-chiatry since he is the one most threatened by any sexual crisis I may undergo, the target most at hand for hostilities against men, and the most disturbed by the instability that comes with my trying to readjust the bal-ance of my mind.

This letter goes to the heart of the matter. I found it deeply disturbing. For what is really at stake is unbelief in the woman as artist, as creator. K no longer sees her talent as relevant or valid, language itself as a masculine invention. That certainly closes the door with a bang! But I believe it will open because the thrust of a talent as real as hers must finally break through an intellectual formula and assert what she now denies. What she writes eventually will be in her own voice. Every now and then I meet a person whose speaking voice appears to be placed artificially, to come not from the center of the person, but form an unnatural reg-ister. I am thinking especially of women with high, strained voices. I know noth-ing about voice placement in a technical sense, but I have longed to say, "For God's sake, get down to earth and speak in your own voice!" This is not so much a matter of honesty, perhaps (K is excruciatingly honest), as of self-assurance: I am who I am. . . .

February 9

It is rather like living in a vast cosmic mood swing here now. I managed to get the car out yesterday and did some quick errands because another storm was in the air. It came, all right, with strong wind, snow, then lashing rain, temperature just above freezing. I woke to trees iced in silver and an April sky, sunlight breaking through clouds. Now in the last half hour it has suddenly become ominously dark, all clouded over, the clouds nearly black. The wind is back.

And it is the same inside me—violent mood swings. It would be a real deprivation to have no phone here, but on the other hand how devastating a voice can be! I feel myself sucked down into the quicksand that isolation sometimes creates, a sense of drowning, of being literally engulfed. When it comes to the important things, one is always alone, and it may be that the virtue or possible insight I get from being so obliviously alone—being physically and in every way absolutely alone much of the time—is a way into the universal state of man. The way in which one handles this absolute aloneness is the way in which one grows up, is the great psychic journey of everyman. At what price would total independence be bought? That's the rub! I am conscious of the fruitful tensions set up between me and anyone for whom I care—Anne Woodson for instance, X of course. I learn by being *in relation to.*

When one is alone a lot as I am, this becomes true even of such an apparently passive relation as that between me and four bowls of daffodils I am growing on the windowsill of the guest room. Whether or not a flower or plant is doing well becomes of singular importance. When I get up in the morning, it matters what tone of voice Punch uses. A happy scream as I lift the lid off the cage and he is free to climb out and sit on a rod outside to admire himself in a mirror makes me laugh with joy. When he is silent, as he was today, I feel it, as I feel for the wild cat who will never be tamed, I fear, but comes every afternoon for milk and food and stares at me intently with her round green eyes. I have wept with anxiety more than once when she was not there. It is absurd. Yet, how, without such intimate relations, keep alive at all? Every relation challenges, every relation asks me to be something, do something, respond. Close off response and what is left? Bearing . . . enduring . . . waiting.

The sun has suddenly come out and there is a bright blue sky—all this happened while I wrote a few words! Astonishing!

I have begun again to play two Schubert impromptus that Louise Bogan gave me—opus 90 and opus 142, Gieseking.

I have said elsewhere that we have to make myths of our lives, the point being that if we do, then every grief or inexplicable seizure by weather, woe, or work can—if we discipline ourselves and think hard enough—be turned to account, be made to yield further insight into what it is to be alive, to be a human being, what the hazards are of a fairly usual, everyday kind. We go up to Heaven and down to

Hell a dozen times a day—at least, I do. And the discipline of work provides an exercise bar, so that the wild, irrational motions of the soul become formal and creative. It literally keeps one from falling on one's face.

That is one way to keep alive in a self-made solitary confinement. I have found it useful also these past days to say to myself, "What if I were not alone? What if I had ten children to get off to school every morning and a massive wash to do before they get home? What if two of them were in bed with flu, cross and at a loose end?" That is enough to send me back to solitude as if it were—as it truly is—a fabulous gift from the gods.

Contrast is one key, and within every day the deliberate creation of diversity. This morning I cheered myself out of depression by saying, "Your reward for the morning's work will be to clean out the liquor cupboard." It is a mess, but a viable mess compared to that of the paper cupboard, despite the rat poison strewn around because I saw a huge rat crawl up the wall in there one day.

Each day, and the living of it, has to be a conscious creation in which discipline and order are relieved with some play and some pure foolishness. God bless Punch, who makes me laugh aloud!

My greatest deprivation is to have no huggable animal around. I miss the two old cats dreadfully.

Upbringing

MOLLY PEACOCK

Bringing yourself up requires long hours alone
to get the nurturing others have felt.
Because of someone else, others have grown up,

so they question why your solitude has grown
so wide, and you wonder at your guilt
that simply being requires these hours alone

with your obstreperous, largely unknown
Being, who only feels and doesn't talk,
whose matted, scaly pelt you've sewn

into what you hope is proper clothing, stock-
still, costumed in a darkness that never melts.
Of course you must take it out when it moans

and let it be naked and chew the bones
and hooves you save for it, after it bolts
around the room and falls, exhausted, down

into the possessed happiness of its selfhood.
This takes hours. As if holding your breath underwater,
you hold in the aboriginal child, attending to the *om*

society seems to breathe that you, a clone,
never seem to understand until you're sick
from something vomiting inside its false home

and the child feels it's done wrong although
it's only an animal. Now you must clean up alone
or you'll both be sick, or one of you will die.

Of course this takes the hours most spend on the phone,
making money, having kids,
or asking why you don't.

About the Authors

ROCHELLE RATNER is the author of two novels, *Bobby's Girl* (1986) and *The Lion's Share* (1991), and several volumes of poetry, including *Practicing to Be a Woman: New and Selected Poems* (1982) and *Someday Songs: Poems Toward a Personal History* (1992). She is executive editor of *American Book Review*. A regular reviewer for several publications, she teaches writing workshops in New York City.

•

PAULETTE BATES ALDEN is the author of the story collection *Feeding the Eagles* (1998) and of the memoir *Crossing the Moon: A Journey Through Infertility* (1998). The recipient of numerous awards, including a Wallace Stegner Fellowship to Stanford, a Loft-McKnight Award, a Bush Foundation Fellowship, and a Minnesota State Arts Board grant, Alden has taught at Stanford University, the University of Minnesota, St. Olaf College, Carleton College, and the Split Rock Arts Program. She lives in Minneapolis and teaches fiction and memoir writing privately.

JULIA ALVAREZ is a poet, essayist, and fiction writer. She spent her early childhood in the Dominican Republic and emigrated to the United States and to the English language at the age of ten. In 1991, she published *How the Garcia Girls Lost Their Accents* (Algonquin Books and Plume paperback), which won a PEN Oakland Award and was selected as a *New York Times* Notable Book and an American Library Book in 1992. Her second novel, *In the Time of the Butterflies* (Algonquin Books and Plume paperback), was a finalist for the National Book Critics Circle Award in 1995. She has also published two books of poems, *The Other Side/ El Otro Lado* (1995) and *Homecoming: New and Collected Poems* (1996). A third novel, *Yo!* (Algonquin Books and Plume paperback) was published in 1997. A collection of essays, *Something To Declare* (Algonquin Books), was published in 1998, and a children's book, *The Secret Footprints* (Alfred A. Knopf) was published in 1999. She lives in Vermont, where she is working on a new novel.

MARGARET ATWOOD was born in Ottawa in 1939 and grew up in northern Quebec and Ontario and later in Toronto. She has lived in numerous other cities in Canada, the United States, and Europe. She is the author of more than twenty-five books—novels, short stories, poetry, literary criticism, social history, and books for children—including the best-selling novels *The Edible Woman* (1969), *The Handmaid's Tale* (1985), *Cat's Eye* (1988), *The Robber Bride* (1983), and *Alias Grace* (1996). Atwood's work has been published around the world and has won many awards and honors, including the Governor General's Award, the Trillium Book Award, the Canadian Authors Association Award, the *Sunday Times* Award for Literary Excellence in the United Kingdom, and the Chevalier dan l'Ordre des Arts et des Letters in France. She lives in Toronto.

BECKY BIRTHA is the author of two volumes of stories, *For Nights Like This One: Stories of Loving Women* (1987) and *Lover's Choice* (1994), as well as a collection of poetry, *The Forbidden Poems* (1991). Her stories have been anthologized in more than twenty college textbooks as well as in such trade anthologies as *Women on Women: An Anthology of Lesbian Short Fiction* and *Daughters of Africa: An International Anthology of Words and Writings by Women of African Descent*. She lives in Washington, D.C.

DEBORAH BOE's first volume of poetry, *Mojave*, was published in 1987. Her poems have also appeared in *Poetry, Poetry Northwest*, and other publications.

SHYLAH BOYD is the author of the best-selling novel *American Made* (1975) and of a collection of short fiction, *A Real Man* (1990). She has also published a book of poems, *American Gypsy*, under the name Frances Whyatt.

DONNA BROOK has been awarded both National Endowment for the Arts and New York Foundation for the Arts Fellowships for her poetry. Her fourth collection, *A More Human Face*, was published in 1998. She is also the author of *The Journey of English*, a history of the English language for younger readers. She lives in Brooklyn, New York.

RITA MAE BROWN was born in Hanover, Pennsylvania, and grew up in Florida. She has a degree in classics and English from New York University and a doctorate in political science from the Institute For Policy Studies in Washington, D.C. Her eleven novels include *Rubyfruit Jungle* (1973) and *Loose Lips* (1990). She has also published several books of poems, five mysteries (with Sneaky Pie), and a writer's manual, and has been twice nominated for Emmy Awards, for her scripts "I Love Liberty" and "The Long Hot Summer." Her autobiography, *Rita Will: Memoir of a Literary Rabble-Rouser*, was published in 1997. She lives outside of Charlottesville, Virginia.

ANA CASTILLO is a Chicago native, born in 1953. Her early collections of poetry include *Zen Makes Me Hungry* (1975), *I Close My Eyes (To See)* (1976), *Otro Canto* (1977), *The Invitation* (1979), and *Women Are Not Roses* (1984), and her selected poems, *My Father Was a Toltec*, was published in 1988. Her first novel, *The Mixquiahula Letters* (1986), won a Before Columbus Foundation American Book Award, her second novel, *Sapogonia* (1990), received an award from the National Endowment for the Arts, and her third novel, *So Far From God* (1993), won the Carl Sandberg Literary Award. Castillo published a collection of critical essays, *Massacre of the Dreamers: Essays on Xicanisma*, in 1994, a collection of short stories, *Loverboys*, in 1996, and another novel, *Peel My Love Like an Onion*, in 1999.

SANDRA CISNEROS was born in Chicago in 1954 and educated in the Midwest. She is the author of two books of poetry, *Bad Boys* (1980) and *My Wicked Wicked Ways* (1987), and two books of fiction, *The House on Mango Street* (1991) and *Woman Hollering Creek* (1991), which was awarded the PEN Center West Award for Best Fiction of 1991, the Quality Paperback Book Club New Voices Award, the Anisfield-Wolf Book Award, and the Lannan Foundation Literary Award, selected as a noteworthy book of the year by the *New York Times* and *Library Journal*, and nominated for Best Book of Fiction by the *Los Angeles Times*. Cisneros's other awards include two National Endowment of the Art Fellowships for fiction and poetry, the Chicano Short Story Award from the University of Arizona, the Before Columbus Foundation American Book Award, and an Illinois Artists Grant. Her books have been translated into ten languages.

TORY DENT graduated from Barnard College and received an M.A. from New York University. Her book of poems, *What Silence Equals*, was published in 1993. Her poetry has also appeared in such periodicals as *Agni, Antioch Review, Kalliope, Kenyon Review, Paris Review, Partisan Review, Pequod*, and *Ploughshares*, and in the anthologies *Life Sentences, The Exact Change Yearbook, In the Company of My Solitude*, and *Things Shaped in Passing*. She has written art criticism for *Arts, Flash Art, Parachute*, and other magazines. Dent has also been a fellow at the Macdowell Colony, Yaddo, and the Virginia Center for the Creative Arts. Her memoir-in-progress is entitled *Many Rivers to Cross: Living with the Challenge of a Life-Threatening Illness.*

NIKKI DILLON is the author of *Scratch: Four Stories*. Her fiction has appeared in numerous literary journals, including *New Letters, The Baffler, Bust*, and *Cimarron Review*, and was nominated for a 1995 Pushcart Prize. Dillon has been involved with the National Coalition Against Censorship, a First Amendment rights group. She lives in New York City, where she is at work on a novel.

DIANE DI PRIMA is the author of thirty-three books of poetry and prose, as well as many plays. Among her recent books are *Pieces of a Song: Selected Poems* (1990), a reprint edition of *Memoirs of a Beatnik* (1998), and a new, expanded edition of her epic poem *Loba* (1998). The first volume of her autobiography, *Recollections of My Life As a Woman*, will be published in 2000. She lives in San Francisco, where she works as a writer, healer, and teacher and studies and practices Tibetan Buddhism.

CHITRA BANERJEE DIVAKARUNI was born in India and emigrated to the United States at age nineteen, settling in the San Francisco Bay Area. She is the author of four collections of poetry, including *Black Candle: Poems About Women from India, Pakistan, and Bangladesh* (1991). Her story collection, *Arranged Marriage* (1995), won the PEN Oakland Josephine Miles Prize for Fiction, the Bay Area Book Reviewers Award for Fiction, and an American Book Award from the Before Columbus Foundation. She is also the author of two novels, the best-selling *The Mistress of Spices* (1997) and *Sister of My Heart* (1999). She now lives in Texas and teaches at the University of Houston.

JODI SH. DOFF, who also publishes under the name Scarlett Fever, first published in the premiere issue of *Bust*. Her work has since been included in *Penthouse, Playgirl, Cosmopolitan, Stim*, and the anthologies *Best American Erotica '95* and *The Bust Guide to the New Girl Order*. She is currently finishing work on both *Chalk Outline*, a memoir about her years in the sex industry, and *Tangled up in Blue*, a crime novel.

DENISE DUHAMEL's most recent volumes of poetry include *Girl Soldier* (1996), *How the Sky Fell* (1996), *Exquisite Politics* (with Maureen Seaton, 1997), *Kinky* (1997), and *The Star-Spangled Banner* (1999), winner of the Crab Orchard Poetry Prize.

JANICE EIDUS has won two O. Henry Prizes and a Pushcart Prize for her short fiction. She is the author of two story collections, *Vito Loves Geraldine* (1990) and *The Celibacy Club* (1997), and two novels, *Faithful Rebecca* (1987) and *Urban Bliss* (1998). She is also co-editor of *It's Only Rock N' Roll: Rock N' Roll Short Stories* (1998). Her work has been widely published in magazines and anthologies throughout the world. She lives in New York City.

PATRICIA FOSTER is editor of the anthologies *Minding the Body: Women Writers On Body and Soul* (1995), *Sister to Sister: Women Write About the Unbreakable Bond* (1995), and *The Healing Circle: Authors Writing of Recovery* (1998). She teaches at the University of Iowa and has just completed a memoir.

DANIELA GIOSEFFI is the author of ten books of poetry and prose, most recently *Word Wounds & Water Flowers* (poems, 1995), and *In Bed with the Exotic Enemy* (stories and a novella, 1997). She conceived and edited the classic feminist anthology *Women on War: International Voices* (1988) and the international compendium of poetry and prose *On Prejudice: A Global Perspective* (1993), which won a Ploughshares World Peace Award. She is also the recipient of an American Book Award from the Before Columbus Foundation. Her poems, stories, and critical prose have appeared for over thirty years in such magazines as the *Paris Review*, the *Nation, Antaeus, Choice, Prairie Schooner*, and *Ms.*, and she edits the E-zine *Wise Women's Web*.

AMY HEMPEL is the author of *Tumble Home* (1997), a novella and short stories, and of the story collections *Reasons To Live* (1995) and *At the Gates of the Animal Kingdom* (1990). She teaches in the Graduate Writing Program at Bennington College and at the New School in New York City.

LINDA HOGAN, whose heritage is Chickasaw, was born in 1947 in Denver, Colorado, and grew up in Oklahoma. In 1991 she was a finalist for the Pulitzer Prize for her novel *Mean Spirit*, and in 1996 she won the Colorado Book Award for her poetry collection *The Book of Medicines*. Her other books of poetry and prose include *Seeing Through the Sun* (1985), *Savings* (1988), *Red Clay: Poems and Stories* (1994), *Dwellings: A Spiritual History of the Living World* (1995), *From Women's Experience to Feminist Theology* (1996), *Solar Storms* (1997), and *Power* (1998).

BELL HOOKS was born in 1952 and published her first book, *Ain't I A Woman: Black Women and Feminism*, when she was nineteen years old. Her books, which integrate postmodern speculations, cultural criticism, neglected literature, and autobiographical disclosure into feminist theory, include *Yearning: Race, Class and Cultural Politics* (1990), *Black Looks: Race and Representation* (1992), *Outlaw Culture: Resisting Representation* (1994), *Art on My Mind: Visual Politics* (1995), *Killing Rage: Ending Racism* (1996), *Bone Black: Memories of Girlhood* (1996), and *Remembered Rapture: The Writer at Work* (1998).

About the Authors

HETTIE JONES is the author of *Drive* (1998), a collection of poems, and two earlier poetry chapbooks, *Having Been Her* and *For Four Hetties*. Her memoir, *How I Became Hettie Jones*, was published in 1990. She is also the editor of *The Trees Stand Shining: Poetry of the North American Indians* (1971) and the author of *Big Star Fallin' Mama: Five Women in Black Music* and of other award-winning books for children and young adults. Jones has taught writing at a dozen institutions, including, currently, Parsons School of Design, Lang College, and the 92nd Street Y Poetry Center. She also runs a writing workshop at the Bedford Hills Correctional Facility and is chair of the PEN Prison Writing Committee.

IRENA KLEPFISZ was born in Warsaw, Poland, in 1941 and emigrated to the United States in 1949. She was a founder of *Conditions*, a feminist magazine emphasizing the writing of lesbians, and co-editor of *A Tribe of Dina: A Jewish Women's Anthology* (1989) and of *A Jewish Women's Call for Peace: A Handbook for Jewish Women on the Israeli/Palestinian Conflict* (1990). She is the author of *A Few Words in the Mother Tongue: Poems Selected and New (1971–1990)* and *Dreams of an Insomniac: Jewish Feminist Essays, Speeches, and Diatribes* (1990).

JOY KOGAWA is a novelist and poet whose books include *A Choice of Dreams* (1974), *Jericho Road* (1977), *Obasan* (1981), *Itsuka* (1994), and *The Rain Ascends* (1995). She is a member of the Order of Canada, and she resides in Toronto.

VICKI LINDNER is the author of a novel, *Outlaw Games* (1982), and co-author of several nonfiction books, including *The Money Mirror: How Money Reflects Women's Dreams, Fears, and Desires* (1996). Her short stories, essays, and articles have appeared in a variety of publications, from *Omni* to the *Kenyon Review*. The recipient of two New York State Fellowships, a National Endowment for the Arts fellowship, and a Wyoming Arts Council fellowship, Lindner teaches writing at the University of Wyoming.

MARY MACKEY graduated from Radcliffe College and received her Ph.D. from the University of Michigan. From 1989 to 1992 she served as chair of the West Coast Branch of PEN American Center. A professor and writer in residence at California State University, Sacramento, she is the author of four collections of poetry and nine novels, including the three volumes of *The Earthsong Trilogy—The Year the Horses Came* (1993), *The Horses at the Gate* (1995), and *The Fires of Spring* (1997)—in which she draws on the research of the late feminist archaeologist Marija Gimbutas.

ELIZABETH MARRAFFINO-REES is the author of close to fifty young adult and middle grade novels, most recently the series *Heart Beats*. Her poetry has been published widely in literary magazines and anthologies, including the *Nation* and *The Dream Book: An Anthology of Writings by Italian American Women*. Her collection of poetry, *Blue Moon for Ruby Tuesday*, was published in 1981.

REBECCA MCCLANAHAN has published three books of poetry, most recently *The Intersection of X and Y* (1996), and a book of creative nonfiction. Her work has appeared in *Georgia Review, Shenandoah, Southern Review, Kenyon Review,*

Boulevard, and elsewhere, and has been aired on National Public Radio's "The Sound of Writing." She has received a Pushcart Prize and a PEN Syndicated Fiction Award.

VALERIE MINER's seven novels include *Blood Sisters* (1982), *Movement* (1982), *Winter's Edge* (1985), *A Walking Fire* (1994), and *Range of Light* (1998). She is also author of a collection of stories, *Trespassing and Other Stories* (1989), and a collection of essays, *Rumors from the Cauldron* (1992). She is professor of English at the University of Minnesota.

KATHLEEN NORRIS is the author of *Dakota* (1993), *The Cloister Walk,* a *New York Times* Notable Book for 1996, *Amazing Grace: A Vocabulary of Faith* (1998) and *Meditations on Mary* (1999). Her most recent book of poetry is *Little Girls in Church* (1995). She lives in South Dakota, and for the last decade has been an oblate of Assumption Abbey in North Dakota.

JUDEE NORTON began writing while an inmate in Arizona State Prison. She now works and writes in a small farm community in southeastern Arizona. She is currently at work on *Slick,* fictional reflections on personal decisions and their consequences.

NAOMI SHIHAB NYE is the author of three books of poems, *Red Suitcase* (1994), *Words Under the Words: Selected Poems* (1995), and *Fuel* (1998). Her recent books include a novel for young readers, *Habbi* (1997), a children's picture book, *Lullaby Raft* (1997), and a volume of essays, *Never in a Hurry* (1996). She has also edited four prize-winning anthologies of poetry for young readers. She was a Guggenheim Fellow for 1997–1998.

JOYCE CAROL OATES is Roger S. Berlind Professor in the Humanities at Princeton University. Her many books include, most recently, the novels *Broke Heart Blues* (1999) and *Man Crazy* (1998), the story collection *The Collector of Hearts* (1998), the volume of collected essays *Where I've Been and Where I'm Going* (1999), and *New Plays* (1998). Her earlier books include *You Must Remember This* (1987), *Because It Is Bitter, and Because It Is My Heart* (1990), and *Foxfire* (1993). Oates is a founding editor of *Ontario Review.*

SUZANNE OSTRO is the author of two books, *Demolition Zone* and *Dream of the Whale.* Her poems and stories have been published in a variety of literary magazines. Her previous work was published under the name Suzanne Zavrian.

GRACE PALEY was born in the Bronx in 1922 and attended public schools. She is the author of three short story collections, *Enormous Changes at the Last Minute* (1974), *Later the Same Day* (1984), and *The Little Disturbances of Man* (1985), now available in one volume as *The Collected Stories* (1995). She is also the author of several volumes of poetry, and her poetry has been collected in *Begin Again: Collected Poems* (1999). Her other works include *Long Walks and Intimate Talks* (with paintings by Vera B. Williams, 1991) and the collection of essays, prefaces, talks, and political reports *Just As I Thought* (1998). Paley has two children and two grandchildren. After living most of her life in New York, she presently lives in Vermont.

MOLLY PEACOCK is the author of *Paradise, Piece by Piece* (1998), a poet's memoir about all her decisions in life, including the decision to be child-free. A Woodrow Wilson fellow and president emerita of the Poetry Society of America, she is the author of *How to Read a Poem—and Start a Poetry Circle* (1999) as well as four books of poems, including *Take Heart* (1989) and *Original Love* (1995).

MARGE PIERCY is the author of fifteen books of poetry, among them *What Are Big Girls Made Of?* (1997). A collection of her early poetry, *Early Grrrl*, and a collection of her Jewish-themed poetry, *The Art of Blessing the Day*, both appeared in 1999. She has written fourteen novels, all still in print, most recently *City of Darkness, City of Light* (1996) and *Storm Tide*, written with her husband, Ira Wood (1998).

MINNIE BRUCE PRATT's second book of poetry, *Crime Against Nature*, was chosen as the 1989 Lamont Poetry Selection by the Academy of American Poets, was nominated for a Pulitzer Prize, and received the American Library Association's Gay and Lesbian Book Award for Literature. She is co-author, with Elly Bulkin and Barbara Smith, of *Yours in Struggle: Three Feminist Perspectives on Anti-Semitism and Racism* (1984). Her other books include the poetry collection *We Say We Love Each Other* (1992), *Rebellion: Essays 1980–1991*, and the story collection *S/HE* (1995). Her most recent book, a collection of long narrative poems, is *Walking Back Up Depot Street* (1999). She lives in Jersey City, New Jersey.

ELISSA RAFFA was born and raised in New York, and currently divides her time between Minneapolis and Greece. Her creative work has appeared in several literary magazines and anthologies and on several Minneapolis stages. She received a 1994 Minnesota State Arts Board Fellowship and a 1995 Astraea Emerging Lesbian Writers Award for *Freeing Vera*, her first novel. She is at work on a second novel.

KIT REED's twelve novels include *Captain Grownup* (1976), *Catholic Girls* (1987), *J. Eden* (1996), and *Seven for the Apocalypse* (1999). She is also author of the collection *Weird Women, Wired Women* (1998). Reed is a Guggenheim fellow and the first U.S. recipient of a five-year literary grant from the Abraham Woursell Foundation. Her stories have appeared in magazines ranging from the *Yale Review* and the *Missouri Review* to the *Magazine of Fantasy and Science Fiction* and *Omni*. She is the mother of three children.

WENDY ROSE has twice been nominated for a Pulitzer Prize in poetry. She has authored eight volumes of poetry and her work has appeared in numerous anthologies. Her eight books of poetry include *Lost Copper* (1980), *The Halfbreed Chronicles* (1986), *Going to War with All My Relations* (1993), *Now Poof She Is Gone* (1994), and *Bone Dance: New and Selected Poems 1965–1993* (1994). Since 1984 she has been the coordinator and an instructor of American Indian Studies at Fresno City College. Her tribal affiliations are Hopi and Miwok.

EVELYN C. ROSSER, a native of Valdosta, Georgia, lives in Athens, Georgia, where she is a high school English teacher and instructor in the Upward Bound Program at the University of Georgia. Her first novel, *Too Late for Tears*, was published in 1994 and her second novel, *Dancing Naked Under Palm Trees*, was published in

1997. Her work has also appeared in *Life Notes: Personal Writings by Contemporary Black Women.*

JANE RULE was born in Plainfield, New Jersey in 1931, but has lived most of her adult life in Canada. Now retired from writing and teaching, she lives on Gailiano Island off the coast of British Columbia. She is the author of numerous novels, short stories, and essays, including *The Desert of the Heart* (1964), *Theme for Diverse Instruments* (1975), *Lesbian Images* (1975), *Memory Board* (1987), and *After the Fire* (1989).

MAY SARTON (1912–1995) published fifteen books of poetry, represented in *Collected Poems, 1930–1993,* and nineteen novels, including *Mrs. Stevens Hears the Mermaids Singing* (1965), *Anger* (1985), and *The Magnificent Spinster* (1985). She is also the author of thirteen volumes of memoir and journal, including *Plant Dreaming Deep* (1968), *Journal of a Solitude* (1973), *Recovering* (1980), *The House by the Sea* (1977), *At Seventy* (1984), *After the Stroke* (1988), and the posthumously published *At Eighty-two (1996).*

LYNDA SCHOR is the author of two books of short fiction, *Appetites* and *True Love & Real Romance.* Her stories and articles have appeared in *Redbook, Ms., Playboy, Mademoiselle,* the *Village Voice, Confrontation, Fiction, Cream City Review,* and other publications. She has won a Baltimore City Arts grant and a Maryland State Arts Council Grant. She lives in Baltimore and New York City and teaches fiction writing at Lang College of the New School for Social Research.

SANDRA SCOFIELD, a native Texan and long-time resident of Oregon, is the author of the novels *Gringa* (1989), *Beyond Deserving* (1991), a finalist for the National Book Award, *Walking Dunes* (1992), *More Than Allies* (1993), *Opal on Dry Ground* (1994), *A Chance to See Egypt* (1996), and *Plain Seeing* (1997).

AMY TAN was born in 1952 in Oakland, California, and grew up in the San Francisco Bay Area. She received her master's degree in linguistics from San Jose State. Her first novel, *The Joy Luck Club* (1989), won the National Book Award and the Los Angeles Times Book Award in 1989. Her other novels are *The Kitchen God's Wife* (1991) and *The Hundred Secret Senses* (1995). She has also written books for children. Tan's work has been translated into twenty languages.

LUCI TAPAHONSO was born in Shiprock, New Mexico, and is a currently professor of English at the University of Arizona. She is the author of two children's books and five books of poetry, including *Blue Horses Rush In: Poems and Stories* (1997), which was awarded the Mountains and Plains Booksellers Association's 1998 Award for poetry. She is the recipient of a number of other awards, including the 1998 Kansas Governor's Art Award and Distinguished Woman awards from the National Association of Women in Education and the Girl Scout Council. She was featured on the Rhino Records CD *In Their Own Voices: A Century of American Poetry* and in the films *The Desert Is No Lady: Art of the Wild,* and *Woven by the Grandmothers: An Exhibition of 19th Century Navajo Textiles,* which were released on PBS stations.

PAMELA WALKER was born in Iowa in 1948. She received an M.F.A. from the University of Iowa Writers Workshop and an M.Ed. from Bank Street College of Education. Her short fiction has appeared in *Hawaii Review* and *Iowa Woman*. She recently moved to California with her husband and daughter.

JOY WILLIAMS is the author of the novels *State of Grace* (1973) and *Breaking and Entering* (1988) and the story collections *Taking Care* (1982) and *Escapes* (1990). She received the Strauss Living Award from the American Academy of Arts and Letters. She lives in Tucson and Key West.

Further Reading

(Compiled by Angelynn King, University of Redlands librarian, with additions by Rochelle Ratner.)

Books

Anton, Linda Hunt. *Never to Be a Mother: A Guide for All Women Who Didn't— or Couldn't— Have Children.* San Francisco: HarperSanFrancisco, 1992.

Bartlett, Jane. *Will You Be a Mother?: Women Who Choose to Say No.* New York: New York University Press, 1995.

Brady, Joan. *I Don't Need a Baby to Be Who I Am: Thoughts and Affirmations on a Fulfilling Life.* New York: Pocket Books, 1998.

Burgwyn, Diana. *Marriage Without Children.* New York: Harper & Row, 1981.

Cameron, Jan. *Without Issue.* Canterbury, New Zealand: Canterbury University Press, 1997.

Campbell, Elaine. *The Childless Marriage: An Exploratory Study of Couples Who Do Not Want Children.* London: Tavistock, 1985.

Carter, Jean W., and Michael Carter. *Sweet Grapes: How to Stop Being Infertile and Start Living Again.* Indianapolis, Indiana: Perspectives Press, 1998.

Casey, Terri. *Pride and Joy: The Lives and Passions of Women Without Children.* Hillboro, Oregon: Beyond Words Publishing, 1998.

Dally, Ann. *Inventing Motherhood: The Consequences of an Ideal.* New York: Schocken Books, 1987.

Dowrick, Stephanie, and Sibyl Grundberg, editors. *Why Children?* London: The Women's Press, 1980.

Elvenstar, Diane. *Children: To Have or Have Not?* San Francisco: Harbor Publishing, 1982.

Engel, Beverly. *The Parenthood Decision: Discovering Whether You Are Ready and Willing to Become a Parent.* New York: Doubleday, 1998.

English, Jane. *Childlessness Transformed: Stories of Alternative Parenting.* Mount Shasta, Calif.: Earth Heart, 1989.

Faux, Marian. *Childless by Choice: Choosing Childlessness in the Eighties.* Garden City, New York: Anchor Press/Doubleday, 1984.

Harper, Kate. *The Childfree Alternative.* Brattleboro, Vermont: Stephen Greene Press, 1980.

Hawkins, Barbara W. *Women Without Children: How to Live Your Choice.* Saratoga, Calif.: R & E Publishers, 1984.

Ireland, Mary S. *Reconceiving Women: Separating Motherhood from Female Identity.* New York: Guilford Press, 1993.

Lafayette, Leslie. *Why Don't You Have Kids?: Living a Full Life Without Parenthood.* New York: Kensington Books, 1995.

Lang, Susan S. *Women Without Children: The Reasons, the Rewards, the Regrets.* New York: Pharos Books, 1991.

Lewis, Berwyn. *No Children by Choice.* Ringwood, Australia: Penguin Books, 1986.

Lisle, Laurie. *Without Child: Challenging the Stigma of Childlessness.* New York: Ballantine Books, 1996.

Marshall, Helen. *Not Having Children.* Melbourne, Australia: Oxford University Press, 1993.

May, Elaine Tyler. *Barren in the Promised Land: Childless Americans and the Pursuit of Happiness.* New York: Basic Books, 1995.

Morell, Carolyn M. *Unwomanly Conduct: The Challenges of Intentional Childlessness.* New York: Routledge, 1994.

Nason, Ellen Mara and Margaret M. Poloma. *Voluntarily Childless Couples: The Emergence of a Variant Lifestyle.* Beverly Hills, Calif.: Sage Publications, 1976.

Peacock, Molly: *Paradise, Piece by Piece.* New York: Riverhead Books, 1998.

Peck, Ellen. *Pronatalism: The Myth of Mom and Apple Pie.* New York: Crowell, 1974.

Reti, Irene, editor. *Childless by Choice: A Feminist Anthology.* Santa Cruz, Calif.: HerBooks, 1992.

Rule, Jane. *The Desert of the Heart.* Tallahassee, Florida: The Naiad Press, 1985.

Russo, Nancy Felipe, editor. *The Motherhood Mandate.* New York: Human Sciences Press, 1979.

Safer, Jeanne, *Beyond Motherhood: Choosing a Life Without Children.* New York: Pocket Books, 1996.

Silverman, Anna, and Arnold Silverman. *The Case Against Having Children.* New York: D. McKay & Co., 1971.

Veevers, J. E. *Childless by Choice.* Toronto: Butterworths, 1980.

Whelan, Dr. Elizabeth. *A Baby? Maybe.* New York: The Bobbs-Merrill Company, 1973, 1980.

Ziman Tobin, Phyllis O., with Barbara Aria. *Motherhood Optional: A Psychological Journey*. Northvale, New Jersey and London: Aronson, Inc., 1998.

Magazines

Particularly over the past decade, there have been numerous articles published in the popular press that explore the issue of childlessness from varying points of view. Listed here are a few of the most enlightening.

Conant, Jennet. "Breaking the Bad News," *Newsweek* (September 1, 1986) 73–76.

Griffin, Katherine. "Childless by Choice," *Health* (March/April 1996) 99–103.

Jacoby, Susan. "The Baby Bandwagon," *Glamour* (September 1987) 388–389, 430–431.

Polaneczky, Ronnie. "To Breed or Not to Breed," *Philadelphia* (October 1992) 81–83, 133–135.

Credits

Rochelle Ratner, "Stork Talk," originally published in an earlier version in *First Intensity* 6, Summer 1997. Copyright © 1997, 1999 by Rochelle Ratner. Used by permission of the author.

Kit Reed, "The Weremother," from *Weird Women, Wired Women*, Wesleyan University Press 1998. Copyright © 1998 by Kit Reed. Reprinted by permission of the author.

Wendy Rose, "Forty, Trembling," from *Now Poof She Is Gone*, Firebrand Books 1994. Copyright © 1994 by Wendy Rose. Reprinted by permission of Firebrand Books.

Evelyn C. Rosser, "January 1953," from "Chocolate Tears and Dreams," originally published in *Life Notes: Personal Writings by Contemporary Black Women*, edited by Patricia Bell Scott, W. W. Norton & Co. 1994. Copyright © 1994 by Evelyn C. Rosser. Used by permission of the author.

Jane Rule, "The Question of Children," from *Hot-Eyed Moderate*, Naiad Press 1985. Copyright © 1985 by Jane Rule. Reprinted by permission of Naiad Press.

May Sarton, excerpt from *Journal of a Solitude*, W.W. Norton & Co. 1973. Copyright © 1973 by May Sarton. Reprinted by permission of W. W. Norton & Co. Inc.

Lynda Schor, "The Arm Baby," originally published in *Maryland Poetry Review* 13, Spring/Summer 1994. Copyright © 1994 by Lynda Schor. Used by permission of the author.

Sandra Scofield, "Cutting My Heart Out: Notes Toward A Novel," originally published in *Left Bank* 5:7, "Borders & Boundaries" (published by Blue Heron Publishing). Copyright © 1994 by Sandra Scofield. Used by permission of the author.

Amy Tan, excerpt from *The Joy Luck Club*, G.P. Putnam's Sons 1989. Copyright © 1989 by Amy Tan. Reprinted by permission of G. P. Putnam's Sons, a division of Penguin Putnam Inc.

Luci Tapahonso, "All the Colors of Sunset," from *Blue Horses Rush In*, University of Arizona Press, 1997. Copyright © 1997 by Luci Tapahonso. Reprinted by permisson of the University of Arizona Press.

Pamela Walker, "The Wash House," originally published in *Hawaii Review* 14:1, Spring 1990. Copyright © 1990 by Pamela Walker. Used by permission of the author.

Joy Williams, "The Case Against Babies," originally published in *Granta* 55, 1996, "The Children," and in *The Best American Essays, 1997*, edited by Ian Frazier. Copyright © 1996 by Joy Williams. Used by permission of the author.